Sport and Exercise Psychology

Topics in Applied Psychology

Andrew M. Lane

HODDER
EDUCATION
PART OF HACHETTE LIVRE UK

First published in Great Britain in 2008 by
Hodder Education, part of Hachette Livre UK, 338 Euston Road, London NW1 3BH

www.hoddereducation.com

© 2008 Andrew M. Lane

British Library Cataloguing in Publication Data
A catalogue record for this book is available from the British Library

Library of Congress Cataloging-in-Publication Data
A catalog record for this book is available from the Library of Congress

ISBN 978 0 340 92894 3

1 2 3 4 5 6 7 8 9 10

Cover & section opener © Kevin Edge Photography/iStockphoto.com

Typeset in 10pt Berling Roman by Servis Filmsetting Ltd., Stockport, Cheshire
Printed and bound in Malta

What do you think about this book? Or any other Hodder
Education title? Please send your comments to the
feedback section on www.hoddereducation.com.

Contents

Contributors

Chris Beedie, Canterbury Christ Church University, UK

Tracey Devonport, University of Wolverhampton, UK

Michael J. Duncan, Newman College of Higher Education, UK

Abby Foad, Canterbury Christ Church University, UK

Kate Hays, Nottingham Trent University, UK

Costas I. Karageorghis, Brunel University, UK

Andrew M. Lane, University of Wolverhampton, UK

Mária Rendi, Semmelweis University, Budapest, Hungary

Adrian Schonfeld, Leeds Metropolitan University, UK

Dave Smith, Manchester Metropolitan University, UK

Attila Szabo, Eötvös Loránd University of Science, Budapest, Hungary, and National Institute for Sport Talent Care and Sport Services, Budapest, Hungary

Richard Thelwell, University of Portsmouth, UK

Mark Uphill, Canterbury Christ Church University, UK

Neil Weston, University of Portsmouth, UK

Caroline Wright, Department of Sport and Exercise Science, University of Chester, UK

Series preface

Psychology is still one of the most popular subjects for study at undergraduate degree level. As well as providing the student with a range of academic and applied skills that are valued by a broad range of employers, a psychology degree also serves as the basis for subsequent training and a career in professional psychology. A substantial proportion of students entering a degree programme in Psychology do so with a subsequent career in applied psychology firmly in mind, and as a result the number of applied psychology courses available at undergraduate level has significantly increased over recent years. In some cases these courses supplement core academic areas and in others they provide the student with a flavour of what they might experience as a professional psychologist.

Topics in Applied Psychology represents a series of six textbooks designed to provide a comprehensive academic and professional insight into specific areas of professional psychology. The texts cover the areas of **Clinical Psychology, Criminal Psychology, Educational Psychology, Health Psychology, Sports and Exercise Psychology**, and **Organizational and Work Psychology**, and each text is written and edited by the foremost professional and academic figures in each of these areas.

Each textbook is based on a similar academic formula which combines a comprehensive review of cutting-edge research and professional knowledge with accessible teaching and learning features. The books are also structured so they can be used as an integrated teaching support for a one-term or one-semester course in each of their relevant areas of applied psychology. Given the increasing importance of applying psychological knowledge across a growing range of areas of practice, we feel this series is timely and comprehensive. We hope you find each book in the series readable, enlightening, accessible and instructive.

Graham Davey
University of Sussex, Brighton, UK
September 2007

Preface

Sport and Exercise Psychology is both an academic subject and a profession. As an academic topic it makes an important contribution to undergraduate degree programmes at all levels. A substantial proportion of undergraduate students applying to read psychology do so because they have a career in applied psychology in mind. As a profession, sport and exercise psychology is an important component of the provision of scientific support aimed at increasing performance for professional and elite athletes of most countries. It is also an important component in terms of increasing and maintaining exercise adoption, working alongside private and public sectors. Professionally-trained Sport and Exercise psychologists carry out an increasing range of duties within those services, including tasks of assessment, intervention and evaluation.

The purpose of this book is to introduce the undergraduate psychology student to both academic and professional aspects of Sport and Exercise Psychology. Individual chapters are written by practitioners with considerable knowledge and professional expertise in their areas of competence. The book begins with a chapter on applied sport psychology to give the reader an insight into the domain of sport psychology, providing an overview of some of the techniques that could be used. The next three chapters focus on cognitive and affective factors that influence performance (mood, anxiety, self-confidence). This leads to four chapters that focus on managing psychological states (coping, performance profiling, imagery and music). The next chapter focuses on leadership. Two chapters focus on the effects of exercise on psychological states, providing a balance between the benefits and potential drawbacks. The final chapter provides an insightful view on the issue of placebo effects. Chapters include information about what Sport and Exercise psychologists do, what research questions and applied issues need addressing, and the importance of conducting theory-led practice.

As with all the books in the *Topics in Applied Psychology* series, this text is written as a support for a one-term or one-semester course in Sport and Exercise Psychology, and contains all the teaching and learning features appropriate to the series including coverage of research methods and ethical issues. Activity boxes provide the student with the opportunity to engage in active learning. Each chapter also ends with extensive support for further reading, including relevant journal articles, books and web-sites, and this should enable the interested student to engage with a topic in some depth.

Finally, the over-arching aim of this book is to provide the undergraduate psychology student with a structured introduction to Sport and Exercise Psychology, covering both academic and professional issues. As such it aims to provide an insight into the theoretical evidence and practical suggestions that underpin what a Sport and Exercise psychologist does.

Andrew M. Lane
University of Wolverhampton, UK
December 2007

1 Applied sport psychology: Enhancing performance using psychological skills training

Richard Thelwell

Given that the stakes in modern day sport are so high and the margins between success and failure so narrow, one might question whether it is strange that some performers do not utilize the services of a sport psychologist. As you will see from the chapters within this book, athletes at the top of the sporting ladder have a number of challenges put before them; these take the form of opponents, environmental conditions and their own mindset, to name but a few. One excellent example of this comes from Steve Harmison, one of England's fastest bowlers who, in July, 2005, started England's Ashes Test Series against Australia at Lords with a hostile and accurate ambush on the Australian top-order batting, and in particular Justin Langer. However, some 18 months later, Harmison bowled the first ball of the 2006–2007 Ashes series in Brisbane to Langer, and instead of bowling a hostile delivery to set the tone for the series, he misdirected the first delivery that went for four wides via second slip! After the events, and unfortunately a very disappointing series for both England and Harmison, he revealed that he had *frozen* before the first ball in the Test match. Harmison commented that this negative experience was driven by the enormity of the occasion which made his entire body tense, leading him to have no rhythm and to perform poorly. Of course, one does not know the extent to which Harmison engaged with a sport psychologist or whether he employed psychological skills, but what we do know is that employing psychological skills increases the chances of positive performance experiences.

With this in mind, the purpose of this chapter is to explore how sport psychologists can help athletes enhance their performance via the use of **psychological skills training (PST)**, which for this chapter will primarily focus on the skills of self-talk, imagery, relaxation and goal-setting. Throughout, we will explore the concept of PST with a specific focus on whether it enhances performance. To enable this to be achieved, we will commence the chapter by reviewing some of the literature that has supported the use of PST in sport and provide suggestions as to why performers have been resistant to the use of such skills. We will then turn our attention to the examination of two models of PST development that link the assessment process to the integration and implementation of psychological skills. Having reviewed the models, the final section of the chapter will focus on the different research approaches that have examined the impact of PST on performance. In addition to the above, throughout this chapter, readers will be asked to reflect on their own experiences with reference to the material presented.

Learning outcomes

When you have completed this chapter you should be able to:

1. Evaluate the literature that has suggested PST to be of benefit to the sports performer.
2. Evaluate some of the models of PST delivery and appraise how such skills can be implemented.
3. Critically evaluate the contemporary approaches to researching PST and performance.

Activity 1.1

Think back to your sporting experiences and the psychological skills that you either do, or could, employ to benefit your performance. As you work through the skills, consider whether you do, or could, use them in training as well as competition. Also, consider how such skills have enhanced your performance when you have used them compared to when you have not.

Skill employed	Training/competition	Impact of using the skill

We would imagine that you, like many athletes, tend to employ psychological skills in a competition environment but not in a training environment, which is strange given that this is where the competition habits are created. Also, I suspect that when you use the psychological skills you have greater perceptions of success, possibly because you feel in control, more confident and more focused compared to when you do not use such skills.

Having considered your own experiences using psychological skills, now read Frey, Laguna and Ravizza (2003) to see how they reported the use of psychological skills and associated perceptions of success in collegiate athletes. Read how they collected their data, how they analysed their data and what they found, and then compare this to what you do.

Should you do anything differently?

Evaluating the literature that has suggested PST to be of benefit to the sports performer

Before exploring the benefits of employing psychological skills, we first need to define exactly what we are referring to. Weinberg and Gould (2007: 250) defined psychological skills as a 'systematic and consistent practice of mental or psychological skills for the purpose of enhancing performance, increasing enjoyment, or achieving greater sport and physical activity self-satisfaction'. Examining psychological skills should be guided by examination of relationships with the three outcomes cited above. Importantly, applied sport psychologists should be able to use interventions that are grounded in a scientific evidence base.

In an attempt to respond to the questions directed towards whether PST interventions are effective, three meta-analyses have been conducted. Each of these included intervention studies that were well controlled and based on performance changes in competitive environments (so as to protect against any reductions in the ecological validity of the studies). The first meta-analysis, conducted by Greenspan and Feltz (1989), reviewed 19 studies that examined the impact of PST on performance in competitive environments. Even though a variety of sports were studied, the results suggested that such interventions positively influenced performance in over 80 per cent of the studies. A further meta-analysis by Vealey (1994) reported that PST studies continued to report the positive impact on performance, with in excess of 75 per cent resulting in performance enhancement in both individual and team sports. Finally, Weinberg and Comar (1994) advanced Vealey's study by reporting an additional 10 intervention-based studies where, once again, positive effects on performance were reported. Taken together, prior to 1994 an approximate success rate of 85 per cent was reported in studies that examined the impacts of PST on performance, suggesting that such skills are of benefit to the performer. Unfortunately, there is no up-to-date meta-analysis of PST intervention studies despite a marked increase in the number of such studies conducted within the past 15 years.

Allied to the meta-analytical results discussed above are a number of more recent studies that have examined Olympic athletes' use of psychological skills. For example, when comparing athletes who performed to their potential to those who did not, Gould et al (1999) suggested that higher level achievers were more effective at coping with disruptions, had well-developed performance plans and engaged in performance evaluation, all of which drew upon their psychological skills resources. They also tended to set appropriate goals, employ positive imagery and have higher levels of confidence that enabled them to perform to their potential. Similarly, Greenleaf, Gould and Dieffenbach (2001) interviewed a number of Olympic athletes and found that over 85 per cent of them employed psychological skills to enhance performance. Further, such skills were employed on a regular basis both in training and competition.

More recently, the effectiveness of PST has been documented within the emerging research area of mental toughness, which is now widely regarded as a fundamental prerequisite for successful performance (Gould et al, 2002a; Jones

Figure 1.1 The Olympic Games. For some athletes seeing the Olympic stadium will be an exciting thought; for other athletes, it represents the cauldron of anxiety.

Source: Photograph courtesy of Professor Greg Whyte.

et al, 2007). Although to date the definitions of mental toughness have been varied, recent researchers (e.g. Jones et al, 2002; Thelwell et al, 2005) have contended that it includes attributes such as an athlete's ability to recover from setbacks, persistence when faced with failure, maintaining focus despite performance (and other) distractions and an ability to cope with excessive pressure. Further to this, recent research by Connaughton et al (2008) examining the *development* and *maintenance* of mental toughness has indicated the use of PST to be critical for both aspects. Therefore, with mental toughness contributing to the attainment of sporting success and PST enabling the development of mental toughness, this provides further justification to the benefits of employing such skills.

Given that the above presents an evidence-based argument for PST enhancing performance, it seems perplexing that there are many athletes who choose not to practise such skills. The following serves to provide an insight to why this might be the case.

First, many athletes neglect PST due to simply misunderstanding it. This is a concern on a number of levels, the first being that many athletes perceive PST (and as such mental toughness) to be inherent rather than developed. This is an awkward assumption given that even the most talented individuals in the sporting world spend endless hours practising their skills, even though they may have been blessed with a high level of innate talent. Another misunderstanding is that many athletes expect immediate success following the implementation of an intervention and as such do not understand that, like physical skills, psychological skills require a great deal of time and practice to develop.

A further reason why athletes may neglect psychological skills has to do with time. Specifically, many athletes struggle with not being able to devote enough time to the development of physical skills let alone psychological skills. This was one of the key findings reported by Gould et al (1999b) who examined some of the roadblocks to the development of psychological skills from the perceptions of junior tennis coaches. This does, however, seem counter-intuitive given that many of the reasons provided for performance failure are attributed to psychological factors. For example, how many times have you finished a performance and then said 'I felt too tense before the shot' or 'I just bottled it, just couldn't get it right at that crucial time … my confidence had gone'? As a result, one could suggest that even though psychological skills may impact quite significantly on performance, they do not appear to be of utmost importance to the athletes in terms of the time allocated; hence they become neglected.

There are also some myths that pervade athletes' use of PST (Weinberg & Gould, 2007) such as suggestions that psychological skills are for 'athletes with problems' or only for 'elite athletes'. The vast majority of athletes use a sport psychologist for educational rather than clinical purposes. Despite this, there is still sometimes a negative stigma associated with consulting a sport psychologist, the main issue here being the view that if you need to see a sport psychologist, then you are unable to cope with the climate and demands of elite sport (see Chapter 5). This view was demonstrated by Australian fast bowler Glenn McGrath who, prior to the 2006–2007 Ashes series, heard that the new English spin bowler Monty Panesar was seeing a sport psychologist. McGrath commented that it was ridiculous that Panesar was seeking such support prior to the series and that he must be 'soft'. Conversely, England football goalkeeper David James argues that the benefits of seeing a sport psychologist outweigh any negative public perception. James contends that psychology is one of the building bricks to being a top athlete, so it should be normal for athletes to use such expert support. In James' experience, developing athletes should work with psychologists. With regard to PST being for elite athletes only, it may be that support is most readily available to those with funding (i.e. through governing bodies, bursaries etc.), but this is not to say that young, recreational athletes or athletes with disabilities are not able to seek such support. A further myth associated with PST is that it provides 'overnight' performance solutions. Obviously, the achievement of this accelerated success is not possible due to the time required to develop the skills in a variety of pressurized environments, prior to being employed within competition.

Evaluating some of the models of PST delivery and how such skills can be implemented

Although we are aware of the potential benefits of PST and some of the reasons why athletes neglect their use, the debate about how best to deliver and integrate such skills remains. As such, this section will review two models of psychological skill delivery, while also providing an insight to how each approach might impact on sports performance.

Sinclair and Sinclair's (1994) mental management

The first model, **Sinclair and Sinclair's mental management** (1994), advocated an approach that enabled athletes to develop their psychological skills alongside physical, technical and tactical skills rather than being viewed as an 'add-on' that occurs when athletes experience performance difficulties. The basic premise for the model stemmed from the authors' experiences with a number of athletes. They recognized that while effective psychological skills were beneficial to enhancing performance, they were only developed when athletes started to experience performance difficulties. As a consequence, they contended that athletes are placed in a position of 'crisis management' where a sport psychologist is brought in and expected to bring about a change in the athletes' psychological condition immediately (which we know from learning outcome 1 is highly unlikely). In respect of this approach, it could be construed that the development of psychological skills is seen as an 'add-on' rather than an inclusive feature of performance.

In an attempt to resolve the 'add-on' issue, Sinclair and Sinclair (1994) developed their 'mental management' model that incorporated Norman's (1988) 'action cycle' where the two key aspects of *execution* (doing something) and *evaluation* (where someone is now and where they want to get to) were central to the process. These two aspects are then split into seven action stages: setting goals, perceiving the current situation, interpreting the situation, evaluating interpretations, making intentions to act, selecting a sequence of actions and executing the action sequence. Norman contends that, as with many sporting situations, the whole process is driven by a goal. The goal then requires the individual to develop a set of internal commands that can be completed to achieve it. As such, Norman suggests that the whole process is in essence a mental process given that the action sequence comes into play at the final stage.

In transferring the process to the sporting environment where athletes are able to develop their psychological skills alongside their physical and technical skills in the training and competition environment, Sinclair and Sinclair (1994) advocate a seven-step approach. Each step will now be worked through prior to Activity box 1.2 where you will have an opportunity to develop the seven steps for a skill of your choice.

Step 1: Goal-setting

Before any action takes place, it is necessary to identify the objective that is being targeted. Goal-setting requires specific, realistic and measurable goals.

Step 2: Identifying relevant cues

Focusing skills. For any skill that athletes conduct, there will be a number of cues that they may focus on. Unfortunately, many of the cues may be irrelevant. Accordingly, this step is about trying to select the appropriate cue. For example, when working on bowling in cricket, the coach may demonstrate the skill and verbalize some of the key cues that players need to focus on. Some of the cues might include 'smooth run-up', 'nice approach to the wicket', 'high bound', 'head up and looking at the batter', 'drive through with the arms' and 'follow through'. As the bowlers become more proficient at bowling, the cues will become more refined to a point at which only a couple of 'key words' are used.

In addition to focusing skills, *refocusing skills* may also be developed. For example, if a bowler has bowled a poor delivery or has not achieved the intended goal, each delivery will require a refocus to consistently achieve the desired outcome. If task-irrelevant cues are being focused on, an appropriate prompt from the coach can make the player aware of how their attention has shifted inappropriately.

Step 3: Developing a motor plan

Having set a goal and become aware of the cues that will facilitate achievement of this goal, the player must make an appropriate performance plan. This may require the development of imagery skills wherein the athlete can develop all sensory modalities to recreate the experience. Here the bowler would think through the execution of a successful delivery while also using the cues established in step 2. For a full review of imagery theory and research see Chapter 8.

Step 4: Executing the skill

Having set the goal, identified relevant cues and imaged themselves performing, this step requires the athlete to have a go at the skill. Inevitably, there will be occasions where the skill is not performed to the aspired level. For example, the ball may be a 'short delivery' rather than a 'good length delivery', which may be attributed to tension. Here focus may be directed towards self-awareness and how the athlete felt (both physically and emotionally) before and during the delivery.

Step 5: Evaluation and feedback

Having attempted the skill, the next step is to evaluate the degree to which success was achieved. Often this process commences with athletes being very negative and evaluating in a dysfunctional manner. However, through appropriate guidance, self-awareness and rationalization skills can be developed. Also, in this stage, athletes may become more aware of the self-talk that they engage in. We know from much of the recent self-talk literature that positive self-talk is more effective than negative self-talk (see Hardy, 2006) but being able to transfer negative into positive self-talk is a skill that requires attention and time. For example, while it is not uncommon for a bowler to berate themselves following a poor delivery, it is not always the case that the athlete will know the potential debilitating effect of the self-talk. Therefore, facilitating increased self-awareness of what they are saying will be of use.

Step 6: Revising the motor plan

Here, the procedures advocated in step 3 would be encouraged.

Step 7: Execute the skill (again and again)

Here, the procedures advocated in step 4 would be encouraged, followed by the remainder of the cycle before going back to step 3 and so on.

As indicated herein, the mental management approach advocated by Sinclair and Sinclair (1994) enables performers to develop all aspects of performance in a formal and systematic manner. Importantly, the development of fundamental psychological skills (goal-setting, focusing, arousal regulation, imagery, self-talk) is embedded within the overall skill development/learning process. Although a brief insight to the mental management model is presented here, you are encouraged to read Sinclair and Sinclair's work for a fuller description of how psychological skills can be continually reinforced and developed throughout the learning process.

Activity 1.2

Think of a physical/technical skill that you conduct that would benefit from additional psychological skills. Consider how you learnt the skill and how you would develop it if you had worked on your psychological skills at the same time. When thinking about the skill, work through the seven steps and identify the psychological skills you would attempt to develop and how they would fit into the overall development of the skill.

Step	Psychological skill	Reason for developing skill
1.		
2.		
3.		
4.		
5.		
6.		
7.		

When reviewing Sinclair and Sinclair's (1994) model, would the overall skill be enhanced via the 'add-on' approach or via effective mental management throughout the long-term development of the skill?

Taylor's conceptual model

A second approach to the development and integration of PST comes from the conceptual model of Taylor (1995). Taylor posits that the development of PST interventions and subsequent delivery of the skills will depend on the integration of the demands of the sport and the athletes' needs. Specifically, all sports have varying physical, logistical and technical demands that will influence the psychological needs for success in the sport. Sport psychologists need to be aware of these demands and develop appropriate psychological skills interventions. Take for example the 10,000 m run and golf. While both events are relatively long in duration, they have very different physical demands. They also have very different skill requirements: golf is a sport requiring precision while the 10,000 m requires gross motor movements. Alternatively, consider a 100 m swimmer who requires explosive power. Evidently, each sport has contrasting demands, especially in terms of their time, physical and technical characteristics, which, according to Taylor, will influence the psychological demands placed on the athletes. For example, because the 10,000 m is long in duration, uses gross motor movements and is aerobic in nature, the psychological priorities may be to overcome low motivation, pain control and boredom-related issues. As such, the psychological skills may include key words (motivational/focus/instructional), relaxation strategies and goal-setting, each of which is specific to the demands of the sport (see Lane, 2006). The golfer, for example, may have psychological priorities that are driven by the need to maintain concentration and intensity levels, possibly due to the length of a round where the performance time is minimal and the idle periods between shots could be lengthy. Accordingly, skills such as arousal regulation, imagery and a variety of skills put together to develop pre- and post-shot routines would be of benefit.

Of course, while the above psychological priorities and advocated skills represent only a guide, it is the responsibility of the practitioner to assess the demands of the sport and the athlete's needs prior to developing any ensuing intervention. That said, Taylor's (1995) work is appropriate in suggesting that not all individuals and sports can be addressed with the same skills in the same manner.

Activity 1.3

Consider three sports of your choice and work through **Taylor's (1995) conceptual model**. In doing so, consider the physical demands of each sport, the psychological priorities and the psychological skills that will be most appropriate. To enable you to complete this task you may wish to read the associated paper.

Sport	Physical demands	Psychological priorities	Psychological skills
1.			
2.			
3.			

Having worked through the three sports, you should now be able to see that it is not advisable to approach all three sports in the same manner, especially because we have not considered the specific needs of the athletes.

> **Focus 1.1**
>
> There are differing approaches to how PST can be delivered and implemented. Despite the contrasts in the two models discussed, the key messages are summarized as follows:
>
> 1. Psychological skills are best developed alongside physical and technical skills.
>
> 2. Psychological skills need to be evaluated and developed over time.
>
> 3. Sports have varying physical and technical demands, therefore we need to be aware of the differing psychological demands.
>
> 4. Practitioners need to be aware of the athlete's needs when developing PST.

Critically evaluating the contemporary approaches to researching PST and performance

We will now explore how researchers are examining the PST–performance relationship. Understanding such approaches and the subsequent findings is vital for the applied practitioner given that our work is based on sound theoretical and research evidence.

What we do know is that in recent years the applied sport psychology literature has seen an increase in the number of experimental studies examining the impacts that PST can have on performance. We also know that while many skills and strategies have been employed, the four most commonly researched are self-talk, imagery, relaxation and goal-setting. Examples of such research stem from both questionnaire-based studies (e.g. Fletcher and Hanton, 2001; Harwood et al, 2004) and the more applied-based studies (e.g. Filby et al, 1999). Among the studies examining the four skills, there have been debates regarding (a) whether psychological skills should be examined singularly or within a package, and (b) developments in the experimental designs employed.

Should psychological skills be examined singularly or within a package?

Taking the first point, several researchers have advocated that to fully understand the impact of psychological skills on performance, they should be examined individually. For example, the wealth of literature examining self-talk (e.g. Johnson et al, 2004; Hatzigeorgiadis et al, 2007) has identified varying forms of self-talk (e.g. instructional, motivational) and has shown how each form can influence functions of performance (e.g. psychological states or overall performance) in a variety of sports. Similarly, studies focusing on the effectiveness of imagery (e.g. Cumming and Ste-Marie, 2001; Gregg et al, 2005) have reported its varying forms (instructional, motivational, facilitative, debilitative) and how they influence sporting performance. Although the single-skill studies examining self-talk and imagery have been more numerous in recent years, studies examining the effectiveness of relaxation or goal-setting strategies on performance are less frequent. Maynard, Hemmings and Warwick-Evans (1995) reported the positive impacts of a relaxation intervention on competitive state anxiety and performance relationships in soccer. Swain and Jones (1995) examined the impacts of a goal-setting intervention on specific basketball components. Here they reported goal-setting to be of benefit in enhancing targeted performance behaviours. Few studies have followed a similar design, and this represents a gap in the literature.

The above represent some studies that have adopted a single-skill approach. Together, they have undoubtedly provided practitioners with a wealth of knowledge on the merits of developing a single skill over time to enhance performance. However, there are also a number of potential shortfalls to the adoption of such approaches. For example, it is common to find that several skills benefit each other. This has been reported on numerous occasions: Rushall (1984), Zeigler (1987) and Rushall et al (1988) all concluded that self-talk, when combined with imagery, enhanced performance in rowing, tennis and cross-country skiing, respectively. Ostensibly, self-talk allowed performers to focus on relevant and correct cues during the imagery session. Other researchers (e.g. Kirschenbaum and Bale, 1984; Hamilton and Fremouw, 1985) have acknowledged the success of relaxation and self-talk when combined with other mental skills, such as imagery, modelling, attentional focus, game plans and feedback mechanisms.

More recently, researchers have combined skills and reported positive effects in ice hockey (Rogerson and Hrycaiko, 2002: centering and self-talk) and darts performance (Cumming et al, 2006: imagery and self-talk). A further potential shortfall of single-skill interventions is that many sports require multiple skills, which was clearly articulated earlier in the discussion of both Sinclair and Sinclair's (1994) and Taylor's (1995) models of psychological skill delivery and implementation. Much of the research now tends to adopt a 'package' approach to the study of psychological skills (e.g. Thelwell and Maynard, 2003; Barwood et al, 2007) which brings with it a different set of concerns. The most notable of these is the uncertainty surrounding the order in which skills should be developed and how they interact with each other to provide an 'additive' effect towards performance improvement. It is fair to say that the 'jury is still out' with regard to this matter and although this remains a challenge for future research, one thing that practitioners can argue with some confidence is that individual differences here will often dictate the effectiveness of certain skills.

How should experiments be designed?

The second development within applied-based research revolves around experimental designs. Although a historical account is not provided here, it is important to note that researchers several years ago foresaw changes. For example, when writing about the development of sport psychology, Alderman (1984: 53) stated that '… in the field of sport psychology over the next 20 years, research will become more applied, clinical, and technique-oriented'. This statement has now become reality as researchers have tended to prefer the use of **single-subject designs** (that enable the tracking of an individual's performance both pre- and post-intervention to detect small changes in performance) rather than more traditional group designs where the effects of interventions may be masked by the use of statistics. On this point, it is also important to note that at an elite level, performance changes may be very subtle and as such may not be apparent within a group design. Also, even though the performance changes may be relatively small, at the higher level of performance, these small changes are mostly significant. Finally, the role of applied sport psychologists is to provide an intervention based on the person and sport in question. To facilitate this, research designs have progressed to enable practitioners to link research to practice, which itself was commented on some 20 years ago by Frank (1986: 24) who stated 'nomothetic science can never escape the individual ... its findings must [eventually] be applied to the individual'.

In short, the benefits of single-subject design are that a participant's behaviour is observed prior to any experimental condition which means that each participant has their own 'control' and 'treatment' condition. There are a number of single-subject design approaches and although only the multiple-baseline across participants approach will be mentioned here, interested readers are directed to Martin and Pear (2003) or Martin, Thompson and Regehr (2004) for a detailed review of alternative approaches.

Another development in the recent research is related to the fact that the majority of applied studies have focused on the measurement of performance outcomes alone, and have neglected performance subcomponents. Although it is acknowledged that this is not always appropriate, there are a number of sports where a more detailed insight of performance subcomponents may give a better understanding of overall performance achievement. One such study was conducted by Thelwell, Greenlees and Weston (2006) who examined the impact of a soccer, midfielder-specific psychological skills intervention on position-specific performance measures (first-touch percentage, pass completion percentage and tackle success percentage). In this particular study, a total of five participants had their performances monitored across nine competitive matches where each, in turn, received the intervention. The results indicated that the intervention, designed with specific positional roles in mind, enabled at least small improvements on the three performance measures for each participant. In discussing the findings, the authors reinforced the potential benefits of using not just sport-, but position-specific interventions that examine position-specific measures.

Conclusions

We have seen that there is a wealth of literature suggesting that psychological skills can be beneficial to athletic performance. Evidence is drawn from studies using successful professional and Olympic athletes combined with experimental research examining either single-skill or package interventions. It is also evident that there is no exact way in which psychological skills should be delivered, and although there are more 'desirable' approaches, practitioners are encouraged to gauge the situation while also being aware of the appropriate underpinning research evidence. We have outlined the proposed benefits of psychological skills, the models for their development, and the contemporary research that has demonstrated the efficacy of such skills. The tasks that have been set were designed to reinforce each of the three learning outcomes while also enabling a more detailed understanding of the psychological skills–performance relationship. It is hoped that this will facilitate an enhanced understanding of applied sport psychology with specific reference to psychological skills, and in particular to their effectiveness, their delivery and how they are researched.

Research methods 1.1

The single-subject multiple-baseline across individuals research design is becoming increasingly used within applied research. The basic premise of the design is that each of the participants has their baseline (control) data collected concurrently before receiving the intervention (treatment) in a staggered fashion. This normally takes place when a stable baseline of the dependent variable is achieved, or when performance moves in a direction opposite to that expected following the intervention.

In the two figures below, we can see data for two participants who had their five minute running performance assessed over a 10 session/week period (the blocked line reports actual performance while the dotted line is the average performance). The first participant had their baseline period for sessions 1 to 4, when they then received the intervention. The post-intervention period for participant 1 was from sessions 5 to 10 where it can be seen that the intervention enabled an improvement in performance (denoted by actual and average performance). The second participant received the intervention after five baseline sessions, and again the post-intervention performance effects were positive.

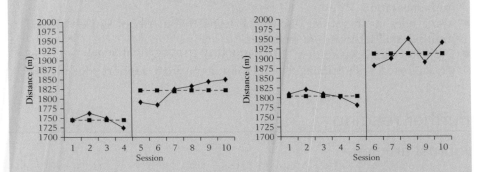

To fully understand the findings, we need to be aware of how single-subject data are analysed. Martin and Pear (2003) have suggested that

Continued . . .

. . . Continued

visual inspection of data should look for the following: the number of overlapping data points between pre- and post-intervention phases (the fewer the number, the greater the intervention effect); the immediacy of the effect; the size of the effect after intervention; the number of times the findings are replicated across participants (the greater the number, the greater chance that the intervention will work irrespective of when it is delivered, thus giving some external validity); and, the consistency around the mean. Although the first four approaches to visual inspection of data are critical, the final approach is important for the practitioner in a different way. For example, it may be that while there is no discernable improvement in average performance, the actual performance may become more consistent and closer to the mean scores. Ideally, though, we would like to see improvements in actual performance, average performance and consistency of performance, post intervention. However, for some performers, achieving greater consistency is often a difficult hurdle and practitioners should be encouraged to monitor this.

Key concepts and terms

Psychological skills training
Sinclair and Sinclair's (1994)
  mental management

Single-subject designs
Taylor's (1995) conceptual
  model

Sample essay titles

- Critically examine the role that psychological skills have in the development and maintenance of mental toughness.
- With reference to appropriate examples, critically appraise the effectiveness of two models of psychological skills delivery and implementation.
- Using relevant literature, discuss the respective merits of single-skill and multiple-skill intervention strategies.
- Evaluate the development of experimental designs for the study of psychological skills training. Use relevant literature to support your answer.

Further reading

Journal articles

Fletcher, D., and Hanton, S. (2001). The relationship between psychological skills usage and competitive anxiety responses. *Psychology of Sport and Exercise*, 2, 89–101.

Frey, M., Laguna, P.L., and Ravizza, K. (2003). Collegiate athletes' mental skill use and perceptions of success: An exploration of the practice and competition settings. *Journal of Applied Sport Psychology*, 15, 115–128.

Gould, D., Guinan, D., Greenleaf, C., Medbury, R., and Peterson, K. (1999a). Factors affecting Olympic performance. Perceptions of athletes and coaches from more and less successful teams. *The Sport Psychologist*, 13, 371–394.

Greenleaf, C., Gould, D., and Dieffenbach, K. (2001). Factors influencing Olympic performance: Interviews with Atlanta and Nagano U.S. Olympians. *Journal of Applied Sport Psychology*, 13, 154–184.

Sinclair, G.D., and Sinclair, D.A. (1994). Developing reflective performers by integrating mental management skills with the learning process. *The Sport Psychologist*, 8, 13–27.

Taylor, J. (1995). A conceptual model for integrating athletes' needs and sport demands in the development of competitive mental preparation strategies. *The Sport Psychologist*, 9, 339–357.

Thelwell, R.C., Greenlees, I.A., and Weston, N. (2006). Using psychological skills training to develop soccer performance. *Journal of Applied Sport Psychology*, 18, 254–270.

1 | Cognitive and affective factors

2 Mood and sport performance

Andrew M. Lane

Focus 2.1

Definition of mood

Lane and Terry (2000: 16) defined **mood** as 'a set of feelings, ephemeral in nature, varying in intensity and duration, and usually involving more than one emotion' (*Journal of Applied Sport Psychology*).

Parkinson et al (1996: 216) proposed that 'mood reflects changing non-specific psychological dispositions to evaluate, interpret, and act on past, current, or future concerns in certain patterned ways', a definition used in Lane et al (2005a) in response to issues raised by Mellalieu (2003).

Definition of emotion

Lazarus (2000b: 230) defined **emotion** as 'an organized psychophysiological reaction to ongoing relationships with the environment ... what mediates emotions psychologically is an evaluation, referred to as an appraisal, of the personal significance for the well-being that a person attributes to this relationship (... relational meaning), and the process'.

Anecdotal quotes from athletes, coaches and fans allude to playing and watching sport being an emotional experience. The elation of celebrating players is matched by the despair of losing. In the UK, national elation followed regaining the Ashes in 2005 and winning the rugby World Cup in 2003; disappointment, upset and anger followed exiting the soccer 2006 World Cup. Winning athletes typically refer to experiencing intense emotions during competition, and it is their ability to control these emotions that helps bring about success.

I was involved in a discussion on the role of mood and emotions in sport performance on BBC Radio 5 Live, the Simon Mayo show (21 November 2006). The programme involved discussion between experts and callers who were listening to the show. In the space of two conversations, anxiety was described as helpful and harmful for sport performance. Former England cricket captain Mike Gatting described feelings of nervousness when batting that gave him an edge. He suggested his concentration would not be so sharp without experiencing these feelings. Following this, a caller described a situation in which a Manchester United player looked nervous in the tunnel before an important Premier League game. He argued that high anxiety led to defeat. I responded by trying to reconcile these seemingly differing positions using theory and empirical evidence to guide my answer. Sport psychologists should be able to offer reasonable explanations on why mood states influence sport performance, and practising sport psychologists should be able to help athletes develop emotional control techniques.

Figure 2.1 Emotional control is a key ingredient of sports success.

Source: Photograph courtesy of Professor Greg Whyte.

The aims of this chapter are twofold. The first aim is to describe mood–performance relationships in the literature. Evidence indicates that mood–performance relationships are strong in some studies and weak in others. A second aim is to describe and evaluate a conceptual model of mood–performance relationships. At least two important themes run throughout this chapter, the first being measurement issues: how mood is assessed has an important bearing on subsequent mood–performance relationships. If the methods we use are not valid and reliable, results using the methods should be interpreted cautiously. The second theme running through the chapter is ethical issues. Researchers and practitioners should care for their participants and use methods that minimize possible harm.

Learning outcomes

When you have completed this chapter you should be able to:

1. Evaluate mood–performance relationships and methodological factors that influence this relationship.
2. Evaluate the conceptual model of Lane and Terry (2000) and describe the revised conceptual model proposed by Lane (2007a).
3. Be aware of relevant ethical issues in either the research or practical application of mood and performance.

Activity 2.1

Think carefully about when you participated in an important competition. Select one situation or competition that was personally important to you. This should be a competition where performance really mattered. Now think back to that situation, try to remember what was around you, who was with you, and try to see these images as clearly as possible. Now try to recall the sounds, hear them as clearly as possible, try to sharpen the sounds so that they are crystal clear, as if you are there. Now remember how you felt before the competition started, consider how you felt physically, what you were thinking about and what emotions you experienced.

Write down all the emotions you can recall experiencing. Use single words such as nervous, calm, excited, downhearted, happy, sad, vigorous or tired. Use a sentence if you wish. 'I was excited because I thought I would perform well' ... 'I was sad because I knew I would not meet my expectations'. When you have completed this list, rate the extent to which you experienced these emotions as either 'a little', 'somewhat', 'moderately', or 'very much so'.

I suspect your list will contain a mixture of pleasant and unpleasant emotions. Athletes can feel excited (pleasant) and nervous (unpleasant) before an important competition. Athletes usually feel a number of intense emotions.

Read Lane (2007a) and Jones et al (2005) for the emotions experienced before competition and the impact of these on performance. Compare the emotional states you listed with those reported by Jones et al. Read how Jones et al summarized these emotions and, importantly, note that words sometimes considered as emotions (feeling motivated, confident) were not considered to be an emotion using the criterion specified.

Evaluating mood–performance relationships and methodological factors that influence this relationship

Mood and performance: The evidence

'The iceberg has melted'

The mood–performance relationship has been extensively researched, even featuring as the topic for a special edition of the *Journal of Applied Sport Psychology* in March 2000. Text books have also focused on mood and emotions, namely in the 17 chapters in my book *Mood and Performance: Conceptual, Measurement, and Applied Issues* (Lane, 2007b). A search on the database SportDiscus™ using the key word 'mood' reveals over 1000 articles that could be accessed. There is no shortage of commentary on mood, enabling students to access information with relative ease.

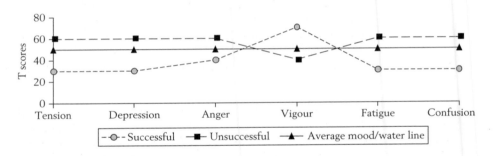

Figure 2.2 The iceberg profile: successful (iceberg) and unsuccessful (inverse iceberg) athletes as proposed by Morgan (1980).

Activity 2.2

Go back to those emotions listed for the task in Activity box 1.1. Develop a profile associated with success, and a profile associated with failure. Pay close attention to unpleasant emotional terms such as 'angry' and 'downhearted'. Based on your experiences, is anger or anxiety helpful for performance, or are these unpleasant affective states harmful to your performance. Consider how you control your emotions when you feel anxious before performance. What do you do? By writing these experiences down you will start to learn about how you experience mood, how you control mood states that could hamper performance, or how you psych yourself up to perform successfully.

Mood research in sport has concentrated around an examination of the **iceberg profile**. The iceberg profile is a mood constellation characterized by above average vigour with below average anger, tension, confusion, depression and fatigue (see Figure 2.2; Morgan, 1980). Mood researchers tend to use the Profile of Mood States (POMS; McNair et al, 1971) or derivates of the POMS such as the Brunel Mood Scale (Terry et al, 1999) to assess the six psychological states. Morgan (1980) proposed that the POMS was the 'test of champions' based on evidence showing it was associated with performance. Examination of whether successful performance was associated with an iceberg profile provided the impetus for much of the ensuing research.

By 1995, there was considerable debate concerning the utility of mood states (Renger, 1993; Rowley et al, 1995; Terry, 1995a). In a narrative review, Renger (1993) questioned the utility of iceberg profiling, citing studies where elite athletes did not uniformly report an iceberg profile, or non-athletes that showed an iceberg profile. Renger argued that the POMS was a poor tool in distinguishing elite from non-elite athletes or from distinguishing athletes from non-athletes. In a **meta-analysis** (a method of re-analysing data that seeks to answer a similar research question), Rowley et al found that POMS measures accounted for approximately 1 per cent of the variance in performance. With 99 per cent of performance variance unexplained, Rowley et al suggested that researchers 'abandon the POMS'. They argued that despite over 200 studies published, evidence was so equivocal that a more fruitful line of investigation lay elsewhere.

While both research groups (Renger, 1993; Rowley et al, 1995) are critical of evidence pertaining to POMS–performance relationships, neither article asks the question 'why should mood states relate to sport performance?' A second review of mood literature in 1995 by Peter Terry (1995a) outlined methodological reasons to explain inconsistent mood–performance relationship. Terry considered why mood states might predict performance and demonstrated that mood is an effective predictor of performance under certain conditions. Terry argued that mood states predict performance in cross-sectional studies when a self-reference measure of performance was used, and when participants were similar in skill and fitness. He argued that mood has a subtle influence on performance and that the research design needs to account for this. Beedie, Terry and Lane (2000) conducted an updated meta-analysis to test Terry's proposals.

'A tale of two questions'

Terry (1995a) argued that mood is an effective predictor of performance when certain conditions are met. He emphasized the commonly understood point among psychologists and laypeople alike that mood states are transitory in nature and vary from situation to situation. Terry (1995a) questioned the validity of using mood to compare elite athletes against non-elite athletes or comparing mood states of athletes against non-athletes. A research design to compare mood states of different groups in different situations effectively treats mood states as a stable construct. Lane (2007a) describes a hypothetical situation that could characterize the methods used to answer this question. He indicated that many studies have posted the POMS to the athlete. The athlete was asked to complete the POMS using a *'past month'* response timeframe, that is, to think back over the previous month and provide a single score that summarized these feelings. However, no consideration of situational factors was undertaken. The athlete completed the POMS, indicated their level of athletic ability and posted this information back to the researcher. Consider the following example to illustrate the problem as reported by Lane (2007a). Athlete A, who is a club level athlete, receives the POMS in the post on a day when he also receives an enormous gas bill (negative mood). Athlete B, who is an elite athlete, receives the POMS in the post on a day when he receives a huge tax rebate (positive mood). If both complete the POMS when they receive it, athlete A should report a negative mood and athlete B should report a positive mood. If we compare mood with performance, it would show that elite athletes report more positive mood states than non-elite athletes. Clearly, mood states were influenced by what was in the post. If the researchers do not know the situation in which the measure was completed, then they will not know what factors influenced mood at the time of completion. Given the number of factors that influence mood, what might be more surprising is that mood has predicted performance in some studies. The following section offers further methodological limitations of some of the early studies.

How you ask the question shapes the answer you receive: A case for looking at the response timeframe

Mood states vary from situation to situation. Therefore, researchers should use a response timeframe of 'how do you feel right now?' to assess the transient nature of mood. The POMS has two principal response timeframes: 'How have you been feeling over the past week?' including 'today' and 'right now'. A great deal of mood research used the 'past week' response timeframe, or did not specify the response timeframe used. Lane and Terry (2000) highlighted problems with using a 'past week' response timeframe. Consider the issue through the example contained in Table 2.1. Both athletes report the same score for anger scores over the past week; however, one athlete is feeling angry at the time of testing, whereas the other athlete is recalling feelings of anger from memory.

The key point is that mood states are transitory, and research that explores mood–performance relationships should ideally assess mood during competition. However, this is difficult and ethically inappropriate as it could interfere with an athlete's performance. The most appropriate time to collect mood data is approximately one hour before competition using the response timeframe 'how do you feel right now?'. Mood researchers should seek to capture the mood states experienced before competition and so should not use the past month response timeframe which assesses memories of mood across multiple situations. Taking psychological state assessments one hour before competition is the standard approach in anxiety research (see Martens et al, 1990) and should be applied to mood (see Lane, 2007a). Many of the studies in the meta-analysis by Rowley et al (1995) do not report the response timeframe used, which is a major limitation of the early work in this area.

Day	Anger score on the BRUMS (raw score from 0 to 16)	
	Person A	Person B
Monday	0	6
Tuesday	0	0
Wednesday	0	0
Thursday	0	0
Friday	0	0
Saturday	1	0
Sunday: How do you feel right now?	4	0
Sunday: How have you been feeling over the past week including today?	2	2

Table 2.1 Anger scores using different response timeframes.

Activity 2.3

Measurement issues

Both Athlete A and Athlete B have the same mood profile for the past week response timeframe. Athlete A is angry at the time of testing and Athlete B is not, and the mood states currently being experienced will be more influential than mood states stored in the memory in terms of their relation with behaviour in this situation. However, anger scores are identical for the past week response timeframe, so using this timeframe leads to an unclear measure as the individual could be angry at the time of testing, or recalling a memory of a mood, and these affect behaviour and cognition differently. If both people are exposed to the same set of frustrations, Athlete A is more likely to respond in an angry manner as he or she is currently angry.

With reference to your own mood states, consider which would affect your behaviour more:

a) Feeling angry immediately before performance? *or*
b) Feeling angry during the week and having a memory of feeling angry?

Mood and team performance

Terry (1995a) argued that mood states will have a relatively subtle influence on performance. Researchers need to design studies that acknowledge this effect size and thus control for potentially confounding variables. It is unrealistic to expect mood states to predict team performance if we assess an individual's mood (and not the team's) and analyse performance by win/loss. For example, a soccer goalkeeper performing in a negative mood may perform badly but not concede any goals due to good performances from the surrounding defenders, or they may concede three goals but their team scores four. It is also unrealistic to expect mood states to predict objective measures of performance in cross-sectional research where participants are heterogeneous in terms of skill and ability. Consider the following example to illustrate this point.

There are two track athletes competing in a 100 m race. Athlete A, an elite sprinter with a personal best time of 10.00 seconds, reports a negative mood before the present race. Athlete B, a club sprinter with a personal best time of 11.00 seconds, reports a positive mood before the same race. If both athletes run 10.5 seconds and no consideration is given to the relative quality of their performances, then results would indicate no relationship between mood and performance. Contrastingly, if the same elite athlete is compared to another elite athlete, with the same personal best, who reports a positive mood before the present race and runs 10.00 seconds, the result would suggest that mood and performance are related. It is therefore important to develop a self-referenced measure of performance to detect the relatively subtle influence of mood on performance (see Terry, 1993). Using the example of the elite and club sprinters cited above, a self-referenced measure of performance, e.g. comparing current performance against previous performance, would show that the elite athlete underperformed and the novice athlete performed above expectation, and this is reflected by variations in mood.

Activity 2.4

Anger and/or performance relationships

Think carefully about when you have played your sport. What goals did you set for yourself? What standard of performance would you be happy with? Now imagine yourself playing in a competition, try to remember how you felt. Write down the emotions you felt and rate these emotions as either 'a little', 'somewhat', 'moderately', or 'very much so'. Think of how well you performed. Rate whether you performed to expectation or underperformed. Performing to expectation should be related to positive mood states and underperformance should be associated with negative mood states. It might be that you experienced anger and anxiety when performing successfully. We will look at the nature of anger and anxiety later in the chapter.

Mood and performance in elite athletes

Research that has investigated mood–performance relationships in elite samples that uses a self-referenced measure usually shows significant relationships. Elite athletes tend to be similar in terms of skill and fitness levels, whereas non-elite athletes vary greatly in the amount of training conducted. It is reasonable to expect that training and physiological fitness will have a stronger relationship with performance than mood. With reference to the two athletes described above, Athlete A is almost always likely to beat Athlete B regardless of mood states as physiological factors will be more salient than psychological factors. However, if Athlete A races another athlete with the same personal best, psychological factors such as mood tend to predict variances in performance. Terry (1995a) reported some impressive figures for mood performance research. He found that 100 per cent of performers were correctly classified as either successful or unsuccessful in rowing (Hall and Terry, 1995), 92 per cent of performers were correctly classified in karate (Terry and Slade, 1995) and 71 per cent of performers correctly classified in bobsleigh (Terry, 1993).

POMS Research: 'The baby and the bathwater' (Lane, 2007a)

Lane (2007a) described the state of affairs for prospective mood researchers considering starting a project in 1995. He contended that students planning to study mood would have been unclear on how to investigate mood–performance relationships given inconsistent evidence presented in the literature. Two research articles attempted to address this confusion. Beedie et al (2000) conducted two meta-analyses with each analysis producing vastly different results. The first meta-analysis summarized findings from studies that sought to link mood and athletic achievement by comparing the mood responses of elite and non-elite athletes. The value of this research question is questionable, that is, we would not expect the mood of an elite athlete and a club athlete to differ in any predictable way. The overall effect size (ES) was very small, a finding consistent with the previous meta-analysis by Rowley et al (1995). The second meta-analysis completed by Beedie et al included studies that examined the relationship between pre-competition mood and subsequent performance. This is arguably a more productive line of enquiry given that we would expect an athlete's mood to influence their performance.

Beedie et al concluded the following from their meta-analysis:

- Vigour is associated with facilitated performance, while confusion, fatigue and depression are associated with debilitated performance.

- Anger and tension were associated with facilitated performance in some studies and debilitated performance in others.

- Effects were very small for the debilitative effects of fatigue.

Application 2.1

Meta-analysis results of Beedie et al (2000)

Question: Can mood predict athletes of different levels of achievement, or do elite athletes have a monopoly on good mood?

Continued . . .

. . . Continued

Answer: No. The mean effect size was 0.10, suggesting that the relationship between mood and achievement was minimal. This concurs with 1 per cent of variance of performance that could be explained by variations in mood found by Rowley et al (1995).

Question: Can mood states predict performance when assessed shortly before competition?

Answer: Yes. A mean effect size = 0.31 indicates that mood measures assessed before a single performance have some predictive validity.

The conceptual model of Lane and Terry (2000) and the revised conceptual model proposed by Lane (2007a)

Focus 2.2

Lane and Terry's (2000) conceptual model

A theoretical model based on the mood states assessed by the Profile of Mood States in which depression is proposed to moderate relationships with performance for anger and tension. In the presence of depression, anger and tension are linked with poor performance, whereas in the absence of depression, anger and tension can be helpful for performance.

Why do mood states predict performance?

The nature of mood: Development of a theoretical model with a focus on depression

After identifying that mood states can predict performance, researchers continue to pose the question 'why do mood states predict performance?'. What is it about the nature of mood that influences performance? If mood states influence performance, how can intervention strategies lead to enhanced mood states before competition? (see Chapters 1 and 7). Turning to theoretical perspectives on the nature of mood, Lane and Terry (2000) developed a conceptual model around the mood states assessed in the POMS. A theory should offer a clear definition of what the construct is, and what it is not. A surprising feature of mood research in sport and exercise is the absence of a definition in the literature. Few authors offer a definition. To address this limitation, Lane and Terry (2000: 16) offered a tentative definition of mood as 'a set of feelings, ephemeral in nature, varying in intensity and duration, and usually involving more than one emotion'. Lane et al. (2005a) recently acknowledged a limitation of this definition in that emotion and mood are defined by each other (see Chapter 3 for further discussion). Lane et al accepted that measurement issues drove their early definition of mood. Lane et al used definitions of mood and emotion from the general psychology literature. Lazarus (2000b: 230) offered the following definition of emotion as 'an organized psycho-physiological reaction to ongoing relationships with the environment ... what mediates emotions psychologically is an evaluation, referred to as an appraisal, of the personal significance for the well-being that a person attributes to this relationship (... relational meaning), and the process'. Parkinson et al (1996: 216) proposed that 'mood reflects changing non-specific psychological dispositions to evaluate, interpret, and act on past, current, or future concerns in certain patterned ways'. Beedie et al (2005) discuss issues related to mood and emotion distinctions. These discussions are extensive and the interested reader is referred to this work. A key part of the definition forwarded by Lane and Terry (2000) was to demonstrate the transient nature of mood and argue that mood–performance research in sport should assess mood states before competition using the 'right now' response timeframe.

Lane and Terry (2000) explored the nature of each mood state assessed in the POMS. They offered a definition on the nature of each construct, identifying its antecedents and correlates, and describing its relationship with performance. After exploring the nature of each mood state in the POMS, Lane and Terry proposed that depressed mood should have the strongest influence on sport performance. Depressed mood is characterized by themes such as hopelessness, sadness and feeling miserable. Sport performance requires athletes to persevere in the face of adversity, drawing on personal resources to maximize their potential – in other words, depression is the antithesis of a mindset needed to bring about optimal performance. However, meta-analysis results of Beedie et al (2000) indicate a weak relationship between depression and performance.

In an attempt to address the issue of weak depression–performance relationships, data from several published studies were re-analysed (see Lane, 2007a, for a review), focusing on the depression scores. Following a close inspection of raw scores for depression, a pattern emerged which indicated that the modal score for depression from athletes close to competition was zero for all items. Around 50 per cent of athletes report zero for all items in the depression scale, therefore depressed mood data have variance in only half the participants in the sample. As performance scores would vary in all participants, around 50 per cent of data would show a zero correlation. The result of this is that the overall correlation would be weak (see Lane et al 2005b for a discussion on how the range in data influences the size of a correlation coefficient). Quite simply, correlation results tend to increase when the variance in data is large. Lane and Terry (1999) reported that only 39 per cent of athletes from a sample of 1317 athletes reported a depressed mood score of 1 or more on a 16-point scale. Depressed mood data dichotomize into two groups: a no-depression group, and participants scoring one or more on the depression scale. Lane and Terry (2000) labelled this latter group the depressed mood group.

A second key issue regarding the nature of mood–performance relationships concerned inconsistent results for anger and tension (Beedie et al, 2000). Anger/tension was associated with successful performance in some studies (Cockerill et al, 1991; Terry and Slade, 1995) and unsuccessful performance in other studies (Morgan, 1980). Lane and Terry (2000) hypothesized that anger and/or tension can be either facilitative or debilitative of performance, depending on interactions with depressed mood. Lane and Terry proposed that individuals in a depressed mood tend to direct feelings of anger internally, leading to suppression, self-blame and, ultimately, performance decrements (Spielberger, 1991). Similarly, such individuals tend to transfer tension into feelings of threat and worry, also leading to performance decrements. Conversely, in the absence of depressed mood, the arousal component of anger and tension can serve a functional role by signalling the need for positive action (see Lane, 2007a, for a review). Specifically, anger is likely to be expressed outwardly at the source of the original frustration (or displaced toward another object or person) and may be channelled productively into determination to succeed, and symptoms of tension are more likely to be interpreted as indicating a readiness to perform and be seen as facilitative of performance.

Lane and Terry (2000) proposed four main hypotheses. The first hypothesis is that anger, confusion, fatigue and tension will be higher and vigour will be lower among athletes experiencing depressed mood. The second hypothesis is that interrelationships among anger, confusion, fatigue, tension and vigour will be stronger for athletes experiencing depressed mood. The third hypothesis is that vigour will facilitate performance, and confusion and fatigue will debilitate performance regardless of the presence or absence of depressed mood. The fourth hypothesis is that anger and tension will be associated with debilitated performance among individuals reporting symptoms of depression, whereas anger and tension will show a curvilinear relationship with performance among individuals reporting no symptoms of depression.

Review of Lane and Terry's model

Lane (2007a) reported the 17 studies that tested the Lane and Terry (2000) model. All provided strong support for the hypothesis that participants in the depressed mood group would simultaneously report higher scores for anger, confusion, fatigue, and tension but lower vigour scores. The mean effect sizes (Cohen's d) for these mood dimensions were in the moderate to large categories – Anger: $M = 0.85$, SD = 0.25; Confusion: $M = 0.93$, SD = 0.25; Fatigue: $M = 0.79$, SD = 0.37; Tension: $M = 0.61$, SD = 0.27; and Vigour: $M = 0.51$, SD = 0.34. In terms of mood–performance relationships, results lend support for the switching effect for anger and tension. Anger and tension were positively related to performance in the no-depression group, and negatively related to performance in the depressed mood group. The switching effect was significant for both anger and tension but was clearly greater for anger. Vigour showed a moderate positive relationship with performance in both groups, whereas confusion and fatigue showed weak negative relationships. These findings support the notion that depressed mood moderates mood–performance relationships for anger and tension but not for confusion, fatigue and vigour, as hypothesized by Lane and Terry (2000).

When viewed collectively, studies testing Lane and Terry's model offer reasonable support for the central hypotheses (see Mellalieu, 2003, vs. Lane et al, 2005a, for a detailed discussion on the utility of the model). The model may represent a plausible theoretical explanation for the apparently contradictory findings highlighted in previous reviews of the mood–performance research. Second, the model provides testable hypotheses relevant to the POMS, a measure that despite much controversy is still widely used by researchers and applied sport psychologists.

Although the conceptual model has arguably advanced POMS-based research, Lane et al (2005a) highlighted that the POMS assesses a limited range of mood states (see Figure 2.3). The revised model included calmness and happiness and removed confusion. Confusion was removed because it is more of a cognitive state than a mood state. Confusion is arguably a manifestation of a mood disorder, rather than a mood state itself. The decision to include a greater number of positive mood states stems from applied work in which mood state responses were monitored among biathletes training at altitude (Lane et al, 2003, 2005c). Given the proposed influence of depressed mood, special attention was given to its detection. Self-reported happiness data helped detect maladaptive responses to training. Athletes reported high scores on the happiness scale and simultaneously reported zero on the depressed mood scale. When an athlete was not coping with training successfully, happiness scores deteriorated and fatigue scores increased. As happiness scores gradually deteriorated, the athlete started reporting some symptoms of depressed mood. Depressed mood was accompanied by confusion and anger. It appeared that reductions in happiness offered an early indicator to a possible rise in depression symptoms. Reductions in happiness over time could be used to monitor effective adaptation. Calmness was included not only to increase the range of positive mood states but also because it could offer insight into the nature of tension and anger when experienced in the absence of depressed mood. It is argued that if athletes are using anger and tension to motivate behaviour, and are in control of these states, athletes should report feeling calm, angry and tense.

The revised model focuses on the influence and interaction between pleasant mood states, unpleasant mood states and performance. Happiness is proposed to show a curvilinear relationship with performance. It is argued that happiness is associated with the superficial processing of information, which can have negative performance effects (Sinclair and Mark, 1992). Happiness is also proposed to increase the accessibility of positive material in the memory and, according to Hirt et al (1996), often leads to the recall of sufficient information to fill cognitive capacity, thereby debilitating performance through attentional overload. By contrast, happiness could be linked with high self-efficacy and therefore associated with enhanced performance through similar mechanisms. Therefore, it is argued that two additional hypotheses be included. The first is that happiness will show a curvilinear relationship with performance; the second is that calmness will show facilitative performance effects.

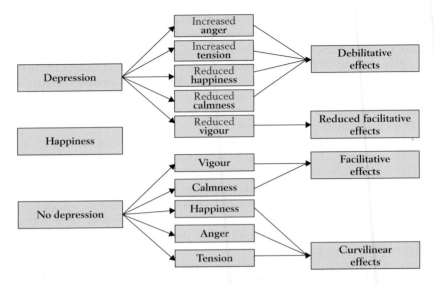

Figure 2.3 Revised conceptual model of mood and performance (see Lane, 2007a).

Ethical issues in research or practical application of mood and performance

Lane (2007b) in his chapter *Developing and Validating Psychometric Tests for Use in High Performance Settings* described and discussed ethical issues when testing athletes in high-performance settings. He indicated that a prospective research methodology that is sensitive to the range of psychological states experienced by individuals performing under stress needs to be developed for such a purpose. It is important to recognize that the act of data collection intrudes on the typical preparation of individuals in such situations. The act of completing a psychological inventory can make participants aware of how they feel. For example, asking a soccer penalty taker how anxious they feel before shooting could raise anxiety as the researcher has made the participant sensitive to how anxious they are feeling. What could follow from this is that the player, who is likely to have experienced anxiety previously, will make self-regulatory efforts to reduce anxiety. Theoretically, researchers do not wish to change the construct they are seeking to assess, and if such research has damaging effects on participants beyond the benefits of conducting the research, then the study is unethical. Research teams need to consider the research skills of data collectors and investigate the extent to which asking the question leads participants to becoming aware of how they are feeling, and possibly engaging in strategies to change how they feel.

Conclusions

Athletes commonly report that emotional states influence thoughts and behaviour during competition. Research that has used appropriate methods has found support for the notion that mood states influence performance. A great deal of research investigated whether mood states of athletes were different to the mood states of non-athletes, or whether elite athletes have a better mood than non-elite athletes. I have argued that there is no theoretical basis for this research question and that it is not surprising that mood–performance relationships are weak. Lane and Terry (2000) developed a conceptual model for mood–performance relationships that emphasized the importance of depressed mood in interpreting POMS scores. Terry et al (1999) developed a valid and internally reliable scale for assessing athletes before competition, and thus between the studies, theoretical and methodological issues were clarified. Lane (2007a) reviews studies that have tested Lane and Terry's model and found support for the switching effect for anger–performance relationships.

Key concepts and terms

Emotion
Iceberg profile
Lane and Terry's (2000)
   conceptual model

Meta-analysis
Mood

Sample essay titles

- Sport psychology should 'abandon the POMS'. With reference to theory and empirical evidence discuss this proposition.
- Terry (1995a) proposed that mood states predict performance when certain methodological conditions are met. Describe and evaluate these methodological conditions with reference to theory and research.
- The POMS offers an overly narrow conceptualization of mood. Discuss this finding with reference to Lane and Terry's (2000) conceptual model of mood–performance relationships.
- Critically evaluate Lane and Terry's (2000) conceptual model. Use theory and research to support your ideas.

Further reading

Books

Lane, A.M. (2007a). 'The rise and fall of the iceberg: Development of a conceptual model of mood-performance relationships.' In: A.M. Lane (Ed.), *Mood and Human Performance: Conceptual, Measurement, and Applied Issues.* Hauppauge, NY: Nova Science, 1–34.

Lane, A.M. (2007b). *Mood and Human Performance: Conceptual, Measurement, and Applied Issues.* Hauppauge, NY: Nova Science.

Lane, A.M. (2007c). 'Developing and validating psychometric tests for use in high performance settings.' In: L. Boyar (Ed.), *Psychological Tests and Testing Research*. Hauppauge, NY: Nova Science, 203–213.

Parkinson, B., Totterdell, P., Briner, R.B., and Reynolds, S. (1996). *Changing Moods: The Psychology of Mood and Mood Regulation*. London: Longman.

Journal articles

Beedie, C.J., Terry, P.C., and Lane, A.M. (2000). The profile of mood states and athletic performance: Two meta-analyses. *Journal of Applied Sport Psychology*, 12, 49–68.

Beedie, C.J., Terry, P.C., and Lane, A.M. (2005). Distinguishing mood from emotion. *Cognition and Emotion*, 19, 847–878.

Lane, A.M., and Terry, P.C. (2000). The nature of mood: Development of a conceptual model with a focus on depression. *Journal of Applied Sport Psychology*, 12, 16–33.

Lane, A.M., Beedie, C.J., and Stevens, M.J. (2005a). Mood matters: A response to Mellalieu. *Journal of Applied Sport Psychology*, 17, 319–325.

Mellalieu, S.D. (2003). Mood matters: But how much? A comment on Lane and Terry (2000). *Journal of Applied Sport Psychology*, 15, 99–114.

Rowley, A.J., Landers, D.M., Kyllo, L.B., and Etnier, J.L. (1995). Does the Iceberg Profile discriminate between successful and less successful athletes? A meta-analysis. *Journal of Sport & Exercise Psychology*, 16, 185–199.

Terry, P.C. (1995a). The efficacy of mood state profiling among elite competitors: A review and synthesis. *The Sport Psychologist*, 9, 309–324.

3 Anxiety in sport: Should we be worried or excited?

Mark Uphill

Although research illustrates that athletes experience a range of emotions (e.g. Hanin, 2000; Uphill and Jones, 2007a), it has predominantly focused on the antecedents (causes) and consequences of anxiety (Woodman and Hardy, 2001a). To illustrate sport researchers' interest, a literature search limited to the term 'anxiety' using SportDiscus™ revealed 489, 1026 and 1207 articles published on anxiety during the periods 1970–79, 1980–89, and 1990–99, respectively. During the period 2000–06, an average of 161 articles per year were published. This chapter begins by exploring the characteristics, antecedents and consequences of anxiety. By identifying contemporary and contentious issues, it is intended that the reader will develop a thorough understanding of this fascinating area of study.

Learning outcomes

When you have completed this chapter you should be able to:

1. Describe the main characteristics and causes of anxiety.
2. Discuss the strengths and weaknesses of anxiety measures.
3. Evaluate theories that address the anxiety–performance relationship.
4. Describe some strategies that an applied sport psychologist might use to help athletes deal with anxiety.

Defining anxiety

An enduring problem in sport psychology research has been the inconsistent and imprecise use of the terms 'arousal', 'stress' and 'anxiety' (cf. Woodman and Hardy, 2001a). Given that inconsistent definitions are likely to lead to divergent conclusions, it is important to be clear about the terminology used. Anxiety refers to an unpleasant emotion which is characterized by vague but persistent feelings of apprehension and dread (Cashmore, 2002). According to Frederickson (2001), there is consensus that an emotion is a cognitively appraised response to an event, either conscious or unconscious. This is likely to 'trigger a cascade of response tendencies across loosely-coupled component systems, such as subjective experience, facial expression, cognitive processing and physiological changes' (Frederickson, 2001: 218).

Frederickson's (2001) definition reflects several key aspects of competition anxiety. First, anxiety is a multifaceted response (e.g. it has cognitive and somatic symptoms). Second, the notion that an emotion is a reaction to an event has often been used to differentiate emotion from the related construct of mood (see Chapter 2). In practice, it may be difficult to differentiate anxiety as an emotion from the mood state of anxiety. For example, Lane and Terry (2000) contended that it may be difficult for athletes to differentiate between feelings that arise in relation to a specific stimulus and those that may already be present as part of an underlying mood state. While the response stem 'please rate how you are feeling in relation to the upcoming competition' may help to differentiate emotion from mood (e.g. Jones et al, 2005), difficulties nevertheless remain.

Arousal has been defined as 'the extent of release of potential energy, stored in the tissues of the organism, as this is shown in activity or response' (Duffy, 1962: 179). Such a response has been viewed as lying on a continuum from deep sleep to extreme excitement. This rather vague and imprecise definition of arousal has given way to increasingly sophisticated conceptualizations. For example, rather than arousal being considered a unitary response, evidence suggests that at least three different forms of arousal can be differentiated (Woodman and Hardy, 2001a): electro-cortical activity (electrical activity measured in the cortex via an electro-encephalogram, or EEG), autonomic activity (physiological indices such as galvanic skin response, heart rate or blood pressure) or behavioural activity (overt activity).

Stress has sometimes been viewed as being synonymous with anxiety. However, stress is arguably a broader construct than anxiety (e.g. Lazarus, 1999). Jones (1990) described stress as a state in which some demand is placed on an individual who is required to cope with the demands of the situation. Stress, then, may or may not place a 'strain' on athletes (e.g. Lazarus, 1966); it will be influenced by the **appraisal** (or evaluation) of one's ability to cope (see Chapter 5). Importantly, and as alluded to above, how athletes appraise particular situations is believed to impact the emotions experienced (e.g. Lazarus, 2000a; Uphill and Jones, 2007a). If an athlete perceives a stressor (e.g. a footballer taking a penalty kick) as a threat, and doubts their ability to succeed, then the most likely emotion elicited will be anxiety. If one accepts that anxiety is an emotion and that some type of cognitive evaluation necessarily precedes an emotion (see Ochsner and Gross, 2007), then to understand how anxiety arises it is imperative to examine the cognitive precursors to anxiety.

Activity 3.1

We all know how it feels to be anxious, don't we? Think about an important competition, one in which your sport performance really mattered. Think about the days leading up to the event, the day of the competition, and the minutes immediately prior to competition. How do you feel when you become anxious? What thoughts do you have? Do you notice any bodily sensations? How do you behave? Write down all the symptoms of anxiety that you can recall, whether it be single adjectives (e.g. uneasy, nervous) or complete sentences (e.g. 'I was pacing round the living room on the morning of the event' or 'I couldn't keep still'). What, if anything, changed as competition approached? How easy is it for you to recall how you felt and how valid do you think such descriptions are? Compare your responses to the items listed in the Competitive State Anxiety Inventory-2 (CSAI-2; Martens et al, 1990). Do you think this measurement instrument possesses 'face validity' (i.e. adequately captures what you perceive to be anxiety?).

Measurement of anxiety

Since Spielberger's (1966) seminal work distinguishing between trait and state anxiety, several scales to measure these constructs have been developed. While state anxiety concerns an individual's response to a specific situation, trait anxiety represents a general disposition to respond to a variety of situations with heightened levels of state anxiety (e.g. Martens et al, 1990). A 15-item Sport Competition Anxiety Test (SCAT; Martens, 1977) has historically been used to measure a person's level of trait anxiety in sport. This *unidimensional* measure (i.e. assuming that trait anxiety has a single dimension) has however been superseded by the Sport Anxiety Scale (SAS; Smith et al, 1990a). In contrast to the SCAT, the SAS is a **multidimensional** (anxiety is comprised of several facets) instrument comprising 21 items grouped into three sub-scales: worry, **somatic anxiety** (one's perception of physiological symptoms associated with the anxiety experience) and concentration disruption.

Several studies have indicated that the SAS has at least three items that illustrate measurement shortcomings (e.g. Prapavessis et al, 2005), particularly when administered to child athletes. Accordingly, Smith et al (2006) developed a revised version of the SAS, the Sport Anxiety Scale-2. The SAS-2 has 15 items which load onto three sub-scales each comprising five items: somatic anxiety (e.g. 'My body feels tense'), worry (e.g. 'I worry that I will not play well') and concentration disruption (e.g. 'It is hard to concentrate on the game'), which, on initial testing, has been demonstrated to possess adequate validity and reliability.

The Competitive State Anxiety Inventory-2 (CSAI-2; Martens et al, 1990) has largely been the instrument of choice for measuring competitive *state* anxiety. The CSAI-2 comprises 27 items measuring the *intensity* of **cognitive anxiety** (symptoms such as worry and negative expectations associated with the anxiety experience), somatic anxiety and self-confidence. Nine items are contained within each sub-scale with each item rated on a four-point Likert scale ranging from 1 (*not at all*) to 4 (*very much so*). Although the CSAI-2 has been, and remains, a popular research and applied tool it has attracted a number of criticisms.

Criticisms and limitations of the CSAI-2

First, concerns have been raised about the validity of the cognitive anxiety sub-scale. Although Martens et al (1990) defined cognitive anxiety as reflecting negative expectations about performance, Lane et al (1999) suggested that only one item ('I have self-doubts') genuinely assesses cognitive anxiety. The remaining items (e.g. 'I am concerned about this competition') may not necessarily reflect cognitive anxiety, but rather a perception of the importance of the event. Limitations have also been identified with the somatic anxiety sub-scale. Martens et al (1990: 121) defined somatic anxiety as the 'physiological and affective elements of the anxiety experience that develop directly from autonomic arousal'. Kerr (1997) suggested that increases in physiological arousal may accompany other emotions (e.g. excitement). Thus, if items on the somatic anxiety scale (e.g. 'my heart is racing') are assessing perceptions of athletes' physiological state, it is conceivable that high scores on this scale may not necessarily be indicative of heightened anxiety. Indeed, Schachter (1964) proposed that emotion is a product of individuals' cognitive appraisal of physiological arousal. To illustrate, heightened physiological arousal could be interpreted as excitement if an athlete is competing against an athlete they have long admired, or fear if they are about to go scuba diving for the first time for example. Although Cox, Martens and Russell (2003) have developed a revised CSAI-2 (CSAI-2R) which addresses some of the concerns highlighted by Lane et al (1999a), it also arguably shares limitations of construct validity highlighted above.

Besides measuring the intensity of anxiety symptoms, researchers have also highlighted the necessity of measuring the frequency (Swain and Jones, 1993) and 'direction' (Jones et al, 1993) of anxiety symptoms. With regards to the former, Swain and Jones (1993) appended a frequency scale to each item of the CSAI-2 asking 'How frequently do you experience this thought or feeling?' on a scale of 1 (*not at all*) through to 7 (*all the time*). Although intensity and frequency components are related, they should nonetheless be viewed as independent dimensions which individually contribute to athletes' affective (e.g. anxiety) experience (Diener et al, 1991). Indeed, compared to the intensity of symptoms, individuals may report frequency components of the emotion response with greater accuracy and less recall bias (Diener et al, 1991).

In sport, Mahoney and Avener (1977) first documented that anxiety could be interpreted in different ways by athletes. A measure to assess the 'direction' of anxiety – the CSAI-2(d) – was developed by Jones and Swain (1992). Similar to assessing the frequency of anxiety symptoms, Jones and Swain attached a scale (ranging from −3, through 0 to 3) to each item of the CSAI-2, asking performers to rate the extent to which they perceive each thought or feeling to either debilitate or facilitate performance respectively. Indeed, a model of facilitative and debilitative anxiety (Jones, 1995; Figure 3.1) presents coping and goal attainment as important mediators of anxiety interpretation.

The addition of the directional dimension has arguably conferred some advantages. For instance, Jones et al (1993) observed no differences between

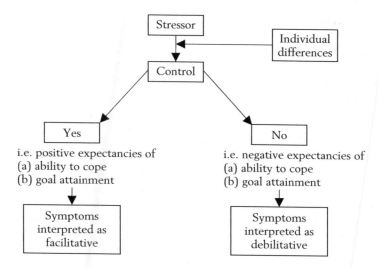

Figure 3.1 A model of facilitative and debilitative anxiety.

high-performance and low-performance gymnasts in cognitive anxiety intensity, somatic anxiety intensity and somatic anxiety direction. However, high-performance gymnasts reported their cognitive anxiety symptoms as more facilitative to performance than their low-performance counterparts. The differentiation of the measurement of anxiety into separate components has also been recently supported by Hanton, Jones and Maynard (2004), who indicated that patterning of the intensity, frequency and directional interpretation of anxiety differed as the time approached competition. Finally, on a practical note, it could be argued that changes in the frequency and direction of reported anxiety symptoms are useful indicators of intervention effectiveness independent of any change in anxiety intensity (cf. Uphill and Jones, 2007b).

Activity 3.2

The three scoring systems of the MRF are provided. Based on your understanding of anxiety, decide which instrument you would be most likely to use, and justify why. Having done this, you may wish to refer to the original article by Krane (1994), and perhaps consider whether by combining the approaches an MRF-4 might be viable! Use the MRF to plot your responses 2 weeks, 1 week, 1 day, and 30 minutes prior to a forthcoming sport competition. What do you think will happen to your scores and why? Some articles you may wish to refer to are Butt et al, 2003 and Hanton et al, 2004.

Krane, V. (1994). The Mental Readiness Form as a measure of competitive state anxiety. *The Sport Psychologist*, 8, 189–202.

Continued . . .

. . . Continued

Original MRF

My thoughts are:

Calm _____ Worried

My body feels:

Relaxed _____ Tense

I am feeling:

Confident _____ Scared

(Scores are obtained by measuring in millimetres the mark on the line corresponding to how you feel. Scores range from 0 to 100 for each item.)

MRF Likert

My thoughts are:

1	2	3	4	5	6	7	8	9	10	11
Calm   Worried

My body feels:

1	2	3	4	5	6	7	8	9	10	11
Relaxed   Tense

I am feeling:

1	2	3	4	5	6	7	8	9	10	11
Confident   Scared

MRF-3

My thoughts are:

1	2	3	4	5	6	7	8	9	10	11
Worried   Not worried

My body feels:

1	2	3	4	5	6	7	8	9	10	11
Tense   Not tense

I am feeling:

1	2	3	4	5	6	7	8	9	10	11
Confident   Not confident

Increasing debate continues regarding the concept of 'facilitative anxiety'. Burton and Naylor (1997) suggested that 'anxiety' symptoms that are interpreted as facilitative are unlikely to be labelled as anxiety. Further, researchers mislabel positive emotions (e.g. excitement) as facilitative anxiety. Re-phrased, if anxiety is defined and characterized by uncertainty regarding goal attainment and perceived threat, a state in which individuals hold positive beliefs in their ability to cope with the situation and achieve their goals, by definition cannot be anxiety (cf. Jones and Uphill, 2004)!

Based on this measurement conundrum, Jones and Uphill (2004) contended that researchers can adopt three different perspectives regarding the use of the modified CSAI-2(d). First, symptoms reported on the intensity sub-scales assess the intensity of anxiety, and the direction scale assesses athletes' beliefs about the way these symptoms impact performance. A second perspective holds that high scores on the intensity sub-scales may be representative of some state other than anxiety (e.g., excitement) and the perception sub-scales assess athletes' beliefs about the way these symptoms impact performance. Finally, even if the intensity sub-scales may be reflective of more than one emotional state, it might be possible to distinguish anxiety (perception that these symptoms debilitate performance) from other states (perception that the symptoms improve performance) on the basis of the directional scale. Jones and Uphill (2004) asked athletes to complete the modified CSAI-2 as if they were either anxious or excited prior to the most important game of the season. Results suggested that participants in the anxious group reported significantly higher scores on the intensity sub-scales compared to the excited group, while the excited group reported a more facilitative perception of their symptoms on the somatic anxiety sub-scale. However, the magnitude of differences was typically small, with about one in three participants being incorrectly classified as excited or anxious on the basis of scores from the CSAI-2(d). Given such criticisms, some caution is needed when interpreting data derived from the CSAI-2.

The CSAI-2, the CSAI-2R and the CSAI-2(d) are relatively long instruments for athletes to complete prior to, or during, competition. The Mental Readiness Form was developed by Murphy et al (1989) as a brief instrument that could potentially be used immediately prior to, or even during, competition. Krane (1994) later extended the MRF by examining three different methods of scoring the instrument (see Activity box 3.2). Indeed a five-item measure of anxiety is contained within the recently validated Sport Emotion Questionnaire (SEQ; Jones et al, 2005). Although researchers (and practitioners) are not short of instruments that purportedly assess anxiety, several of these instruments possess a number of limitations that, at the least, demand a healthy dose of scepticism when interpreting the results.

Sources of anxiety

According to Gould, Petlichkof and Weinberg (1984), if sport psychologists could identify the antecedents of anxiety in a competitive situation then appropriate interventions could be designed to help athletes. Owing to the

Focus 3.1

Understanding the challenge of facilitative anxiety

Based on the issues reviewed, there are a number of challenges confronting researchers of anxiety in sport. Conceptually, there appears to be a consensus that an emotional state that is *felt as unpleasant* may not necessarily be associated with negative impacts on performance (e.g. Woodman and Hardy, 2001a). (As an aside, positive emotional states, although felt as pleasant, need not necessarily or always be associated with adaptive response to competition either!) There is the theoretical challenge of explaining how anxiety (or any other emotional state for that matter) may confer both advantages and disadvantages for sport performance. In addition there is the methodological and measurement challenge of differentiating an affective state (i.e. anxiety) from *athletes' perceptions* of the impact of that affective state on performance, and the *actual* impact on performance. With emotion being seen as a state that is influenced by athletes' appraisals, beliefs or evaluations about the impact of that state upon performance will theoretically impact the affective state itself (e.g. Lazarus, 2000b; Jones and Uphill, 2004). It is disentangling this issue that has arguably generated much of the controversy surrounding 'facilitative anxiety' to date.

ethical issues associated with the manipulation of variables that are hypothesized to cause anxiety, researchers have tended to examine correlations between factors that are thought to cause anxiety and the intensity of the anxiety response (cf. Woodman and Hardy, 2001a). A brief selection of personal and situational antecedents of anxiety is reported below.

Trait anxiety

Athletes who exhibit high levels of trait anxiety are more likely to interpret sports situations as threatening compared to their less trait-anxious counterparts (e.g. Spielberger, 1966). 'High' and 'low' trait-anxious individuals may not represent homogeneous groups. Based on the seminal work of Weinberger, Schwarz and Davidson (1979), some individuals exhibit physiological and behavioural reactions that are not compatible with a paper and pencil test of trait anxiety. Individuals who display this response are defined by (a) low scores on trait anxiety, and (b) high scores on a measure of defensiveness (the Marlowe–Crowne social desirability scale). This subgroup of low trait-anxious individuals are labelled as 'repressors' in such research and are distinguished from the 'truly low anxious', who score low on both measures of trait anxiety and defensiveness (e.g. Brosschot et al, 1999). There is the suggestion that repressors are in fact high anxious individuals (and may not necessarily be cognisant of their symptoms) who claim not to be anxious on self-report measures. Similarly, high trait-anxious individuals may also be subdivided into groups based on their defensiveness scores. Most researchers in sport have not acknowledged this distinction.

Perfectionism

How perfectionism influences sport performance is subject to considerable debate. On the one hand, although some view perfectionism as a trait that makes Olympic champions (e.g. Gould et al, 2002a), others see perfectionism as a characteristic that undermines rather than facilitates performance (Anshel and Mansouri, 2005; Flett and Hewitt, 2005). This apparent paradox has been evidenced in several studies (e.g. Stoeber et al, 2007). Stoeber et al suggested that perfectionism is a multifaceted construct, and while some dimensions may be harmful or maladaptive, others may be benign or adaptive. The maladaptive dimensions have the potential to adversely influence cognitive processes and, by extension, the anxiety response (Stoeber et al, 2007).

Self-handicapping

Self-handicapping is a term used to describe the process of proactively reducing effort and creating performance excuses to protect oneself from potentially negative feedback in evaluative environments such as sport (Berglas and Jones, 1978). According to Berglas and Jones (1978: 406), self-handicapping involves 'any action or choice of performance setting that enhances the opportunity to externalize (or excuse) failure and to internalize (reasonably accept credit for) success'. For example, a rugby player might buy a take-away meal the night before a big game, making the excuse that, in the event of a poor performance it is attributable to poor nutrition as opposed to any deficit in personal ability. However, should a positive performance ensue, such a self-handicap affords the opportunity to enhance one's self-esteem (e.g. I must be a good rugby player if I can perform well after eating what I did!)

The adoption of self-handicapping strategies may serve both self-protection and self-enhancement motives then (Tice, 1991). Although self-handicapping affords athletes the opportunity to externalize a poor performance (and thereby protect self-esteem), it also increases the likelihood of failure (cf. Kuczka and Treasure, 2004). With regards to anxiety, it is proposed that self-handicapping is most likely when an individual perceives a threat to their self-esteem (Prapavessis and Grove, 1998) or feels uncertain about their ability (Berglas and Jones, 1978).

Characteristics of sport event

The type of competition (e.g. individual vs. team sports or contact vs. non-contact sports) has been associated with differences in state anxiety, with individual and contact sport participants reporting higher levels of anxiety than their team and non-contact sport counterparts (Simon and Martens, 1977). The importance of the event has also been associated with changes in anxiety; more important events are associated with a heightened anxiety response (Dowthwaite and Armstrong, 1984).

Time to competition

Studies using the 'time-to-event' paradigm (i.e. measuring competitive state anxiety in the time leading up to competition) support the multidimensional conceptualization of anxiety in that different patterns of responding in cognitive anxiety and somatic anxiety are observed. Specifically, whereas cognitive anxiety remains high and stable in the period leading up to competition, somatic anxiety remains fairly low up until one or two days prior to competition and then increases steadily until the point at which the competition commences (e.g. Gould et al, 1984).

Appraisal

The basic premise of appraisal theories of emotion is straightforward: emotions appear to be related to how people evaluate events in their lives (Parrott, 2001). For example, imagine that you have just lost a hockey match by a single goal and one of your parents is criticising you for poor positioning, which allowed your opponent to score the critical goal. What emotion(s) would you experience in response to this situation? Perhaps you would respond angrily if you consider the criticism to be unjustified and that you were in a poor position because a team-mate had lost possession. Alternatively, if you consider that your error directly impacted upon the result you may feel guilty or disappointed. Several appraisal theories (e.g. Lazarus, 1991; Roseman, 1991; Smith and Ellsworth, 1985), although differing slightly in their detail, attempt to understand the role of appraisal in the generation of emotion. One appraisal theory in particular, cognitive motivational relational theory (CMR; Lazarus, 1991) has been purported to be applicable to sport (Lazarus, 2000a), is increasingly being used to inform research (e.g. Skinner and Brewer, 2004) and has received support for some of its tenets (Hammermeister and Burton, 2001; Uphill and Jones, 2007a). However, in general there is a need for more research examining the relationships between appraisal components and anxiety in athletes.

Effects of anxiety on sport performance

Early approaches to the investigation of the anxiety–performance relationship such as drive theory and the inverted-U hypothesis (see Woodman and Hardy, 2001a) were based upon unidimensional conceptualizations of *physiological arousal* and are now largely ignored by anxiety researchers (see Jones, 1995; Woodman and Hardy, 2001a, for the limitations of these models).

The multidimensional examination of the anxiety–performance relationship was propagated by multidimensional anxiety theory (Martens et al, 1990). Martens et al predicted that cognitive anxiety would exhibit a negative linear relationship with performance, because worrying depleted a limited capacity attentional resource. A curvilinear (inverted-U) relationship was postulated between physiologically-based somatic anxiety and performance.

Somewhat equivocal support has been obtained for Martens et al's predictions regarding components of anxiety and performance (Burton, 1988; Gould et al, 1984). Indeed, recent meta-analyses (Craft et al, 2003; Woodman and Hardy, 2003) are similarly inconclusive. Importantly, Hardy and Parfitt (1991) observe that multidimensional anxiety theory attempts to explain the three-dimensional relationship between cognitive anxiety, somatic anxiety and performance in terms of a series of two-dimensional relationships.

Catastrophe models extend multidimensional anxiety theory by making predictions about the *interactive* effects of cognitive anxiety and physiological arousal on performance. Two catastrophe models of the anxiety–performance relationship have been related to sport: the 'butterfly catastrophe', and, more commonly, the 'cusp catastrophe'. The **cusp catastrophe** model (see Figure 3.2) is used to describe the interactive effects of cognitive anxiety and physiological arousal on performance and makes several assertions with regard to the anxiety–performance relationship. Specifically, at low levels of cognitive anxiety, changes in physiological arousal should lead to small, continuous changes in performance. Second, when physiological arousal is high, a negative correlation is postulated between cognitive anxiety and performance. Finally, when cognitive anxiety is high, the effect of physiological arousal upon performance may be either positive or negative (Hardy and Parfitt, 1991). Indeed, some support for the predictions made by the cusp catastrophe model has been obtained (e.g. Hardy and Parfitt, 1991; Hardy et al, 1994).

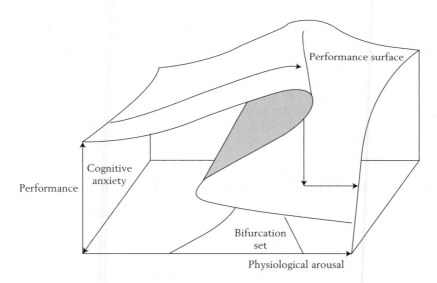

Figure 3.2 Cusp catastrophe model of anxiety.

Source: Fazey and Hardy, 1988: 25.

The butterfly catastrophe model (Hardy, 1990) contains the addition of two further dimensions: a *bias* factor and a *butterfly* factor. A detailed consideration of the butterfly catastrophe model is beyond the scope of the present chapter, as it remains largely untested within sport (see Hardy, 1996b for an exception). The inclusion of a bias factor is reported to have the effect of swinging the front edge to the right or left. Although this is quite difficult to visualize, according to this contention, under high levels of cognitive anxiety, highly self-confident performers would be hypothesized to withstand a greater intensity of physiological arousal before experiencing a decrement in performance than their less confident counterparts (Hardy, 1990). Some initial support for this proposition has been obtained by Hardy and colleagues (Hardy, 1996b; Hardy et al, 2004).

Although catastrophe models generally seem advantageous in that they account for some of the inconsistencies in previous research and model multiple factors in describing the impact of anxiety, they do not explain *how* anxiety impacts performance. A number of explanations about how anxiety impacts performance are described briefly below.

Processing efficiency theory

Processing efficiency theory (Eysenck and Calvo, 1992) predicts that worry (i.e. cognitive anxiety) depletes the processing and storage capacity of working memory, effectively diverting attention from task-relevant cues. Processing efficiency theory also predicts that worry may stimulate on-task effort. Specifically, to avoid aversive consequences associated with poor performance, anxious individuals may allocate additional processing resources to the task. This acts to (a) reduce processing efficiency (described as performance effectiveness divided by the processing resources required for the task) and, crucially, (b) maintain performance levels by increasing working memory capacity. Williams, Vickers and Rodriguez (2002) examined participants' performance in a table-tennis accuracy task when under high and low cognitive load. Although cognitive anxiety impaired performance under both high and low cognitive load, its impact on processing efficiency was less in the low mental load condition. Processing efficiency theory as an explanation of how anxiety impacts performance, then, is beginning to receive some support within sport psychology (e.g. Murray and Janelle, 2003; Wilson et al, 2006), and may help to explain why anxiety may sometimes lead to improved performance (i.e. motivating performers to exert more effort on a task).

Conscious processing (or reinvestment) hypothesis

The conscious processing hypothesis suggests that a reinvestment of controlled processing or a tendency to induce conscious control over a typically automated movement causes the sudden degradation of skilled performance when a performer is anxious (e.g. Baumeister, 1984; Masters, 1992). This is ostensibly an extension of the 'paralysis-by-analysis' phenomenon, whereby anxiety 'encourages' athletes to turn attention to the skill processes underlying performance, and may in extreme cases lead to 'choking' (see also Moran, 2004). In a recent comparison of self-focus versus processing efficiency explanations of anxiety–performance associations, Wilson et al (2007) asked participants to perform a simulated rally driving task. Conditions were manipulated to direct the focus of attention towards the explicit monitoring of driving or a secondary task, and each condition was performed under evaluative and non-evaluative conditions (designed to manipulate anxiety). Results showed little change in driving performance in the high-threat explicit monitoring condition compared with either the low-threat or the high-threat distraction conditions. Compared to conditions of low threat, mental effort increased in both the high-threat conditions (i.e. when directing attention towards versus away from the primary task). Performance effectiveness was maintained under threat although this was at the expense of reduced processing efficiency, lending stronger support to the predictions of processing efficiency theory. Besides these cognitive accounts of how anxiety impacts performance, it is possible that the physiological arousal associated with anxiety could impact directly upon performance (cf. Jones and Uphill, 2004).

Physiological arousal and performance

High levels of arousal accompanying anxiety may enhance performance on simple tasks (Parfitt et al, 1995). Parfitt et al (1995), for example, found that increased physiological arousal was positively related to height jumped in university age basketball players. However, there are few if any sport tasks whereby success is determined solely by strength; even skills such as weightlifting require attention and coordination to be successful.

Enhanced arousal then could increase muscular tension, leading to a decrement in fine motor control (Parfitt et al, 1990). Indeed, Noteboom and colleagues (2001a,b) observed that performance on a sub-maximal isometric pinch task was characterized by a decrease in steadiness under conditions of high arousal. In sport, Collins et al (2001) reported a change in the movement pattern of soldiers required to perform a stepping task on two parallel bars 20 metres off the ground and weightlifters performing the snatch lift.

What does this mean for practice?

Several strategies have been used or recommended to influence athletes' anxiety (e.g. Hanton and Jones, 1999; Jones, 2003). Typically, multimodal interventions (i.e. comprising a number of strategies) are used to either reduce the intensity of symptoms or encourage athletes to evaluate their symptoms more positively (e.g. Uphill and Jones, 2007b). Although space precludes a full consideration of these techniques, a number of exercises are illustrated below (see also Chapter 1). First, applied practitioners might encourage athletes to recognize the distinction between what media commentators might describe as 'pressure situations' and pressure responses (see also Moran, 2004). Because anxiety is believed to arise as a consequence of how one appraises a situation, we might not be able to influence the situations in which we find ourselves, but we can exert some control over how we think and behave in response to it.

Application 3.1

'What if' scenarios

If anxiety is associated with uncertainty, then using a strategy to reduce athletes' uncertainty would be predicted to attenuate their anxiety. Indeed, in a qualitative study by Uphill and Jones (2004), athletes reported using 'prospective coping' or planning to minimize anxiety. One sailor remarked, 'I

Continued . . .

... *Continued*

make sure everything that's surrounding my campaign is in decent shape ... then I make a plan for the next day. If the race starts at 11 o'clock we'll be there at 9 o'clock to rig the boat ...' (Uphill and Jones, 2004: 85).

Using 'what if' scenarios encourages athletes to (a) identify as many as possible situations or events that might 'go wrong' prior to or during competition, and (b) identify solutions to these difficulties. For example, what if your contact lens falls out while playing rugby? What if the wicket keeper starts to 'sledge' (or verbally distract) me during the innings? Think of your own 'what ifs ...?' in relation to the sport that you participate in, and try to identify solutions to the issues that you identify.

Thinking critically about simulation training

Miller (Miller, B., 1997) described how the Australian women's hockey team practised under adverse conditions (e.g. gamesmanship, 'poor' umpiring decisions) as part of their preparation for the 1988 Olympics. Why might simulation training reduce athletes' anxiety? Using SportDiscus™ or PsycInfo™ can you locate any articles that report the use of simulation training to help athletes cope with anxiety? How confident can you be that any reduction in anxiety can be attributed to the technique of simulation training? Why do you reach this conclusion?

Application 3.2

Cognitive restructuring

Because anxiety is associated with worry, and appraising a situation or event in a threatening manner, restructuring such thoughts would be expected to help athletes control their anxiety. This exercise is intended to illustrate how an applied sport psychologist may help an athlete modify a threatening situation (adapted from Moran, 2004). To begin, think carefully of a situation in your sport or daily life that typically makes you feel anxious. Now describe this scenario by completing the following sentence:

'I hate the pressure of ....,'

For example, you might write, 'I hate the pressure of trying to meet tight deadlines, when I've not done enough preparation', or 'I hate the pressure of my parents watching me perform a new gymnastics routine for the first time'. Now recall that pressure situation again. On this occasion, however, think about the situation in a different light, and attempt to complete the following sentence:

'I love the challenge of ....,'

Rather than merely repeating what you wrote above, you have to focus on something else besides the fear of making a mistake in front of your parents in the above example.

Implications and further directions

Anxiety is a multifaceted response that may help and/or hinder performance. Based on the preceding discourse, it can be suggested that researchers are faced with a number of challenges. First, differentiating the measurement of anxiety from its consequences arguably represents one important avenue for substantial progression in the field to occur. The multifaceted nature of anxiety may require a multifaceted explanation of how anxiety impacts performance. Much might be gained from the thoughtful integration of existing approaches as well as the development of new theories and models. With regard to the former, Hardy, Beattie and Woodman (2007) have 'merged' processing efficiency theory with the cusp catastrophe model to examine the association between anxiety and performance, albeit in a non-sport-related task. With regard to the latter, developments may be made by building bridges between sport and other areas of psychology. For example, Gross and colleagues have indicated that how individuals regulate their emotions can have divergent physiological, cognitive and experiential consequences (e.g. Gross, 1998). Attempts to suppress emotions, for instance, have been associated with a heightened physiological response and reduced memory compared to reappraisal.

Cerin et al (2000) highlighted that much of the research on competitive emotions has examined emotions (including anxiety) pre-competitively. Because athletes' emotional state may fluctuate during competition, assessing the impact of emotions during performance represents something of a 'holy grail' (see Focus box 3.2). There are a number of interesting avenues beyond the anxiety–performance relationship for researchers to explore, however. Although the progression of science has been described as 'standing on the shoulders of giants', researchers not only need to follow the well-trodden paths made by these giants, but also be brave enough to walk in less well charted territory.

Focus 3.2

Ethical issues involved in examining the emotion–performance relationship

If the 'holy grail' of anxiety research is being able to understand the processes or mechanisms by which anxiety impacts performance when it arguably matters most (i.e. at the height of competition), what ethical issues are researchers confronted with when investigating this relationship? Having identified what you perceive to be the ethical issues associated with this type of research, consider the strategies that researchers could use to circumvent these problems. How would you attempt to examine the anxiety–performance relationship, and why would you go about it in this way?

Examining *athletes'* anxiety is a well-trodden path. There remain many other populations such as coaches, sports officials, even spectators, for whom understanding something about their anxiety might yield important advances. In coaches or spectators, for example, how might the experience of chronic anxiety relate to various health implications?

Much has been done in relation to examining athletes' emotions at different times in relation to competition (e.g. Butt et al, 2003). There remains the possibility of examining not only individuals' current experience of anxiety but also their retrospective and prospective evaluations of their anxiety levels. Specifically, individuals may exhibit systematic biases insofar as they are inclined to anticipate that future negative experiences will last longer and be more intense than in fact they are (e.g. Gilbert et al, 2002). If such a finding were to be documented in athletes, educating athletes about such biases may be important in enhancing the efficacy of interventions, perhaps through changing participants' beliefs regarding emotion (e.g. Ochsner and Gross, 2007) or self-confidence (Mellalieu et al, 2003).

In summary, although sport anxiety researchers face some challenges, there are also indications that anxiety research will continue to flourish in the foreseeable future. Should we be worried or excited about the state of anxiety research? You decide!

Key concepts and terms

Appraisal
Cognitive anxiety
Cusp catastrophe

Multidimensional
Somatic anxiety

Sample essay titles

- With reference to theory and research, discuss the proposition that anxiety may not necessarily impair performance.
- 'Facilitative anxiety is excitement mislabelled.' Discuss this statement with reference to theory and research.
- Describe two strategies that you would use to help an athlete cope with their anxiety. Use theory and research to explain why you believe these strategies would be effective.

Further reading

Books

Lavallee, D., Kremer, J., Moran, A.P., and Williams, M. (2004). *Sport psychology: Contemporary themes*. New York: Palgrave MacMillan.

Uphill, M.A., and Jones, M.V. (2007b). '"When running is something you dread": A cognitive-behavioural intervention with a club runner.' In: A.M. Lane (Ed.), *Mood and human performance: Conceptual, measurement and applied issues.* New York: Nova Science, 271–295.

Woodman, T., and Hardy, L. (2001). 'Stress and anxiety.' In: R.N. Singer, H.A. Hausenblas, and C.M. Janelle (Eds), *Handbook of sport psychology*, (2nd Ed.). Chichester: Wiley, 290–318.

Journal articles

Lane, A.M., Sewell, D.F., Terry, P.C., Bartram, D., and Nesti, M.S. (1999). Confirmatory factor analysis of the Competitive State Anxiety Inventory-2. *Journal of Sports Sciences*, 17, 505–512.

Mellalieu, S.D., Hanton, S., and Jones, G. (2003). Emotional labelling and competitive anxiety in preparation and competition. *The Sport Psychologist*, 17, 157–174.

Uphill, M.A., and Jones, M.V. (2007a) Antecedents of emotions in elite athletes: A cognitive motivational relational perspective. *Research Quarterly for Exercise and Sport*, 78, 79–89.

4 Self-confidence in a sporting context

Kate Hays

One of the most consistent findings in the peak performance literature is the direct correlation between high levels of self-confidence and successful sporting performance (Zinsser et al, 2001). Many great athletes attribute their successes to elevated levels of self-belief, and their failures to a lack thereof, as illustrated here by Great Britain javelin thrower Steve Backley, 'if you're slightly down and doubting yourself then you've lost … you've lost that battle with yourself to create a highly skilled performance' (Jones and Hardy, 1990: 273).

While most athletes believe that **sport confidence** is critical to performance, even the most successful athletes can be susceptible to wavering levels of confidence. Given that self-confidence in sport is so important, and yet seemingly so fragile, it is perhaps unsurprising that the study of self-confidence has figured prominently in the sport psychology research literature. This chapter will explore the integrative model of self-confidence (Vealey, 2001), focusing on the mechanisms through which confidence influences performance. There will be a strong emphasis on the application of this research, particularly in relation to sources of confidence and confidence assessment.

Learning outcomes

When you have completed this chapter you should be able to:

1. Describe and evaluate the integrative model of sport confidence (Vealey, 2001).
2. Identify the sources and types of confidence utilized by athletes.
3. Propose confidence profiling as an assessment method.

Describe and evaluate the integrative model of sport confidence

The integrative model of sport confidence (Vealey, 2001; Figure 4.1) was designed to provide a framework from which meaningful extensions to the confidence literature could be generated, and from which interventions designed to enhance confidence in athletes could be developed. Sport confidence was defined as 'the degree of certainty individuals possess about their ability to be successful in sport' (Vealey, 2001: 556). As such, sport confidence is a more general conceptualization of self-confidence.

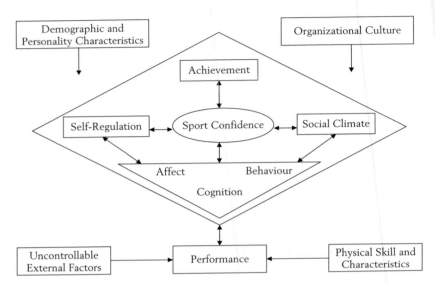

Figure 4.1 *The integrative model of sport confidence.*

Source: Vealey, 2001.

The dimension 'organizational culture' was included in the model to represent the cultural forces that shape human behaviour (e.g. competitive level, motivational climate, and the goals and structural expectations of sport programmes) and their influence on the sources and levels of sport confidence experienced by athletes. In addition, the physical skill and characteristics of the athlete and uncontrollable factors such as weather and opponents were recognized as important influences on performance. However, the centre of the model contained the core constructs and processes that Vealey predicted to most directly influence sport performance, specifically the sport confidence construct, the three domains representing sources of confidence (achievement, self-regulation and social climate), and the ABC's of psychology (affect, behaviour and cognition). The ABC triangle is viewed as the most critical link in the model since it illustrates the importance of understanding how sport confidence influences performance through its effect on how athletes feel about (affect), respond to (behaviour) and think about (cognition) everything that happens to them in sport.

Affect

Confidence has been consistently associated with positive emotions such as excitement and happiness, whereas a lack of confidence has been associated with anxiety, worry and depression (e.g. Hays et al, 2005). Self-confidence has also been identified as a moderating factor in the interpretation of pre-competition anxiety symptoms. These propositions seem to accord with reports of athletes performing exceptionally well when they are feeling both anxious and self-confident. Conversely, performers who experience high anxiety without the accompanying feelings of confidence may suffer performance decrements (Jones and Hanton, 2001).

Behaviour

Self-confidence has also been linked to productive achievement behaviours such as increased effort and persistence. Research would seem to suggest that athletes will exert maximum effort in the pursuit of their goals, but only if they believe they have a reasonable chance of success. A strong sense of confidence has also been associated with challenging goals being set and the expenditure of maximal effort and persistence in the achievement of those goals (Bandura, 1997). Thus, athletes that are high in confidence are likely to succeed due to their productive achievement behaviours.

Cognition

Confident individuals have also been found to be more skilled and efficient in using the cognitive resources necessary for sporting success (Vealey, 2001). For example, Bandura and Wood (1989) found that confident individuals remain task-diagnostic when faced with obstacles and seek process solutions to problems, whereas less confident individuals become self-diagnostic and focus on their inadequacies. Furthermore, confidence has been found to influence the coping processes of athletes. More specifically, athletes who possess a strong belief in their ability have reported being able to peak under pressure and cope successfully with adverse situations during competition (Cresswell and Hodge, 2004).

Identify the sources and types of confidence utilized by athletes

Vealey et al (1998) proposed that athletes rely on sources of confidence influenced by the specific context in which they find themselves immersed. Psychometric evidence obtained from over 500 high school and collegiate athletes from a variety of sports identified nine sources of confidence in athletes. These were mastery (i.e. mastering or improving personal skills); demonstration of ability (i.e. exhibiting skills or demonstrating superiority to opposition); physical/mental preparation (i.e. optimal physical and mental preparation); physical self-presentation (i.e. an athlete's perception of their physical self); social support (i.e. positive feedback and encouragement from coaches, team-mates and/or friends); vicarious experience (i.e. seeing someone else perform successfully); coach's leadership (i.e. an athlete's belief in the coach's skills in decision making and leadership); environmental comfort (i.e. feeling comfortable in the competitive environment) and situational favourableness (i.e. the athlete perceives something has happened in the sporting situation to increase their chances of success).

Beyond the identification of sources of sport confidence, Vealey et al (1998) also sought to identify which sources were the best predictors of sport confidence levels. Synonymous with previous research (e.g. Gill, 1988; Jones et al, 1991), athlete characteristics and the organizational culture of competitive sport were found to influence the development and manifestation of confidence in athletes. For example, social support was a more important source of confidence for female athletes than males. Physical self-presentation was also identified as more important for female college athletes than males, whereas male and female high school athletes reported that physical self-presentation was the least important source of their confidence.

The notion that confidence levels may vary as a function of gender is a relatively consistent finding in the research literature (e.g. Lirgg, 1991). Vealey et al (1998) suggest that this might be a function of the sources upon which that confidence is based. Consequently, by further examining the antecedents of confidence in different athlete groups, we might achieve a better understanding of the way in which organizational culture and individual differences influence the development of sport confidence. Indeed, since Vealey's sport confidence models and preliminary sources of sport confidence were based upon perceptions of high school and collegiate athletes, they cannot be readily generalized to other athlete groups.

In a recent study conducted by Hays et al (2007), nine sources of confidence were identified by world class athletes: preparation, performance accomplishments, coaching, innate factors, social support, experience, competitive advantage, self-awareness and trust. Athletes could distinguish between where they derived their confidence from (i.e. sources of sport confidence) and what they were confident about (i.e. types of sport confidence) without difficulty, providing a solid conceptual foundation for the existence of different types of sport confidence. Four salient types of sport confidence were identified by male and female athletes: skill execution, achievement, physical factors and psychological factors. Superiority to opposition and tactical awareness emerged as types of confidence identified by the male athletes only.

Whereas the preliminary sources of sport confidence identified by Vealey et al (1998) were based upon a review of literature and deductions by the investigators, the sources and types of sport confidence identified by the world class athletes were allowed to emerge inductively through qualitative interviews. This approach resulted in the identification of additional sources of sport confidence not highlighted by Vealey et al. For example, all athletes identified preparation as an important source of their sport confidence. However, responses were categorized into physical, mental and holistic preparation. A holistic approach to competition is a confidence source unique to this study and included video analysis, vision training, nutritional advice, arranging hotels and transport, and getting treatment (i.e. massages) when needed. Ultimate physical training included responses pertaining to effort, good physical training/condition, programme and skill repetition, whereas mental preparation referred to the use of several mental training strategies. Evidence of progressive performance accomplishments further facilitated the athletes' feelings of confidence and training logs were an integral source of their confidence since they enabled them to look back over the months of hard training that they had done and reinforced their improvement from season to season (see Hays et al, 2007 for an example).

Gender variations were evident in the sources of sport confidence utilized by the world class athletes. For example, male athletes seemed to focus more on competition outcomes, whereas female athletes identified good personal performances as a source of their confidence. These findings are synonymous with research that has identified different antecedents predict self-confidence in males and females, and might be used to inform goal-setting interventions. For example, world class athletes might be encouraged to identify and focus on the aspects of their competition which facilitate their confidence (i.e. performance for females and outcome for males). In addition to possible gender differences in goal orientation, male and female athletes derived confidence from their coach in different ways. Females were found to derive confidence primarily from their coach's encouragement, positive feedback/reinforcement and compliments. In contrast, male athletes tended to derive confidence from a belief in their coach to establish an appropriate training programme.

Gender was also found to influence the types of confidence identified by the athletes. For example, superiority to opposition was identified as a type of confidence by six of the seven male athletes, as opposed to only one of the seven female athletes. This type of confidence related to the athlete's belief that they were better than their opposition and included technical, physical and psychological factors. By contrast, female athletes derived confidence from perceived competitive advantages such as seeing their competitors perform badly, or crack under the pressure of competition.

It was evident that the sources of confidence identified by world class athletes might influence the types of confidence they possess. The majority of athletes were confident about 'skill execution', their ability to perform sport-specific skills technically correctly and fulfil the requirements of their sport or position. It would seem logical then to view types of sport confidence as evidence-based belief systems grounded in athletes' sources of sport confidence. Thus, for an athlete to develop a robust sense of sport confidence, they would perhaps be best advised to derive their types of confidence from several sources, as one Olympic medallist highlighted:

As I grew up I was told that I was naturally a great athlete. That gave me confidence but when I lost why couldn't I just turn it around? Because that bubble had burst, I hadn't won ... So the confidence has obviously got to be coming from lots of places otherwise it's very easily broken just by not winning once. (Hays et al, 2007: 449)

Activity 4.1

Compare the sources of sport confidence identified by the world class athletes to the sources of sport confidence identified by the high school and collegiate athletes in Vealey et al's (1998) study. What conclusions can you draw about the organizational culture of these two different athlete groups?

To further explore the relationship between confidence and performance at the world class level, Hays et al (2005) conducted an additional study to explore the role of confidence in world class sport performance. Synonymous with substantial anecdotal evidence and empirical research, results revealed that all athletes interviewed associated feeling self-confident with successful sporting performance. Further, when experiencing low levels of sport confidence, the athletes tended to underperform. Participants indicated that they were aware of their confidence before and during competition and identified several factors that influenced the stability of their confidence. These factors were seemingly related to the sources from which their confidence was based. For example, preparation, performance accomplishments and coaching have been identified as the primary sources of sport confidence used by world class athletes. In this study, poor performances, poor preparation, issues relating to coaching and illness/injury emerged as factors responsible for debilitating sport confidence. Gender also seemed to influence the stability of the athletes' sport confidence. For example, injury/illness was the primary factor identified by the male athletes as debilitative to their confidence, and poor performance was the only other factor identified. In contrast, the female athletes identified poor performances, poor preparation, issues relating to coaching, and pressure and expectations as the primary factors responsible for reducing their feelings of confidence, although psychological factors and injury were also highlighted. Hays et al (2007) concluded that since female athletes tend to be situationally dependent on external information in establishing performance expectations, they might be more susceptible to external confidence debilitating factors such as the organizational stressors associated with world class sports performance.

Consistent with Vealey's (2001) contentions, high sport confidence was congruent with positive thinking, an effective competition focus and effective decision-making. In contrast, low confidence was synonymous with negative thinking and distracted thought patterns. These findings are particularly pertinent given that Hays et al (2005) found athletes perceived strategies designed to enhance sport confidence to be ineffective when implemented in the pressurized environment of world class sport competition. If athletes were not feeling confident going into an important competition, they were seemingly unable to raise their confidence levels once they were there. This highlights the importance of helping athletes to develop and maintain their confidence in competition preparation phases. Finally, with regard to performance appraisals, the athletes attributed both successful and unsuccessful performances either to internal factors or a combination of internal and external factors, as one athlete stated:

> The first thing I'll always blame is me, I always look to me first but if I think 'no it wasn't me there was something else', then I look to what else was going on ... So yeah, we try to be as objective as possible and as honest as possible, if I've got something wrong I've got to admit it ... we've got to be very careful that we don't undo ourselves like that (Hays et al, 2005: 1290).

Thus in accordance with Bandura's (1997) contentions, identifying the true culprit for underperformance and identifying improved strategies, rather than

attributing unsuccessful performances externally, would seem the most effective way to maintain confidence and improve performance.

Summary of research directed towards the study of self-confidence in sport

The positive relationship between high confidence levels and successful sporting performance is well documented (see Feltz and Lirgg, 2001 for a review). On examination of the processes and mechanisms underlying confidence effects, high sport confidence is associated with emotional control, effective competition behaviours and effective competition focus. In contrast, low sport confidence is associated with negative affect, ineffective competition behaviours and an insufficient competition focus. Furthermore, strategies employed by athletes to enhance low feelings of sport confidence have been found to be ineffective in the context of world class sport competition.

Taken collectively, evidence suggests that protecting and maintaining high sport confidence levels in the lead-up to competition is desirable. Since research has shown that the factors responsible for debilitating an athlete's sport confidence are associated with the sources from which they derive their confidence, the most successful interventions might involve identifying an athlete's particular sources and types of confidence, and ensuring that these are intact during competition preparation phases. However, since demographic and organizational factors influence the sources and types of sport confidence utilized by athletes, and the factors responsible for debilitating their confidence levels, these factors need to be considered when assessing the confidence of sport performers.

Describe and evaluate confidence assessment measures in sport

Measuring confidence in sport

Several inventories have been developed to measure sport confidence per se. For example, Vealey (1986) developed a dispositional and a state measure of sport confidence named the Trait Sport-Confidence Inventory (TSCI) and the State Sport-Confidence Inventory (SSCI) respectively. Both the TSCI and the SSCI are 13-item inventories assessing sport confidence on a nine-point Likert scale (1 = low and 9 = high). Total scores are obtained by summing the items. The TSCI asks athletes to think about how confident they 'generally feel' when competing in sport, in comparison to 'the most confident athlete' they know. In contrast, the SSCI requires athletes to think about how confident they feel 'right now' about performing in an upcoming competition, in comparison to 'the most confident athlete' they know. The 13 items assess sport as a unidimensional construct and address various abilities that an athlete typically displays during competition (e.g. skill execution, performing under pressure, making critical decisions). Since recent research with world class athletes has evidenced the existence of different types of sport confidence, new sport confidence assessment measures are needed to reflect this.

In addition to the TSCI and SSCI, Vealey et al (1998) developed the Sources of Sport Confidence Questionnaire (SSCQ) to measure nine sources of confidence particularly salient to athletes in competitive sport (41 items divided into nine sub-scales). The SSCQ is at present the only questionnaire designed specifically to assess athletes' sources of sport confidence. However, validation of the SSCQ is based upon high school and collegiate athletes and cannot be generalized to any other athlete group. In a study examining the sources of sport confidence in master athletes, Wilson et al (2004) failed to replicate the proposed nine-factor structure of the SSCQ (Vealey et al, 1998), suggesting potential inconsistencies between different athlete groups. Their exploratory factor analyses revealed an eight-factor structure with similar factors to the SSCQ, but with fewer items and the elimination of the situational favourableness factor. Thus, demographic and organizational factors need to be considered when assessing the confidence of sport performers.

Towards practical confidence assessment measures

The vast majority of research on self-confidence in sport has used quantitative, **nomothetic research approaches** in which numbers are used to represent athletes' perceived sport confidence (usually on a Likert scale). The nomothetic approach (Allport, 1937) to the study of confidence in sport assumes that all people can be characterized by the same set of descriptors or dimensions. To address some of the limitations associated with adopting nomothetic measures in applied sport psychology practice, Vealey and Garner-Holman (1998) proposed that more ideographic approaches to measurement should be adopted. Eliciting information which is important to the performer, in contrast to tests or questionnaires that plot the performer against predetermined axes, is in accordance with personal construct theory (PCT: Kelly, 1955)[1]. The performance profile (Butler, 1989) is a natural application of Kelly's (1955) PCT and enables performers to construct a picture of themselves rather than forcing them to respond to fixed measures (see Chapter 6).

Hays et al (2006) adapted performance profiling to sport confidence specifically to provide a confidence assessment measure for use within an applied context. In contrast to traditional nomothetic measures developed to assess athletes' sport confidence in research settings, each athlete is encouraged to give an accurate account of their sources and types of confidence, and identify the factors that are debilitative to their confidence levels. This more idiographic approach to the measurement of sport confidence allows the confidence needs of athletes to be assessed at the individual level, regardless of demographics, sport classification or competitive status. **Idiographic research approaches** utilize verbal descriptions as opposed to numbers and allow individual differences in confidence to emerge.

---

[1] Originally developed within the realm of clinical psychology, the central tenet of PCT is that individuals strive to make sense of themselves and their environment by devising theories about their world, testing these theories against reality and then retaining or revising their theories depending upon their predictive accuracy (Fransella, 1981).

Profiling confidence for sport

Following the basic method of performance profiling advocated by Butler and Hardy (1992), the confidence profiling process adheres to three main stages: 1) introducing the idea, 2) eliciting constructs and 3) assessment. See Activity box 4.2 for the consultancy schedule that can be used to facilitate this process.

Stage 1: Introducing the idea. Introductory comments pertaining to sport confidence and the influence of sport confidence on sport performance provide the athlete with an understanding of the importance of effectively assessing their sport confidence levels.

Stage 2: Eliciting constructs. The athlete's sources and types of sport confidence are elicited by adopting the questions used by Hays et al (2007) to identify sources and types of sport confidence utilized by world class sport performers. Essentially, the athlete is asked 'what are you confident about?' to elicit confidence types. These types of sport confidence are then entered onto a visual sport confidence profile. Once all types of confidence have been exhausted, the athlete is asked to identify the source from which the type of confidence is derived. These sources of confidence are then added to their profile.

Encouraging the athlete to identify a time in their career when they had felt particularly confident often enables them to construct their types and sources of sport confidence more easily. The athlete is also asked to recall the time that they had felt least confident going into an important competition and highlight the factors responsible for debilitating their sport confidence, which are also recorded. Finally, the athlete is given the opportunity to add any other important information that might have been overlooked during the process. Any additional sources and/or types of confidence generated from this discussion are also entered into the athlete's sport confidence profile.

Stage 3: Assessment. Each athlete is asked to rate himself or herself on each of their types of sport confidence and these ratings are also recorded on their sport confidence profile. For each type of confidence, the athlete is asked to rate how confident they currently perceive themselves to be. However, rather than use the traditional Likert rating scale adopted by Butler and Hardy (1992), the questioning style commonly adopted during motivational interviewing (MI: Miller and Rollnick, 2002) is incorporated into the process. The athlete is asked on a scale of 1–10, with 1 being 'not at all confident' and 10 being 'extremely confident', 'How confident are you about your ability to remain calm under pressure (for example)?' If the athlete indicates a low level of confidence, a 4 for example, this question is followed with 'Why do you feel that you are a 4 on that rather than a 0?'. Regardless of how low the athlete's ratings of confidence, when compared with 0, they would probably be able to identify at least one source of their identified confidence type, supplementing the in-depth exploration of their current confidence profile. Further motivational strategies are utilized along with the scaling ruler to identify reasons why confidence might be low and to help problem solve to increase confidence (Velasquez et al, 2005). For example, an athlete with a confidence rating of 4 for a particular confidence type might be

asked 'What changes do you think you would have to make in order to be a 6 or a 7?', 'How might you go about making these changes?' and 'What would be a good first step?'. Thus, the athlete is prompted to make an accurate evaluation of their current confidence levels and identify possible strategies using a client-centred approach to change (see Focus box 4.1)

Focus 4.1

A mini case study example to contextualize the confidence profiling process

Sandy is a female middle distance runner who competes at a national level. In a recent consultancy session with her sport psychologist she identified nine types of sport confidence which were related to a range of physical, technical and psychological factors (see Figure 4.2 below). The sources from which Sandy derives her sport confidence are training (e.g. running times obtained and her performance in comparison to that of her team mates), competition performances/experience, feedback from significant others, early success, a hard work ethic, a strong desire to do well and low opposition level. In addition to her sources and types of confidence, Sandy also identified several confidence debilitators. For example, she recognized that she felt less confident and was unable to control her nerves in competitions in which she faced strong opposition. This caused her to tighten up during the race, particularly in her shoulders, impacting upon her running style.

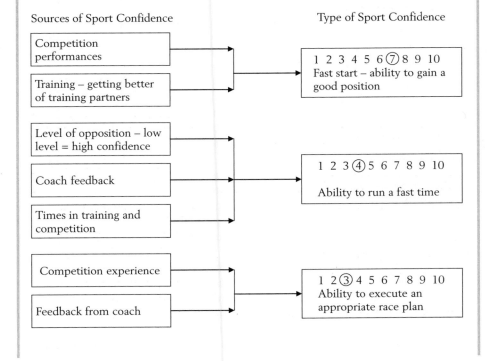

Sources of Sport Confidence   Type of Sport Confidence

Competition performances
Training – getting better of training partners

1 2 3 4 5 6 ⑦ 8 9 10
Fast start – ability to gain a good position

Level of opposition – low level = high confidence
Coach feedback
Times in training and competition

1 2 3 ④ 5 6 7 8 9 10

Ability to run a fast time

Competition experience
Feedback from coach

1 2 ③ 4 5 6 7 8 9 10
Ability to execute an appropriate race plan

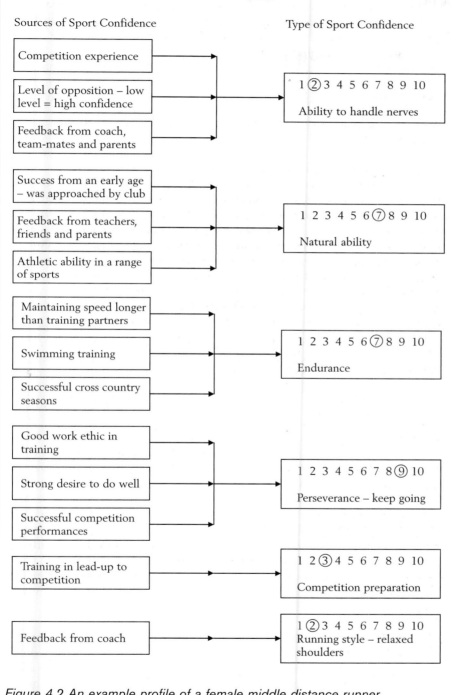

Figure 4.2 An example profile of a female middle distance runner.

Continued . . .

. . . Continued

While Sandy has a moderate level of confidence in some technical and physical abilities, reflected by ratings of 7 for her race start, natural ability and endurance, her confidence relating to her psychological abilities is much lower. For example, Sandy recognized that she is not sufficiently prepared for competition, finds it difficult to control her nerves in the competitive environment and is unable to develop and execute an appropriate race plan.

The implementation of scaling rulers enabled this athlete to assess her current sport confidence levels, but also to begin to generate her own strategies to help enhance her sport confidence. For example, when asked how she might move from a self-assessment score of 3 to a score 6 or 7 for her competition preparation, she identified that in collaboration with her coach she needed to generate a plan and associated goals for every race. The athlete felt that this might prevent her becoming distracted by her opposition. Furthermore, when asked about how she might move from a score of 2 to a score 5 or 6 for her ability to handle nerves, she recognized that with the help of a sport psychologist she needed to develop a method of controlling her physical (muscle tightening) and psychological (negative thoughts) anxiety symptoms.

On evaluation of Sandy's confidence profile, it could be concluded that she is over-reliant on external and uncontrollable factors to source her confidence, for example, feedback from significant others and training/competition outcomes. She seems to be finding it difficult to control her nerves in pressure situations, which is having a negative impact upon her performances. This is perhaps due to her lack of competition preparation.

The confidence profiling process enables athletes to give an accurate and in-depth account of their sources and types of confidence, and consider how these might influence their levels of confidence and subsequent competition performance. Enabling athletes to talk about their confidence in context (i.e. why they had felt confident on a particular day, or what had happened in the lead-up to an event that had facilitated/debilitated their confidence) ensures that they are able to identify their sources and types of sport confidence with ease. The identification of confidence debilitators is a particularly important part of the confidence profiling process, since the factors responsible for debilitating the athlete's sport confidence seem to provide the basis from which intervention strategies might be explored.

The resulting profiles are specific to the individual athlete and also specific to the sport in which they compete. Consequently, the confidence profiling process enables individual differences in confidence to emerge. For example, one athlete might exhibit low confidence in several areas, whereas another might exhibit high confidence but be over-reliant on specific sources and types of confidence. Each of these examples would require a different intervention strategy. For example, sport psychology support might be targeted towards increasing the range of sources and types of confidence utilized, or enhancing confidence in the areas already identified, depending upon the individual confidence needs of the athlete.

Activity 4.2

Using the confidence profiling process described above (and the consultancy schedule provided below), conduct a role play consultation with a classmate to assess their confidence in sport. Reflect upon your consultancy experience and try to identify any positive and/or negative aspects of the confidence profiling process. Consider how the information obtained through this applied approach might differ from information obtained through more traditional confidence inventories. Can you think of any way in which confidence profiling might be modified or improved to best meet the needs of an athlete, sport psychologist and/or coach?

Consultancy schedule

Stage 1: Introducing the idea

1. Explain to the athlete the important relationship between sport confidence and performance.

2. Explain the multidimensional nature of sport confidence and the importance of assessment at the individual level.

3. Explain that the purpose of the session is to identify the athlete's types and sources of sport confidence and produce an individualized confidence profile.

4. Explain what is meant by a source and type of confidence.

5. Show the athlete the profile which will be completed during the consultancy and explain.

Stage 2: Eliciting constructs (sample questions)

1. Can you tell me what you need to be confident about to perform successfully in your sport?

2. What are you confident about?

3. Where do you think that type of confidence in yourself as an athlete comes from?

Specific probe questions: What makes you confident?

4. Can you think of the time that you felt most confident going into an important competition? This may not be the time when you produced your best ever performance.

5. What were you confident about as you stepped onto the track, rink, poolside, etc? What were you confident about on that day?

6. Can you tell me about anything that happened or any factors that influenced your feelings of confidence during the lead-up to competition?

Continued . . .

. . . Continued

7. Can you tell me about anything that happened or any factors that influenced your levels of confidence on the day of competition?

Identifying sport confidence debilitators

8. Please could you describe to me the time when you felt least confident going into an important competition? This may not be a time when you performed unsuccessfully.

9. Can you tell me about anything that happened or any factors that affected your feelings of confidence during the lead-up to competition?

10. Can you tell me about anything that happened or any factors that affected your levels of confidence on the day of competition?
    Specific probe questions: 'What do you think was the main factor responsible for your low levels of confidence?', 'What do you think were the most important factors affecting your confidence?'

11. Are there any areas that you think we have failed to cover relating to your confidence in sport?

Stage 3: Assessment

Ask the athlete to rate themselves on each of their identified types of sport confidence.

1. On a scale of 1–10, with 1 being not confident at all and 10 being very confident, how confident are you about your _____ (type of confidence, i.e. skill execution)?

2. Why do you feel that you are a 3 (for example) on that rather than a 7 (for example)?

3. What changes do you think you would have to make in order to be a 7 (for example)?

4. How might you go about making these changes?

5. What would be a good first step?

6. Debrief the athlete and end the role play consultation.

Athletes can enhance their feelings of confidence by using strategies to stay positive, even when they are not performing well. Let us consider the case of Sandy. She was unable to handle her nerves and wished to develop a method of controlling her negative thoughts. Cognitive restructuring (Davis et al, 1988) is one such strategy that is used extensively in applied sport psychology consultancy and involves restructuring an athlete's negative thought patterns. The first step would be to ask Sandy to review her self-talk and identify the kind of thinking that she found helpful, any thoughts that appeared to be harmful, her consequential feelings and behaviours, and the situations or events that were associated with her self-talk. Once Sandy had become aware of her maladaptive thoughts, she would be shown how to modify them through a process of countering. Countering is an internal dialogue that uses facts and reasons to refute the underlying beliefs and assumptions that lead to negative thinking (Zinsser et al, 2001). With the help of the sport psychologist, and through a process of self-reflection, Sandy would be required to identify and describe the evidence necessary to change her attitudes and beliefs, and develop a list of alternative positive self-statements to replace her negative cognitions. For example, instead of thinking 'I am nervous, I can't do this', Sandy might think 'I am well prepared and ready to compete'.

Activity 4.3

Repeat the role-play consultation with another classmate and compare the two profiles. What are the similarities/differences between the confidence profiles of the classmates you consulted with?

The sport psychology research literature provides multiple examples of the way in which athletes can manipulate their feelings of competence and self-belief through positive self-talk (e.g. Orlick and Partington, 1988; Feltz and Riessinger, 1990). Based upon the knowledge gained throughout this chapter, make some suggestions for additional intervention strategies targeted towards the specific confidence needs of each individual. Refer back to the information contained within this chapter to help you with this, particularly that which relates to athletes' sources of sport confidence.

Ethics

Before implementing any scientific support programme, or conducting research in sport psychology, it is necessary to consider the ethical implications of such work. For example, while the confidence profiling process encourages athletes to discuss their most confident experiences in sport, they are also asked about times when they were not feeling confident and might have underperformed. It is possible that some athletes might experience a degree of discomfort in answering these questions. Consequently, the consultancy should be structured to ensure that it concludes with the athlete discussing positive sporting experiences. If completing the confidence profiling process with a participant under the age of 18, it is vital that parental consent is obtained and that the consultancy takes place in a public setting where both you and the athlete are in full view of a third party at all times. Finally, the sport psychologist must ensure that the athlete is fully informed of the risks associated with the applied work and completes an informed consent form. It should be made clear to the athlete

Continued . . .

. . . Continued

that they are free to withdraw consent or participation from the consultancy at any time, that they are free to refuse to answer any of the questions put to them, and that no disadvantage would arise from a decision not to complete the consultancy.

Conclusions

There is a magnitude of research and anecdotal evidence pertaining to the important relationship between high sport confidence and successful sport performance. Recent advancements in sport confidence research have provided evidence for the conceptualization of sport confidence as a multidimensional construct derived from several sources and comprising several types. These sources and types are influenced by organizational and demographic factors and, as such, are unique to each individual athlete. This has implications for nomothetic confidence inventories designed and developed as research tools. Consequently, confidence profiling is presented for use in an applied context as an alternative assessment measure and basis for intervention development.

Key concepts and terms

Idiographic research approaches

Nomothetic research approaches

Sport confidence

Sample essay titles

- With reference to relevant theory and research, critically evaluate Vealey's (2001) integrative model of sport confidence.
- Sport confidence research endorses gender differences, not only in confidence levels but also in the sources and types of confidence utilized. Describe these differences and identify the practical implications for support staff working with male and female athletes.
- In developing a confidence intervention for athletes, what considerations should the practitioner make with regard to confidence assessment in sport?

Further reading

Books

Vealey, R.S. (2001). 'Understanding and enhancing self-confidence in athletes.' In: R.N. Singer, H.A. Hausenblas, and C.M. Janelle (Eds), *Handbook of Sport Psychology*. New York: John Wiley and Sons, 550–565.

Zinsser, N., Bunker, L., and Williams, J.M. (2001). 'Cognitive techniques for building confidence and enhancing performance.' In: J.M. Williams (Ed.), *Applied Sport Psychology: Personal Growth to Peak Performance*. Mountain View, California: Mayfield, 284–311.

Journal articles

Butler, R.J., and Hardy, L. (1992). The performance profile: Theory and application. *The Sport Psychologist*, 6, 253–264.

Hays, K., Maynard, I., Thomas, O., and Bawden, M. (2007). Sources and types of confidence identified by world class sport performers. *Journal of Applied Sport Psychology*, 19, 434–456.

Hays, K., Thomas, O., Maynard, I., and Bawden, M. (2005). Sport confidence in successful and unsuccessful world class performances: A comparison of affect, behaviour and cognition. *Journal of Sports Sciences*, 23, 1289–1290.

Vealey, R.S., Hayashi, S.W., Garner-Holman, M., and Giacobbi, P. (1998). Sources of sport-confidence: Conceptualization and instrument development. *Journal of Sport & Exercise Psychology*, 21, 54–80.

2 | Managing psychological states

5 Stress and coping among competitive athletes in sport

Tracey Devonport

The future of sport arguably lies in the extent to which athletes can be nurtured to fulfil their potential. Consider the case of Jennifer Capriati, encouraged and coached to play tennis as a small child by her father, the family then moved to Florida so that 10-year-old Capriati could begin an intense training programme. In her first professional tournament at the age of 13 (Virginia Slims tournament, 1990), she progressed to the finals, losing to Gabriela Sabatini, who at the time was rated second in the world. The following year, at 14 years of age, Jennifer reached the semi-final of the French Open and then won a gold medal at the Barcelona Olympics in 1992. At this point she was experiencing personal difficulties and was reported to say 'I wasn't happy with myself, my tennis, my life, my coaches, my friends ...' (cited in *Hello Magazine*, www.hellomagazine.com/profiles/jennifercapriati/ accessed 8 July 2005). In 1993 she was arrested for shoplifting and in 1994 was arrested for marijuana possession. Jennifer withdrew from the sporting world for two years and did not fully reassert herself on the tennis world until 2001.

High-profile examples such as this could represent the tip of a metaphorical iceberg whereby the pressures of sporting excellence lead to disengagement, unhappiness and ultimately sport withdrawal. The responsibility of researchers and applied practitioners alike is to identify and develop strategies to alleviate these kinds of issues that athletes experience. Enhancing **coping** skills that could be used to manage **stress** in different domains of an athlete's life is a strategy that is worth pursuing.

A criticism of sport and exercise psychology research voiced by academics and sports personnel alike is the lack of applied research that strives to bridge the gap between theory and practice (Lane and Terry, 2000; Lazarus, 2001). Coping theory has the potential to contribute significantly to applied practice (Lazarus, 2000a). If coping competencies are enhanced this should lead to increases in performance (Lazarus, 2000a; Pensgaard and Duda, 2003) and positive experiences (Ntoumanis and Biddle, 1998). Despite such theoretical links, studies testing the utility of coping in sport are scarce.

Figure 5.1 Coping with the pressure of competition.

Source: Photograph courtesy of Mark Pritchard, England Netball.

Focus 5.1

Commonly used definitions of stress, **cognitive appraisal** and coping used in the coping literature are as follows:

Definition of stress

Stress refers to the process by which individuals perceive and respond to particular events, termed stressors, which they appraise as challenging or threatening (Lazarus and Folkman, 1984). Stress is conceptualized as a transaction between a person and the environment.

Definition of cognitive appraisal

Cognitive appraisal has been defined as 'a process through which the person evaluates whether a particular encounter with the environment is relevant to his or her well being, and if so, in what ways' (Folkman et al, 1986: 992).

Definition of coping

Coping refers to 'constantly changing cognitive and behavioural efforts to manage specific external and/or internal demands that are appraised as taxing or exceeding the resources of the person' (Lazarus and Folkman, 1984: 141).

This chapter begins by exploring the sources of sports stressors encountered by competitive athletes. It continues by exploring the potential consequences of stress, reviewing the transactional model of stress and coping (Lazarus and Folkman, 1984). In unpacking this model, the range of coping strategies that may be utilized when anticipating, or in response to stress will be explored. Finally, I examine research which has sought to apply coping interventions. This will include issues relating to their implementation and evaluation. Throughout this chapter, readers will be encouraged to consider the practical application of materials presented.

Learning outcomes

When you have completed this chapter you should be able to:

1. Identify the common antecedents and consequences of stress among athletes.
2. Describe key issues in the transactional model of stress and coping.
3. Describe coping classifications and the features of effective coping.
4. Be familiar with coping interventions and considerations of application.

Identifying the antecedents and consequences of stress among athletes

Focus 5.2

Stress is a common experience in sport

Andrew Murray (18 years old) lost in straight sets to Juan Ignacio Chela in the first round of the Australian Open 2006 (tennis). After making the biggest jump of any player in 2005 as he surged from 514 to number 65 by the end of the year, Murray has been touted as a future champion.

'It's difficult for me to go out there and try and perform to the best that I can when I'm expected to win all these matches. If you guys [the media] expect me to play well every single match and every single tournament then it's not going to happen.'

'You don't think there's any pressure on me?' Murray answered after it was suggested in the media conference that he had received nothing but good press since he arrived on the circuit. 'Well, if you don't think that, then I'm obviously going to disagree on something. If you guys don't think you're putting pressure on me, then that's fine. I'll forget about it.'

http://news.bbc.co.uk/sport1/hi/tennis/4620592.stm (accessed 3 February 2007)

The importance of adaptive coping for long-term adherence, satisfaction and success in domains such as sport, employment and education is well recognized (Lazarus, 2000b). Clearly it is important to identify the sources of stress experienced by athletes so that they may be offered assistance and guidance in developing adaptive coping. Stressors identified to date include excessive pressure (Smoll and Smith, 1996); critical comments (Anshel and Delany, 2001); spectators/selectors (Devonport et al, 2005a; Nicholls et al, 2005); selection issues (Woodman and Hardy, 2001b); overemphasis on winning (Nicholls et al, 2005); training environment (Woodman and Hardy, 2001b); opponents (Anshel and Delany, 2001; Nicholls et al, 2005); coach/team-mate relationships (Gould et al, 1993; Devonport et al, 2005a); physical and mental errors (Holt, 2003; Devonport et al, 2005a); self-doubts about talent (Holt and Dunn, 2004); injury (Devonport et al, 2005a; Smith et al, 1990b); personal goals and expectations (Hatzigeorgiadis, 2006); observing an opponent playing well (Nicholls et al, 2006); and a lack of role clarity or role structure (Woodman and Hardy, 2001b).

A good way of exploring the sources of stress in sport is through introspection. Complete Activity 5.1, and consider whether you agree or disagree that the

Activity 5.1

Reflect on your personal experiences and identify the extent to which you agree with the stressors identified, offering a justification for your decision.

Stressor	Agree	Disagree	Justification
Making a physical error			
Making a mental error			
Opponents			
Difficult weather conditions			
Injury			
Coach/team-mate relations			
Excessive pressure			
Lack of role clarity			
Training environment			
Overemphasis on winning			
Selection issues			
Unresolved issues			
Self doubts about talent			
Spectators			
Critical comments			

stressor identified was in fact stressful for you, offering a brief justification for this decision.

Identifying the possible consequences of stress

Anshel and Delany (2001) suggest stress appraisals can cause significant psychological, physiological, emotional and behavioural responses (see Table 5.1). Experiencing the debilitating effects of stress can affect mood (see Chapter 2), create anxiety (see Chapter 3), and reduce confidence (see Chapter 4). By contrast, some individuals appear to thrive on stress, and while such individuals sometimes experience unpleasant mood and emotional responses (Chapters 2 and 3), these tend not to debilitate performance.

Psychological symptoms	Emotional symptoms	Physical symptoms	Behavioural symptoms
Memory problems	Moody and hypersensitive	Headaches	Eating more or less
Difficulty making decisions	Restlessness and anxiety	Digestive problems	Too much or too little sleep
Inability to concentrate	Depression	Muscle tension and pain	Self imposed isolation
Confusion	Anger and resentment	Sleep disturbances	Neglecting responsibilities
Catastrophizing/ generalizing	Easily irritated	Fatigue	Increased substance use
Repetitive or racing thoughts	Sense of being overwhelmed	Chest pain, irregular heartbeat	Nervous habits (e.g. nail biting, pacing)
Poor judgement	Lack of confidence	High blood pressure	Teeth grinding or jaw clenching
Loss of objectivity	Apathy	Weight gain or loss	Overreacting to unexpected problems
		Skin problems	
		Decreased sex drive	

Table 5.1 Symptoms of stress.

In order to better understand how to anticipate and manage stress appraisals and their consequences, it is necessary to consider and apply theory.

Describe key issues in the transactional model of stress and coping

It has been suggested that the transactional model of stress and coping (TMSC; Lazarus and Folkman, 1984) is the most widely accepted theoretical framework of stress and coping (Frydenberg and Lewis, 2004). The TMSC (Lazarus and Folkman, 1984) suggests that, when an individual is faced with something that is potentially stressful, personal and situational factors interact and ultimately influence the appraisal process (see Figure 5.2). The appraisal process consists of primary and secondary appraisal.

During primary appraisal the individual essentially asks themselves 'What are the implications of this for me? Does it have potential to harm, hinder or benefit?'. Primary appraisal results in an event being interpreted in one of three ways: 1) irrelevant, where there are no implications for well-being, 2) benign/positive where the event is perceived to preserve or enhance well-being, and 3) stressful where there is a perceived harm/loss, threat and/or challenge to well-being. Appraisals of harm/loss are characterized by perceptions that damage has already been sustained. A threat appraisal occurs when harm or loss is possible. A challenge appraisal reflects a perception that there may be an opportunity for mastery and gain (Lazarus and Folkman, 1984). The primary appraisals of harm/loss, threat or challenge are not mutually exclusive, thus it is possible for an individual to appraise an event in more than one way at the same time.

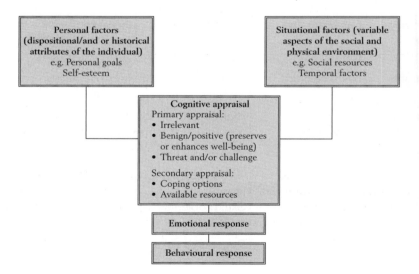

Figure 5.2 Transactional model of stress and coping (adapted from Lazarus and Folkman, 1984).

If the situation is appraised as stressful, the individual then engages secondary appraisal and considers what they can do to prevent or minimize stress. Secondary appraisal focuses on minimizing harm or maximizing gains through coping responses (Lazarus and Folkman, 1984). There is an evaluation of coping options and available resources that may include social, physical, psychological and material assets (Lazarus and Folkman, 1984). Primary and secondary appraisals occur at virtually the same time, and interact to determine the significance and meaning of events with regards to well-being. Depending on how a stressor is perceived, it will have different emotional and behavioural responses. An individual may feel fearful and try to avoid the situation, or may feel challenged and take action to try and remedy the situation.

You can probably recall having experienced stress yourself, and such self-reflection is usually quite revealing in determining the underlying causes of these feelings. There are many factors that may increase the probability of stress perceptions, however it is not possible to review them all within the context of this chapter. As such, those antecedents of stress perceptions that are commonly cited in contemporary coping literature will be reported. These include personal goals, gender and a sample of situational factors.

Personal goals

There is growing acceptance of the importance of establishing the impact of personal goals on stress appraisal, and subsequent coping processes (Lazarus, 1999; Hatzigeorgiadis, 2006). Lazarus (1999) suggests that goal commitment is the most important appraisal variable because, without this, an individual has nothing at stake. Any threat to goal achievement may motivate an individual towards a course of action that can reduce the threat and sustain coping efforts. Carver and Scheier (1998) proposed the control process model of behaviour. This proposes that during the execution of a task, individuals constantly monitor their performance in relation to their goal(s). When discrepancies between a goal and performance are detected (attainment of goal or rate of progress towards goal) the individual experiences worry. When they perceive they can attain a goal, approach-focused coping strategies are adopted (planning, effort increase), whereas when the perception is that they will not attain a goal, avoidance coping strategies (behavioural and mental disengagement) are utilized (Hatzigeorgiadis, 2006).

Research completed with a male elite cricketer (Holt, 2003) and four elite female footballers (Holt and Dunn, 2004) found that stress perceptions occurred when situational demands appeared to threaten seasonal goals. These findings concur with those of Lewthwaite (1990) who found that higher levels of anxiety in sport are encountered when personally relevant goals are believed to be endangered.

Gender

Gender has been well researched in the coping literature as a personal factor that may impact upon coping. Two main hypotheses have been forwarded in an attempt to explain gender differences in coping: the socialization hypothesis and the role-constraint hypothesis (Rosario et al, 1988; Ptacek et al, 1994). The socialization hypothesis predicts that men are socialized to use more active and instrumental coping behaviours, and women are socialized to use more passive and emotion-focused behaviours (Ptacek et al, 1994). The traditional female gender role prescribes dependence, affiliation, emotional expressiveness, a lack of assertiveness and the subordination of personal needs to those of others. The traditional male role prescribes attributes such as autonomy, self-confidence, assertiveness, instrumentality and being goal-oriented. These attributes make it difficult for men to accept and express feelings of weakness, incompetence and fear, while for women it would be more difficult to take a proactive problem-solving stance (Matud, 2004).

The role-constraint hypothesis argues that gender differences in coping may be explained by the likelihood of occupying specific social roles (Rosario et al, 1988). Role occupancy increases exposure to some stressors and diminishes the presence of others, concomitantly influencing role-related resources and opportunities. Women are more likely to identify with the feminine gender role, and men are more likely to identify with the masculine gender role (Matud, 2004). Several studies in community samples report that stress is associated with health and family issues in women, work and finance issues in men (Billings and Moos, 1984).

Situational factors

There are a range of situational factors that may impact upon coping. Lazarus (1999) placed these into the four broad categories of demands, constraints, opportunity and culture. However, within these four categories reside situational factors including novelty of the situation (Nisbett and Ross, 1980), temporal factors (Lazarus and Folkman, 1984), duration of the stressor (Lazarus, 1999) and ambiguity of the situation (Lazarus and Folkman, 1984). The most extensively examined situational factor among coping researchers to date is social resources. The functional support model (Wills, 1990) suggests that resources from an individual's social network, including information, practical assistance and emotional support, can contribute positively to the construction of individual coping strategies. For example, Thoits (1995) suggests that social resources may provide information that can alter perceptions of meaningful aspects of stressful situations. Research also suggests that the connection between social resources and coping is stronger in women and girls than in men and boys. This is partially attributed to cultural influences whereby women, more than men, are expected to be sensitive to the needs of others (Frydenberg and Lewis, 1993).

Cutrona and Russell (1990) suggest that the controllability of a stressor determines support needs. Generally, uncontrollable events would require social support that fosters emotion-focused coping, and controllable events would require social support that fosters problem-focused coping. Rees and Hardy (2004) reinforced this view by highlighting the importance of appropriately matching social support to the needs of the athlete. They also proposed that levels of social support may need to vary over time among athletes who compete away from home.

Activity 5.2

Having explored the transactional model of stress and coping, reflect back on your own experiences. What personal and situational factors do you believe influence your appraisal of stress and subsequent coping?

As an example, previous research has shown that high trait anxious athletes are likely to use avoidance coping (e.g. denial and wishful thinking) significantly more than low trait anxious athletes (Giacobbi and Weinberg, 2000).

Coping classifications and determinants of effective coping

Coping involves cognitive, affective and behavioural efforts to manage a stressor (Lazarus, 1999). The specific skills and strategies used to cope with stressors are typically classified into broad categories that identify the intended purpose of the coping response (Poczwardowski and Conroy, 2002). Some researchers (Gould et al, 1997) suggest that such patterns of coping might not exist and classifying coping may oversimplify the coping process (e.g. problem and emotion-focused coping). For example, Poczwardowski and Conroy (2002) noted that certain coping strategies did not fit neatly into a single category. They felt that the coping strategy 'putting things in perspective' could equally be categorized as both emotion-focused and appraisal-focused. This finding is increasingly noted among coping researchers in sport (Nicholls et al, 2005) and is consistent with the transactional model (Lazarus and Folkman, 1984). Lazarus (2000a) explains that coping functions are determined by the individual's appraisal of the stress, which in turn is influenced by meaning structures developed from personal experiences (Eklund et al, 1993). As such, Lazarus (1999) noted that a single coping strategy may serve multiple functions. However, an understanding of coping functions is useful in considering the development of coping interventions. Table 5.2 presents those coping functions that have been identified within the literature to date.

Coping classification	Description
Problem-focused coping	Intended to alter the circumstances causing distress using strategies directed towards the environment and the self
Emotion-focused coping	Involves the regulation of dysfunctional emotions
Active coping	Taking measures to alleviate the effects of a stressor, including strategies characterized by an orientation towards the threatening aspects of a situation
Avoidance-focused coping	Actions intended to disengage from the stressor and focus attention on alternative tasks

Continued . . .

. . . Continued

Coping classification	Description
Appraisal-focused coping	Appraising or reappraising stressful situations
Reactive coping	Efforts to deal with a stressful encounter that has already happened, or is happening at the present time
Anticipatory coping	Involves coping behaviours intended to deal with a critical event that is certain or fairly certain to occur in the near future
Preventative coping	Concerned with preparation for uncertain events in the more distant future
Proactive coping	Proactive coping is distinguished by three main features: 1) it integrates planning and prevention strategies with proactive self-regulatory goal attainment; 2) it integrates proactive goal attainment with identification and utilization of social resources; and 3) it utilizes proactive emotional coping for self-regulatory goal attainment

Table 5.2 Classification of coping.

There are conditions emerging that are seemingly influential on the outcome of coping efforts. It is important to be aware of these conditions when advising and helping individuals cope with a stressful event. These are as follows:

■ Problem-focused coping which attempts to directly manage the problem or stressor is more suitable in situations that are seen as controllable. Emotion-focused and/or avoidance-focused coping which tries to deal with the emotions resulting from a stressor may be most suitable in response to stressors or problems that are uncontrollable (Lazarus and Folkman, 1984).

■ Those coping strategies used with acute (short-term) stressors may become less effective if the stressor becomes chronic stress (long-term) (Wethington and Kessler, 1991). For example, avoidance strategies may be effective for short-term stressors, but non-avoidant strategies may be effective for long-term stressors.

■ Individuals typically use more than one coping strategy at any point in time (Gould et al, 1993). Research indicates that those individuals who possess a wider range of coping responses adapt more effectively to stress than those with fewer coping options (Gould et al, 1993). However, it should not be assumed that using lots of coping strategies within a short timeframe is adaptive. It may be because the coping strategies individuals try are not effective, and as such they try many different coping strategies (Carver et al, 1993).

■ In order to cope effectively an individual must deal with any emotions resulting from a stressful encounter. Strong emotions may lead to poor performance

(Chapter 2) and inappropriate behaviours such as aggression resulting from anger (Lazarus, 1999).

Coping interventions and considerations of application

Review of coping interventions: Implications for application

Although research concerning the development of coping skills is a relatively new development and papers are few in number, early indications are that individuals can be assisted in the development of their coping skills (Frydenberg and Lewis, 2002). Coping assistance can be provided formally through coping programmes and/or informally using those individuals with whom the individual has frequent contact (Frydenberg and Lewis, 2002). However, the benefit of coping skills programmes that are fully scripted to facilitate implementation is becoming increasingly recognized. An example of such a programme was the *Best of Coping* developed by Frydenberg and Brandon (2002). This was designed to help adolescents cope with daily stressors. The programme comprised ten sessions including the exploration of coping strategies such as thinking optimistically, effective communication skills, steps to effective problem-solving, decision-making, goal-setting and time management. The programme also included a session facilitating the practical use of those coping skills learnt during the programme. In reviewing the *Best of Coping*, the self-efficacy of participants toward dealing with stress increased significantly more than non-participants.

Implication: Scripted, or partially scripted coping interventions facilitate the success of an intervention.

Previous research indicates that the provision of a supportive environment during coping skills training develops an individual's self-efficacy (Bandura, 1997) perceptions regarding their ability to deal with stress (Zeidner, 1990). This is important because individuals with high coping efficacy are more likely to approach problems with the aim of solving them, rather than avoiding them (Frydenberg and Lewis, 2002). Some researchers believe that social support is particularly important for athletes whose coping skills are underdeveloped because it may provide a more positive interpersonal environment, and may act as a buffer against stress (Anshel and Delany, 2001).

Implication: It is important to provide a supportive environment for the development of coping skills.

Smith (1999) suggests that the generalization of coping skills training should become a focal rather than an incidental consideration. A number of factors are believed to enhance the generalizability of coping:

- The extent to which a person believes that a new coping situation calls for the same coping behaviours learned in training will promote the use of the learned coping behaviours in the new situation.

- The extent to which newly acquired coping skills can be successfully applied across a wide range of situations.

- The perceived control of the competencies and relationship with an individual's values and motives.

- The development of global self-regulatory skills.

Implication: It is important that coping interventions work towards the generalization of coping skills.

Types of coping interventions

While there are varied approaches to helping individuals cope with negative events (Sandler et al, 1997; Ntoumanis and Biddle, 1998), a common format does appear to exist. This consists of a) providing recipients with a rationale for the programme; b) modelling or demonstrating the procedure; c) having the participants rehearse or practise the skills; d) motivating the participants to transfer the learning via self-directed activities (Baker, 2001).

Appraisal is an important first step in the coping process (Lazarus and Folkman, 1984; Lazarus, 2000a). As such, any programme that attempts to develop coping skills also needs to teach skills of positive cognitive appraisal. Most recent programmes intended to facilitate the development of coping skills are based upon Lazarus's transaction model of stress (Lazarus and Folkman, 1984) in that the intention is to change an individual's cognition about the nature of stress and their ability to cope with stress (Isrealasvili, 2002). Consequently, all coping interventions carry a cognitive component. These include cognitive behavioural methods, emotional cognitive methods and action theory approaches (Sandler et al, 1997; Isrealasvili, 2002). Each is considered in turn.

Cognitive behavioural approaches

A cognitive behavioural approach to coping skills training is based on the principle that maladaptive emotions and behaviours are influenced by an individual's beliefs, attitudes and perceptions (Cormier and Cormier, 1998). As such, the focus of cognitive behavioural interventions is learning to recognize, interrupt and replace maladaptive cognitions with adaptive ones. For example, Baker (2001) implemented a cognitive behavioural programme that consisted of four 45-minute sessions aimed at identifying self-defeating thoughts and replacing these with self-improving thoughts. Participants were asked to monitor the circumstances surrounding self-defeating thoughts, the level of emotion resulting from this, the self-improving thought used to replace self-defeating thoughts and the level of emotion they felt having made this cognitive change. A 10-page training booklet was also provided to all participants to facilitate self-instruction. A review of the programme revealed improved cognitive self-instruction and decreased state anxiety.

Implication: Teach individuals to recognize, interrupt and replace maladaptive cognitions with adaptive ones.

Emotional cognitive approaches

Studies have found that encouraging positive appraisals leads to improved affect, especially when the participants can choose the exact appraisal to adopt (Wenzlaff and LePage, 2000). Within sport psychology, studies have found that helping athletes think more positively led to reduced performance anxiety during competition (Hanton and Jones, 1999; Arathoon and Malouff, 2004). For example, Arathoon and Malouff (2004) encouraged field hockey players (aged 19–47) to select one of five positive thoughts (e.g. 'something you did well in a game') and one of six coping thoughts (e.g. 'we didn't win but we played well') following loss. This intervention reduced the decrease in positive affect significantly when compared to a control group, supporting the contention that inducing realistic positive cognitions is an effective way to improve affect.

Implication: Encourage positive appraisals so that individuals may be more predisposed to enjoying a challenging situation.

Action theory approach

Action theory addresses not only the cognitive and emotional aspects of stress encounter, but also the motivational, behavioural and contextual aspects (Young and Valach, 2000; Isrealasvili, 2002). Isrealasvili (2002) contends that this offers a more comprehensive strategy to foster a person's ability to confront a stressful episode in life. It does so by addressing three aspects of action: the manifest behaviour of the individual, the conscious recognition that accompanies this manifest behaviour, and the social meaning in which the action is embedded (Young and Valach, 2000). Within action theory, intervention counsellors have the task of helping individuals make sense of their actions. They encourage individuals to evaluate stressful stimuli differently and equip them with a wider range of coping skills.

Isrealasvili (2002) explored the use of this approach with Israeli adolescents facing a school-to-army transition. The programme was implemented by school counsellors with the support of teachers, parents, school graduates and army representatives. The programme addressed anticipated sources of stress in the civilian to basic training transition, and the acquisition of coping skills through group discussion. The intervention also addressed a person's awareness of their goals and of the relationship between these goals and possible ways of coping. The intervention was found to increase enlistees' self-efficacy to adjust to military life. It was concluded that coping is effective only if it adequately relates to the person's goals.

Implication: It is important that coping skills training considers an individual's personal goals to optimize the effectiveness of coping.

In conclusion, a range of coping interventions have been developed and applied in both sport and general psychology. When presenting and reviewing these interventions, key implications for application emerge. These are as follows:

■ Scripted, or partially scripted coping interventions facilitate the success of an intervention.

■ It is important to provide a supportive environment for the development of coping skills.

■ Coping interventions should work towards the generalization of coping skills.

■ Coping interventions should encourage positive appraisals.

■ Coping interventions should teach individuals to recognize, interrupt and replace maladaptive cognitions with adaptive ones.

■ Coping skills training should consider an individual's personal goals to optimize the effectiveness of coping.

With these implications in mind, Devonport et al (2005a) developed a one-year coping intervention for use with nine junior national netball players (aged 15–19), titled the 'The Mentor Programme'. In an attempt to provide a supportive environment for coping skills development, a mentor was identified for participants. Mentoring has been described as a one-to-one developmental relationship where the mentor and mentee work together to establish goals, driven by the needs of the mentee (Linney, 1999). The role of each mentor was to guide players through activities presented in a series of coping packs. These scripted packs were designed to develop five key coping skills including planning and organizational ability, goal-setting, emotional intelligence, problem-solving and communication skills. The planning pack was intended to facilitate preventative and proactive coping by determining an athlete's forthcoming commitments and helping them work towards the attainment of a balanced lifestyle. Goal-setting was incorporated into The Mentor Programme in order to increase an athlete's repertoire of problem-focused coping strategies and facilitate proactive coping. Emotional intelligence was included because of the influence it has on adaptive and emotion-focused coping (Zeidner et al, 2004). The problem-solving pack was designed to develop an athlete's ability to adopt a careful, analytical, planned, and systematic approach to the solution process, thus facilitating problem-focused coping. Finally, the communication pack was designed to enhance the ability of athletes to communicate effectively, and covered skills such as verbalizing ideas and listening effectively to others (Anderson, 1993; Rivers, 2005). This was intended to accrue benefits such as enhancing an athlete's ability to utilize social support.

Within the activities designed for completion in The Mentor Programme, mentors and athletes were encouraged to apply the coping skills addressed across sporting, academic, work and social domains. Smith (1999) suggests that in developing coping skills interventions, the generalization of coping skills training should become a focal rather than an incidental consideration. Applying coping skills in this way may improve coping efficiency and effectiveness, thus encouraging subsequent use. For example, goal-setting can be a time-intensive activity, but with practice an individual is able to set, monitor and adjust goals more efficiently. Furthermore, generalizing the use of goal-setting can help establish a more balanced lifestyle as the individual strives to achieve goals across domains.

It was considered important to address ethical considerations when completing this longitudinal research. It was important to ensure that all individuals working with adolescents had completed a criminal records check, and received certification of approval to work with children. Complying with recommendations of the British Psychological Society, consent for continued involvement in the longitudinal research was secured from mentors and athletes every three months. Finally, as the topic of investigation was stress and coping, it was necessary to ensure that appropriate support mechanisms were in place for individuals evidencing debilitating levels of stress, or demonstrating clinical disorders during the research (e.g. depression, body image dysmorphia). Mentors were asked to refer any emergent issues to the lead researcher who then had access to clinical and counselling support as necessary.

In order to exemplify the impact of The Mentor Programme on participants, a case study of one participant, whose pseudonym is Ellis, is presented (Table 5.3); any other names identified are also pseudonyms. At the start of The Mentor Programme, Ellis, then aged 18 years, demonstrated regular use of adaptive coping strategies (active coping, planning and instrumental support) and infrequent use of maladaptive coping strategies (behavioural disengagement, denial and venting) as measured using the Brief COPE (Carver, 1997). This limited the extent to which an increased or reduced use of specific coping strategies could be demonstrated. However, on completion of The Mentor Programme, she did increase her use of four out of five adaptive coping strategies (see Table 5.3). These were positive thinking (.5), instrumental support (.5), acceptance (.5), and her use of planning increased by one point. In order to interpret the meaning of these changes, her use of planning increased from 'I've been doing this a medium amount' to 'I've been doing this a lot'.

	Baseline	6 months	12 months
Adaptive coping			
Planning	3	3	4
Positive reframing	2.5	3	3
Instrumental support	3	3.5	3.5
Acceptance	2.5	3	3
Active coping	3.5	3.5	3.5
Maladaptive coping			
Venting	2	2	2
Denial	2	1.5	1.5
Distraction	3	2.5	2.5
Behavioural disengagement	1	1	1

Table 5.3 Use of maladaptive and adaptive coping strategies by Ellis over the duration of The Mentor Programme.

Regarding Ellis's use of maladaptive coping strategies (Table 5.3), she evidenced a decrease in the use of denial (.5) and distraction (.5). Her use of venting and behavioural disengagement remained unchanged. Results of the questionnaire representing her use of behavioural disengagement translated as 'I haven't been doing this at all'. As such, the lack of change represented the floor effect whereby it is not possible for the score to be any lower.

Having qualitatively explored the views of Ellis regarding each of the coping packs, she felt they all offered benefits. Ellis set goals to improve her communication on court. These goals were agreed by mentor and mentee, having established during the emotional intelligence pack that her emotional regulation could be improved. Both Ellis and her mentor commented that the resultant improvements had accrued positive effects for her on-court performances. Regarding the planning and time management pack, Ellis surmised 'the wall planner was good ... Jasmine (mentor) set out agendas for me, like we'd do titles of what I wanted to achieve, when by, what I had on that month and how I could sort out what I wanted to achieve and things like that'. When reflecting on the problem-solving pack, Ellis felt this pack structured thinking and increased options, 'she just used to branch off with all these different options and it made me kind of understand like a wider picture'. Finally, regarding the communication pack, Ellis and her mentor would use it to work through 'different scenarios, and also outside of netball things, like how will it affect me? what will I do? ... that was quite good it made me put things more in perspective'. Ellis concluded that The Mentor Programme had been beneficial for her because 'I think I'm a lot more organised ... and again that's 'cause of mentoring where I just had to organise myself and think what am I going to achieve and things like that'.

When considered collectively, the qualitative and quantitative results of all nine participants were complementary. Qualitative results indicated that participants perceived gains to coping, social and emotional competencies following completion of the coping intervention. Quantitative results indicated that the use of four adaptive coping strategies – positive reframing, interpersonal skills, active coping and adaptability – increased, and two avoidance coping strategies reduced over time. Players not on The Mentor Programme demonstrated minimal or no change in their use of coping strategies and socio-emotional competencies over the same timeframe. All participants interviewed recommended that The Mentor Programme be offered to junior national netball players. This view was exemplified by Ellis, 'You're at that level where if you don't plan ... you can find it a bit too much. I think it needs to be asked like individually whether they need it'.

The partially scripted coping intervention devised and applied by Devonport et al (2005) provided a longitudinally supportive environment for the development of coping skills. A key focus, and consequently benefit, of the coping intervention was the generalization of coping skills. In working towards the development of coping competencies, personal goals and the appraisal process were central to intervention activities. This enabled an individualized coping programme to be developed and maintained. The success of the programme was partly attributed to the consideration and implementation of these factors. As such, future coping interventions should strive to devise longitudinal coping interventions, taking into consideration personal idiosyncrasies.

The final activity for this chapter is designed to pull all the preceding information together. Read through the task presented in Activity box 5.3, and then re-read the chapter as necessary, identifying the information that will assist you in its completion.

Activity 5.3

Consider the potential sources of stress, and coping options, for an individual in the following situation:

An athlete is about to play in their first rugby game having returned from injury. What are the possible sources of stress for this individual? What can be done in the months, weeks, days and minutes leading up to the competition to prevent or cope with these potential stressors? What coping strategies can be utilized during and post performance to manage stressors that may occur?

Bear in mind that individuals may use more than one coping strategy at any point in time, and each strategy may have a different purpose. For example, positive self-talk may be used to deal with the emotions of the situation, whereas seeking advice may be used in a direct attempt to change the situation. The combination of coping strategies used may vary accordingly as the event unfolds (e.g. immediately post injury, when discussing rehabilitation, various stages during rehabilitation).

Conclusions

There is a wealth of anecdotal and empirical evidence to suggest that athletes commonly experience the debilitating effects of stress on performance (Hoar et al, 2006). Research has sought to identify the sources of stress typically encountered by athletes, and explore those coping strategies that appear to be effective in the management of such stressors. This chapter has attempted to summarize the stress and coping literature, and explore the coping interventions that have resulted from such research. The main implications for the construction and implementation of coping interventions have been highlighted as the chapter draws to a conclusion. The tasks that have been set are designed around the main contentions of Lazarus and Folkman's transactional model of stress and coping (1984). It is hoped that this will facilitate understanding and subsequent application of this model.

Key concepts and terms

Cognitive appraisal   Stress
Coping

Sample essay titles

- To what extent can the transactional model of stress and coping predict coping behaviours in sport? Discuss with reference to relevant literature.
- Discuss, with reference to relevant literature, those factors that determine the effectiveness of coping.
- In developing a coping intervention for athletes, what considerations should the practitioner make? Explore each consideration with reference to relevant literature.
- With the use of relevant literature, identify the influence that personal and situational factors may have on the appraisal of stress.

Further reading

Books

Frydenberg, E. (2002). *Beyond Coping: Meeting Goals, Visions, and Challenges.* Oxford: Oxford University Press.

Hoar, S.D., Kowalski, K.C., Gadreau, P., and Crocker, P.R.E. (2006). 'A review of coping in sport.' In: S. Hanton, and S. Mellalieu (Eds), *Literature Reviews in Sport Psychology*. Hauppage, NY: Nova Science Publishers, 53–103.

Lazarus, R.S. (1999). *Stress and Emotion: A New Synthesis*. New York: Springer.

Journal articles

Ntoumanis, N., and Biddle, S.J.H. (1998). The relationship of coping and its perceived effectiveness to positive and negative affect in sport. *Personality and Individual Differences*, 24, 773–778.

Rees, T., and Hardy, L. (2004). Matching social support with stressors: Effects on factors underlying performance in tennis. *Psychology of Sport and Exercise*, 5, 319–337.

Woodman, T., and Hardy, L. (2001b). A case study of organisational stress in elite sport. *Journal of Applied Sport Psychology*, 13, 207–238.

6 Performance profiling

Neil Weston

This chapter provides a comprehensive overview of the **performance profiling** technique (Butler and Hardy, 1992). Performance profiling is a client-centred assessment procedure that encourages athletes to identify qualities they deem important to performance and then rate their ability on each of those qualities. The sporting and theoretical origins of profiling will be presented followed by a description of the ways in which profiling can be delivered with individual athletes, coaches and teams. A critical evaluation of the profiling research will then be detailed including a summary of the uses, benefits, impacts and limitations of the technique. The chapter should provide the reader with an insight as to the usefulness of profiling within sports settings.

Learning outcomes

When you have completed this chapter you should be able to:

1. Describe the traditional performance profiling technique and adaptations to this procedure.
2. Describe and explain the theoretical roots of performance profiling.
3. Critically evaluate the profiling literature and outline the uses, impacts and limitations of the technique.

Activity 6.1

In relation to the sport you are currently playing, identify the key attributes or skills that help you to perform in that sport. What are the physical, technical, attitudinal, mental and tactical skills that enable you to play well?

It may help to reflect on a recent best performance. What skills/qualities helped you to perform to a high standard during that performance? Alternatively, reflect on an elite athlete in your sport/position. What skills/qualities/attributes do they possess that enable them to consistently perform at the highest level?

Write down these qualities in the table below:

Continued . . .

. . . Continued

PERFORMANCE QUALITIES				
Physical	**Technical**	**Mental/ attitudinal**	**Tactical**	**Other qualities**
E.g. Strength	*Passing*	*Concentration*	*Game awareness*	*Hydration*

One thing that strikes many athletes when completing this task is how difficult it is to accurately identify the skills that enable them to perform well, perhaps because they are rarely asked to consider what it takes to be good in their sport. Second, the list of qualities that you have identified in this first attempt is rarely a definitive list. Invariably you will need to reflect over time and add to the list of skills before you can be sure that it closely resembles those required for elite performance in your sport. This process of self-reflection and self-awareness is at the heart of Butler's (1989) performance profiling technique and is discussed in more detail in the text.

The traditional performance profiling technique and adaptations to this procedure

Performance profiling technique

The origins of performance profiling

The performance profiling technique was developed and used by Dr Richard Butler while working with the British Olympic Boxing team in the lead-up to the 1988 Seoul Olympics. Butler (1989) surmised that in order to succeed with any intervention a sport psychologist must empathize and understand the athlete's perception of themselves. He interviewed the boxers to understand what they perceived were the essential qualities required to perform successfully and then brought the boxers together as a group to agree upon the 20 most important qualities. Each boxer was finally asked to rate themselves on a scale of 1–7 to help identify their perceived strengths and weaknesses. Butler called the final product a 'self perception map', later termed the **performance profile** (Butler and Hardy, 1992). Following reflection and several years consulting with the British Olympic Boxing team, in 1992 he formalized the performance profiling procedure, detailing specifically how the procedure can be employed within individual and team settings in addition to defining its theoretical roots.

Butler and Hardy's (1992) performance profiling technique

The traditional approach to performance profiling follows three simple phases that can be adapted to suit the athlete(s). In phase one, performance profiling is introduced as a way of helping athletes to become more aware of the attributes necessary for successful performance in their sport and their perceived strengths and weaknesses. The athlete is instructed that there are no right or wrong answers and that an honest appraisal of their ability on the identified qualities can help to design training programmes to improve any areas of weakness. It may help to present an example of a completed profile (see Figure 6.1) so that the athlete gets an idea as to the types of qualities that have been identified and the end product that they will produce. Two main methods of presenting the completed profiles have been adopted in the literature. The first is the circular target (as seen in Figure 6.1) and second a tabular format, examples of which can be viewed in the work of Dale and Wrisberg (1996).

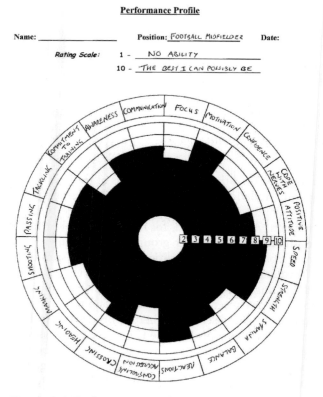

Figure 6.1 Performance profile of a soccer player.

Performance Profile

Name: _____   Sport/Position: _____

Rating Scale: 1 –   10 –

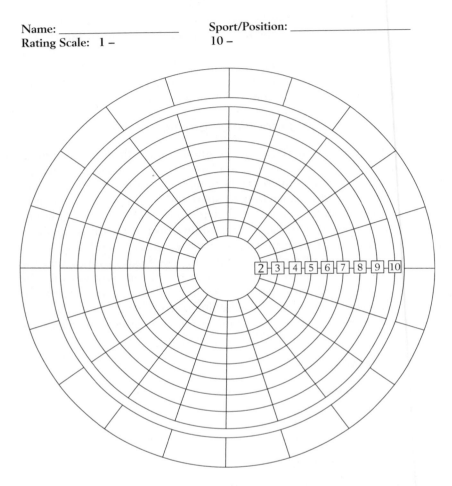

Figure 6.2 Blank performance profile template.

In phase two, when generating the qualities to form the basis of the profile, the procedure differs for group and individual settings. In a group setting, the qualities are developed through brainstorming in small groups that are typically based on positions within the team. A soccer squad, for example, would be split into goalkeeper, defender, midfielder and attacker groups. Each group is then asked to consider 'what in your opinion are the qualities or characteristics of an elite athlete in your sport?' (Butler and Hardy, 1992: 256). Each group would then spend 10–20 minutes discussing and recording the qualities they think are essential for elite performance in their chosen position. Each group then presents their findings back to the whole team with discussion where appropriate. Athletes are then provided with a blank performance profile (see Figure 6.2) and asked to identify, from all the qualities presented by the groups, the 20 most important qualities related to their position and style of play. It is important at this stage that athletes are asked to define each of the qualities. This is particularly important to

	Quality	Meaning
1.		
2.		
3.		
4.		
5.		
6.		
7.		
8.		
9.		
10.		
11.		
12.		
13.		
14.		
15.		
16.		
17.		
18.		
19.		
20.		

Figure 6.2 (continued)

make sure that any future ratings of profile attributes (by athlete and/or coach) are based on the same definition. In doing so, consultants can be more confident in any comparison of profile ratings over time or between athlete and coach.

In an individual setting the athlete elicits the attributes on a one-to-one basis with the help of the sport psychologist. Indeed, in instances when I have conducted this procedure with individual athletes I provide them with an example profile prior to the session and ask them to bring a list of qualities with them which can then be discussed and expanded upon. Video footage of the athlete performing successfully or of an elite athlete in their chosen sport can help initiate discussion.

The third and final profiling phase involves assessment of the qualities chosen by the athlete(s) on a scale of 1 (lowest possible ability) to 10 (ideal level for each quality). The ratings are in relation to the athlete's current perception of their

Activity 6.2

Having identified the list of qualities for your sport in Activity box 6.1, now choose the 20 most important qualities from that list. Using the blank profile provided in Figure 6.2, enter your qualities into each segment on the edge of the circular target and then rate yourself on the scale of 1 (lowest possible ability) to 10 (ideal level for each quality).

One of the key benefits of profiling is that it helps to highlight the specific areas that athletes believe they must improve and thus provides an excellent basis from which athlete-centred goal-setting and training programme implementation can be determined. Therefore, based on your profile, please complete the following table by outlining three key areas that you need to improve, a timeframe for improvement, a proposed new rating goal and a few strategies that will enable you to achieve that goal.

Performance quality	Current rating	Rating goal	Timeframe	Strategies to achieve goal
E.g. Speed	5	8	Next 3 months (by 1st December)	Contact the fitness advisor and arrange for a specific speed programme to be developed over next 3 months Attend each speed session and be 100% committed

Commonly athletes will dwell on areas of weakness and not emphasize those areas that they are good in. It is important that we encourage athletes to be aware of their strengths as much as those areas that they need to improve in order that their confidence is maintained. Therefore, in the table below, please record the top three strengths that you have identified, their ratings, and provide a brief statement, in the final column, to explain what you are going to do to maintain and/or improve these strengths.

Area of strength	Rating	Strategy to maintain/improve this area
Strength	8	To reassess current strength conditioning levels with coach and identify new targets for next three months

ability on each of the qualities. The completed profile then provides a useful visual display of the athlete's strengths and weaknesses which can then be used as a basis for identifying specific goals and training programmes to enhance those areas of weakness.

Variations of the profiling procedure

Since its inception, performance profiling has been employed in a wide variety of both individual and team sports (Doyle and Parfitt, 1997). This has resulted in the original procedure being modified to suit the demands of the particular consultancy situation. The majority of studies (e.g. Butler et al, 1993; Dale and Wrisberg, 1996; Doyle and Parfitt, 1999) have used the basic group profiling procedure outlined by Butler and Hardy (1992) in which a group brainstorming session is followed by the production of individual athlete performance profiles (see Chapter 4). However, variation in the generation of profile qualities, in profile scoring and the implementation of performance profiles has occurred.

Dale and Wrisberg (1996), in their consultancy with a female collegiate volleyball team, produced both coach and team performance profiles in addition to the traditional individual athlete profiles. While the individual athlete profiles adhered to Butler and Hardy's (1992) group profiling, team and coach profiling procedures slightly differed. The authors asked athletes to generate and then come to a consensus as to the qualities reflective of a successful team and ideal coach. Following this, each athlete was asked to rate the team and coach independently on the qualities of each profile on a scale of 1 to 10. A mean score for each attribute was established to determine the team's consensus regarding perceived strengths and weaknesses. At this point the coach was asked to rate independently each of the profiles to provide a comparison between athlete and coach opinions. This was subsequently used as a discussion tool for addressing the key athlete, team and coach performance-related issues.

A synthesis of literature suggests that comparing coach and athlete profile attributes can occur in two different ways (Butler, 1989, 1995; Butler and Hardy, 1992; Butler et al, 1993). The coach and athlete can independently identify the qualities for the athlete, come together and agree upon the 20 most important, separately rate the qualities and then discuss the rating similarities and/or differences. Alternatively, the athlete can determine the qualities and then give them to their coach to rate before coming together to discuss the profile findings.

There are a number of potential benefits and pitfalls with this coach/athlete comparison approach. First, consultants should be wary of how much disparity there is between ratings before getting athlete and coach to discuss the findings. Clearly, if there is already a conflict or clash of personalities between the coach and athlete, getting them to compare ratings may be problematic. Therefore consultants need to use their judgement in determining the suitability for adopting this profiling approach and look for circumstances when such comparisons will facilitate a positive influence on the athlete's performance development.

Jones (1993) provided a useful application of the performance profile when produced in a one-to-one setting. Using a completed profile example and prompts where appropriate, the athlete produced a list of 25 constructs from which to rate her ability. Jones (1993) then employed a variation of the basic rating procedure by asking the athlete to rate each quality on an importance scale of 1 ('not important at all') to 10 ('of crucial importance'). In keeping with the traditional approach (Butler and Hardy, 1992), Jones asked the athlete to determine her ideal score and current level of ability on each of the qualities on a scale of 1 ('couldn't be any worse') to 10 ('couldn't be any better'). Taking the self-assessment score (SAS) away from the ideal (I) and multiplying it by the importance rating (IR) produced a discrepancy score (D): $D = (I - SAS) \times IR$. This provided an indication of the areas requiring the most improvement. Based on this procedure, Jones was able to identify not only areas of weakness but also the most important areas that required immediate attention (see also Doyle and Parfitt, 1996, 1997).

In summary, some variations in the traditional profiling procedures have been adopted. Some have centred on modifying the generation of profile attributes (Butler, 1997; Dale and Wrisberg, 1996) whilst others have attempted to devise innovative approaches to the profile ratings procedure (Doyle and Parfitt, 1996, 1997; Jones, 1993).

Activity 6.3

Based on your profile in Activity box 6.2, it would now be useful to examine how the addition of an importance rating as used by Jones (1993) influences the priority of qualities requiring improvement. Using the table below, firstly record your qualities and their ratings in the first two columns. Then determine an ideal rating for each quality (in most instances this is likely to be 10) and rate the quality as to how important it is for performance (1, not important at all, to 10, extremely important). In the final column, take your current rating away from the ideal and then multiply by the importance rating: the higher the score, the greater the priority for improving the quality.

Quality	Current rating (C)	Ideal rating (ID)	Importance rating (IM)	Overall rating (ID − C × IM)
E.g. Tackling	5	10	8	40

The theoretical roots of performance profiling

Kelly's (1955) personal construct theory

Butler and Hardy (1992), in introducing and describing performance profiling, stated that the technique was based on **Kelly's (1955) personal construct theory (PCT)**. Kelly's theory of personality attempts to explain the way in which people interpret and thus behave in the world. Essentially Kelly believed that people attempt to understand the world by continually developing personal theories. These theories – or constructs, as he later termed them – help an individual to anticipate events in their life and are based on what he termed corollaries (or more simply 'effects'). Constructs can be revised based on athletes' experience of those events over time (the experience corollary). For example, over the course of an athlete's career, a number of assumptions (theories) regarding their sport and their ability (perhaps what they believe contributes to success) may be revised.

Kelly (1955) suggested that individuals will differ in the interpretation of events in their lives (the individuality corollary), and that in order for one to play a role in the 'social process' with another, one must attempt to understand the perceptions of that other person (the sociality corollary). By employing the profiling procedure, sport psychologists are able to understand the individual athlete's perception of performance, discuss such issues more effectively as a result of the increased understanding, and tailor training more closely to the athlete's perceived needs.

Thomas (1979) attempted to extend Kelly's (1955) PCT with the introduction of a self-awareness corollary. He suggested that a person will become more aware of themselves as a result of actively seeking to understand their own thought processes regarding the construction of events. This concept is closely aligned to the performance profiling procedure which asks athletes to organize their own thought processes and become more aware of the important qualities required to perform successfully in their sport and, second, their perceived strengths and weaknesses in relation to those qualities.

In summary, performance profiling provides a direct application of Kelly's (1955) PCT in the sporting environment. The procedure takes account of the fact that each athlete's interpretation of a situation or event will differ (individuality corollary), and provides an opportunity for those alternative views to be displayed to coaches/sport psychologists and thereby help to improve social interaction (sociality corollary). In actively getting athletes to evaluate the essential qualities and then rate themselves on those qualities, profiling can help to enhance an athlete's sporting self-awareness (self-awareness corollary). Moreover, as an individual's interpretation is likely to be revised based on experiences of events (experience corollary), employing the procedure repeatedly over time will help to record any of these changes in opinion.

Deci and Ryan's (1985) cognitive evaluation theory

Besides PCT, Butler and Hardy (1992) cite **Deci and Ryan's (1985) cognitive evaluation theory (CET)** as a theoretical basis for employing the technique. CET proposes that social and environmental factors (e.g. coach behaviour, rewards etc.) which reinforce an individual's perceptions of autonomy (feelings of personal control), competence (confidence in ability) and relatedness (feeling of belonging in a social setting) will facilitate higher levels of intrinsic motivation. Research evidence has shown such self-determined motivation to result in a number of positive consequences within sport/exercise including satisfaction (Frederick et al, 1996), interest (Li, 1999), concentration (Pelletier et al, 1995), pleasure and enjoyment (Beauchamp et al, 1996).

Butler and Hardy (1992) proposed that the autonomy supportive nature of profiling in the initial assessment phase would help to reinforce the athlete's intrinsic motivation for their sport. Furthermore profiling, when repeated over time, could help to reinforce improvements made on key performance attributes, thereby helping to improve athlete perceptions of competence. Finally, the group nature of the profiling procedure could help facilitate greater perceptions of relatedness as athletes communicate, interact and discuss performance-related issues with fellow team-mates and coaching staff.

Despite these assertions, little research has examined the motivational consequences of profiling within sports settings. Weston, Greenlees and Graydon (2004a) examined the impact of a profiling intervention on intrinsic motivation in collegiate soccer players over a six-week period in comparison to two control conditions. In this study, intrinsic motivation for the profiling group was significantly higher compared to the control groups. However, further research is needed to examine a) whether profiling can significantly improve athlete perceptions of autonomy, competence and relatedness, b) how often the procedure needs to be employed to bring about significant improvements, and c) whether any positive affects, cognitions and behaviours accompany these motivational changes.

The profiling literature: Uses, impacts and limitations of the technique

Most research examining the performance profile has been descriptive. Experimental research has tested the construct (Doyle and Parfitt, 1997) and predictive validity (Doyle and Parfitt, 1996) of profiling, in addition to examining the impact of mood state on profile responses (Doyle and Parfitt, 1999), and of repeated profiling on intrinsic motivation (Weston et al, 2004a). Despite the profile's widespread use there remains very little published research examining the efficacy of the technique. This lack of experimental research is surprising given the numerous uses and impacts of profiling that have been proposed in the literature.

Uses and impacts of performance profiling

Figure 6.3 provides a summary of the various impacts of profiling that have been proposed in the literature, some of which will now be discussed.

Enhanced self-awareness

Butler and Hardy (1992), in introducing the performance profile, suggest that the technique increases the athlete's self-awareness by encouraging the athlete to explore the qualities that define a successful performer in their own sport. In an examination of national under-21 netball player perceptions of the profiling procedure, the majority of players indicated that profiling was useful, citing an increase in self-awareness as a reason for its usefulness (Palmer et al, 1996).

Furthermore, Weston et al (2004b) found that 56 British Association of Sport and Exercise Sciences (BASES) accredited sport psychologists strongly believed profiling to be useful in raising athlete self-awareness. Two of the key facilitators come in the identification of the athlete's perceived strengths and also in those areas that they need to improve (Butler and Hardy, 1992; Butler et al, 1993; Weston, 2005). Profiling, specifically within a group environment, provides an additional opportunity to raise athlete awareness. By splitting players up into positional groups, asking them to brainstorm qualities and then presenting those qualities to their fellow team-mates, players can become more aware of the various positional demands within the team (cf. Dale and Wrisberg, 1996; Weston, 2005).

Developing intrinsic motivation

As described above, the performance profiling technique provides athletes with a more dominant role in the decision-making process regarding their future development, and in doing so, helps to maintain or increase athlete intrinsic motivation. Although some research has suggested a possible increase in motivation as a result of a profiling intervention (Jones, 1993; D'Urso et al, 2002), this research has been descriptive in nature and vague in its definition of the motivational changes. However, using an experimental design, Weston et al (2004a) found that a repeated profiling intervention significantly improved soccer players' intrinsic motivation over a six-week in-season period compared to two control conditions.

Developing confidence

Bandura (1997) outlines four sources of efficacy information: performance accomplishments, vicarious experience, verbal persuasion and interpretation of physiological arousal (see also Chapter 4). The use of performance profiling as a monitoring and evaluation technique (see below) could help reinforce a perception of performance accomplishment. For example, Butler et al (1993: 61) suggest that using the performance profile to monitor performance improvements could improve athlete confidence 'in that improvement reinforces a belief in the preparation'. The authors do warn, however, that using the profile to monitor progress could negatively influence an athlete's confidence if their profile ratings fail to improve, particularly in the lead-up to competitions.

Verbal persuasion refers to the use of persuasive techniques by self or other people to influence perceptions of self-efficacy. Examples of such techniques include self-talk, positive imagery, evaluative feedback and verbal persuasion by coaches, parents and peers (Feltz and Lirgg, 2001). Profiling could provide an alternative method to help coaches' feedback and/or reinforce perceptions of athletes' current ability. By employing the coach/athlete comparison of profile ratings procedure (Butler and Hardy, 1992), the coach can reinforce their belief in the ability of the athlete on the integral attributes required for successful performance.

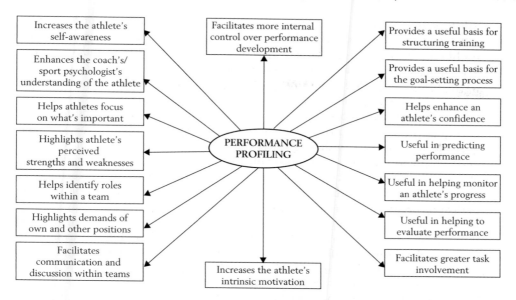

Figure 6.3 A summary of the proposed impacts and uses of performance profiling as suggested in the literature.

Useful basis for goal-setting

Goal-setting has frequently been shown to be a highly consistent and effective strategy in helping to enhance performance across a wide range of general (Locke and Latham, 1990) and sport-related tasks (Burton et al, 2001), particularly when athletes set goals for themselves (Kyllo and Landers, 1995). The profiling procedure of identifying key performance attributes, and then rating the strengths and weaknesses of those attributes, provides a useful template from which performance-related goal-setting can begin (Butler, 1997). The choice corollary of Kelly's (1955) PCT suggests that a person is likely to choose an avenue or alternative that will best facilitate a particular outcome. Thus athletes will choose those goals that they believe will result in the greatest improvements in their performance. Butler (1997) does however warn practitioners that the goals chosen and set by athletes may not always result in the most appropriate goals being set. Hence, while it may be important to get athletes involved in setting goals for themselves, psychologists and coaches should attempt to steer athletes towards choosing more appropriate goals when necessary.

Performance monitoring and evaluation

The monitoring and evaluation of performance is an important component in helping athletes to develop and improve. Repeated profiling over time has been suggested as a beneficial way of monitoring the progress of an athlete (Butler and Hardy, 1992; Doyle and Parfitt, 1997; Weston, 2005). Doyle and Parfitt (1997) experimentally investigated the usefulness of the performance profile in monitoring progress over time, in their examination of the construct validity of the performance profile. The authors suggested that the construct validity of the profile would be shown if a significant decrease in the area of perceived need (ideal score − current score) related to a significant increase in performance over time. Twelve track and field athletes devised and completed their performance profile five times over the course of a training and competitive indoor season. The athletes completed their profile as close to the training session or competition as possible. Other measures taken included the actual performance score (time or distance) and the athlete's and coach's perceptions of performance. Partial support was found for the construct validity of performance profiling. A significant increase in the mean actual performance measure was evident, in accordance with a significant decrease in the mean areas of perceived need profile scores. However, no significant difference was found for either the athletes' or coaches' perception of performance in relation to the perceived need changes. Doyle and Parfitt (1997) concluded that practitioners employing the performance profile as a monitoring tool should be aware that it may only be useful when large changes in performance are likely, either during intense training periods or when recovering from injury. Further research is warranted to examine the profile's utility in this way over longer time periods and across various sporting populations.

Enhanced team communication

In sport, communication has been proposed as an important component in developing team cohesion (Miller B.P., 1997; Carron et al, 2002) and facilitating successful performance (Carron and Hausenblas, 1998; Yukelson, 1998). However, very little literature has been published on the techniques that facilitate effective communication in sport (Yukelson, 1998). Dale and Wrisberg (1996) propose that performance profiling could be a useful technique in opening and enhancing communication channels within teams. Their article described a case study in which a collegiate female volleyball team's head coach asked the consultants to help the team become more united and improve the low communication levels that the coach perceived had developed. Dale and Wrisberg (1996) decided that individual, team and coach performance profiles, produced by the players and then discussed with the coach, would facilitate communication within the team. The process reportedly enabled the athletes to play a more active role in decisions regarding the team's development and helped the athletes to discuss with coaching staff areas in need of improvement. Given the strong relationship that has been found between team cohesion and performance (Carron et al, 2002), collective efficacy (Paskevich, 1995; cited in Paskevich et al, 2001) and work output (Prapavessis and Carron, 1997), identifying strategies that are effective in improving team cohesion is an important consideration for team coaches and psychologists. Further research across a range of team sports is needed to justify the use of profiling interventions to facilitate team cohesion and performance improvements.

Limitations of performance profiling

It is important to be aware of the limitations of profiling in order that practitioners employ the technique in a balanced and appropriate manner. One limitation centres on the identification of the qualities for an athlete's profile. Given that athletes predominantly identify their qualities, problems may emerge in relation to the accuracy of those qualities produced. This may be particularly the case with athletes who have low self-awareness, are new to the sport or are young in age (Weston, 2005). In these instances the practitioner must facilitate coach involvement to enable greater accuracy in the construction of profile attributes. Furthermore, with young athletes in whom brainstorming the key qualities may prove difficult, it would be worthwhile providing them with a list of appropriate qualities from which they can then choose. While not entirely adhering to Butler and Hardy's (1992) suggestions, this process still enables the athletes to feel that they have been involved in the process of developing their profile. A secondary issue relating to profile quality identification is that an athlete's profile rarely captures the true essence of an individual's personal constructs after the first attempt. Indeed, several additional reflections on the profile are needed before an athlete can be reasonably sure that the profile fully represents the necessary qualities needed for successful performance in their sport/position. Thus the profiling procedure can be time consuming, potentially resulting in a lack of engagement from both athlete and coach.

Limitations in the profile can also be found in the rating of profile attributes. First, the subjective nature of athlete rating can result in issues with regard to the accuracy of ability ratings. There may also be issues with athletes being dishonest or self-serving in their ratings. Furthermore, continued rating of the profile over time may result in a decrease in profile ratings, adversely affecting the athletes' confidence. Finally, athletes have voiced concern at rating profiles in preseason or early season when they have little playing experience in order to judge their ability on each quality (Weston, 2005). Given these concerns it is important that practitioners are wary of when (and when not) to profile athletes throughout a season in order that accurate ratings can be produced. It is also important to encourage athletes to choose a rating scale that is meaningful and easily understood so as to increase the accuracy of ratings. Finally, it is critical that athletes are clearly instructed as to the benefits that they will gain through profiling and the confidential nature of the findings so as to encourage greater honesty in profile ratings.

Doyle and Parfitt (1999), in examining the impact of mood state on profile ratings, provide an important consideration when attempting to use the technique. The authors found that a positive mood state prior to profile rating would result in elevated responses to profile constructs whereas negative or neutral mood states did not affect profile responses. Although this is not necessarily a limitation of the profiling procedure, it is important that consultants and coaches are aware that positive mood states prior to profile completion can result in athletes overestimating their ability on profile qualities.

Conclusions

Initial assessment within sport psychology is fundamental to allow the consultant to correctly ascertain an athlete's key strengths and weaknesses and thus determine intervention strategies to aid improvements in performance. Performance profiling has been successfully employed across a range of ages, abilities and sports, providing a useful method of assessment which places the athlete at the centre of the decision-making process regarding their future development. Given the flexible nature of the procedure, it can be employed with individual athletes, coaches, teams and units within teams. Based on the selected principles of Kelly's (1955) PCT, profiling helps to raise athlete awareness as to the qualities essential to elite performance in addition to their perceived strengths and weaknesses. It provides a useful basis for goal-setting and has been found to be useful in evaluating and monitoring performance and facilitating coach/athlete communication, in addition to enhancing communication, interaction and discussion within teams. Given the predominance of descriptive profiling research and lack of empirical research examining the efficacy of the technique within various sports settings, many of the proposed impacts of the technique (e.g. improving confidence, intrinsic motivation and self-awareness) require further investigation. Furthermore, more longitudinal evaluative research, employed during, post and retention measures, is needed to ascertain the efficacy of the technique in order to enhance its credibility.

Key concepts and terms

Deci and Ryan's (1985) cognitive evaluation theory

Kelly's (1955) personal construct theory

Performance profile

Performance profiling

Sample essay titles

- Performance profiling fails to provide a valid and reliable method of performance assessment. Critically evaluate this statement with reference to appropriate literature.
- Critically evaluate the efficacy of Butler and Hardy's (1992) performance profiling technique.
- Critically discuss the uses, impacts and limitations of performance profiling.
- Performance profiling fails to have a strong theoretical and research basis to justify its use. Discuss this statement with reference to relevant literature.

Further reading

Books

Butler, R.J. (1989). 'Psychological preparation of Olympic boxers.' In: J. Kremer, and W. Crawford (Eds), *The Psychology of Sport: Theory and Practice*. Belfast: BPS Northern Ireland Branch, 74–84.

Butler, R. (1997). 'Performance profiling: Assessing the way forward.' In: R.J. Butler (Ed.), *Sports Psychology in Performance*. Oxford: Butterworth-Heinemann, 33–48.

Journal articles

Butler, R.J., and Hardy, L. (1992). The performance profile: Theory and application. *The Sport Psychologist*, 6, 253–264.

Butler, R.J., Smith, M., and Irwin, I. (1993). The performance profile in practice. *Journal of Applied Sport Psychology*, 5, 48–63.

Dale, G.A., and Wrisberg, C.A. (1996). The use of a performance profile technique in a team setting: Getting the athletes and coach on the 'same page'. *The Sport Psychologist*, 10, 261–277.

Doyle, J.M., and Parfitt, G. (1997). Performance profiling and constructive validity. *The Sport Psychologist*, 11, 411–425.

D'Urso, V., Petrosso, A., and Robazza, C. (2002). Emotions, perceived qualities, and performance of rugby players. *The Sport Psychologist*, 16, 173–199.

Jones, G. (1993). The role of performance profiling in cognitive behavioural interventions in sport. *The Sport Psychologist*, 7, 160–172.

7 The scientific application of music in sport and exercise

Costas I. Karageorghis

Neither are the two arts of music and gymnastics really designed, as is often supposed, the one for the training of the soul, the other for training of the body.

What then is the real object of them?

I believe, I said, the teachers of both have in view chiefly the improvement of the soul. (Plato, The Republic)

This chapter describes the science underlying the effects of music in sport and exercise. Recent theoretical advances pertaining to the effects of music in these contexts are discussed, and relevant literature is critically appraised. Also, a new instrument is presented – the Brunel Music Rating Inventory-3 – that can be used to assess the motivational qualities of music in sport and exercise. The chapter is peppered with examples of how music can be applied and concludes with some suggestions for future research.

Learning outcomes

When you have completed this chapter you should be able to:

1. Describe the main constituents of music and its psychological, psychophysical, psychophysiological and ergogenic effects.
2. Present and discuss the conceptual/theoretical models that have been advanced to explain the effects of music in the domain of sport and exercise.
3. Apply an objective method for the selection of music that is appropriate for sport and exercise contexts.
4. Design some basic music-related interventions for athletes or exercise participants.

Introduction: An overview of music in sport and exercise

History books reveal that from the very dawn of civilization, ancient cultures combined sounds in ways that influenced the human psyche. With the passage of time, primitive forms of music evolved into ever-more artistically pleasing arrangements. Accordingly, music came to be used for highly diverse purposes: as an integral part of worship, as a form of entertainment, to aid healing, to lead soldiers into battle and to punctuate civil ceremonies.

A musical composition entails the organization of three primary elements: *melody*, *harmony* and *rhythm*. Melody is the tune of a piece of music – the part you might hum or whistle along to; harmony acts to shape the mood of the music to make you feel happy, sad, edgy or romantic through the meshing of sounds; whereas rhythm has to do with the speed of music and the way in which it is accented. Essentially, rhythm is the element of music that prompts a physical reaction in the listener. Wilson and Davey (2002: 177) observed that even when people sit motionless, 'it is often very difficult to suppress the natural urge to tap the feet or strum the fingers along with the beat of the music'. Moreover, musical rhythm relates to the various periodicities of human functioning such as respiration, heart beat and walking (Bonny, 1987).

During the last two decades, music has become almost ubiquitous in venues associated with physical exercise, sports training or competition. It is played in gymnasiums, athletic stadiums and even through underwater speakers in swimming pools. Is such music played in order to promote greater work output or does it simply make participation in an activity a little more pleasurable? If music does indeed increase work output or enjoyment of an activity, how can we go about maximizing such benefits? These are questions that will be addressed in this chapter using, in part, the author's own research findings and applied practice.

History, tradition and mythology

During the twentieth century, the Olympic Games helped to formalize the association between music and athletic endeavour. Music was incorporated into some Olympic events, such as rhythmic gymnastics and synchronized swimming. Live music was used at the opening and closing ceremonies of the Games. One of the most spectacular examples of this was the opening ceremony of the 1984 Los Angeles Games, at which 84 white baby-grand pianos were played in unison. Also, the national anthem of the winning athlete for each event is played at the medal ceremony, often reducing seasoned competitors to tears as the emotion associated with the occasion overwhelms them.

Music and sport seem to go hand-in-hand at modern-day sporting events with professional deejays often hired to make appropriate selections to rouse the players or engage the crowd. It is rare not to hear music blaring out of soccer stadiums, rugby grounds and basketball arenas around the globe. Most teams have adopted their own anthems or signature tunes. For example, at West Ham United FC it is the classic *I'm Forever Blowing Bubbles*, while the Kop at Anfield reverberates to the anthemic *You'll Never Walk Alone*, which was popularized by Gerry and the Pacemakers in the 1960s.

Through a cursory examination of popular myth and folklore, one might reach the conclusion that music has a profound influence on the human psyche. The Pied Piper of Hamelin took revenge on the town's dishonourable officials by

Application 7.1

Swing Low, Sweet Chariot

The use of anthemic chanting that reverberates around a rugby crowd can be a tremendous source of inspiration to the players. Most great teams have a signature chant or song. For example, England rugby fans sing the rousing negro spiritual *Swing Low, Sweet Chariot*. This was spontaneously adopted in March 1988 during a game against Ireland when Chris Oti, a black player, scored a sensational hat-trick for England. The recital of this hymn, whether in the stands or the players' dressing room, serves to promote feelings of patriotism, unity and pride.

entrancing all of the children with his intoxicating melodies. In Homer's *Odyssey*, Odysseus told of the songs of Sirens, creatures who were half woman and half bird, that cast a spell on sailors whose ships were subsequently dashed against the rocks. He insisted that wax be placed in the ears of each of his men and he himself was tied to the mast of his ship so as not to succumb to the Sirens' songs (see Figure 7.1). In the Old Testament, David's harp playing enabled King Saul to overcome a deep state of depression, and David went on to become the second king of Israel. In more recent history, the 12-bar blues emerged through the work songs of enslaved African Americans. Their work movements were made smoother and more efficient by the directing force of group singing (Farnsworth, 1969). Such songs also gave the slaves hope of a future free of oppression and exploitation.

Figure 7.1 Odysseus and the Sirens.

Source: From the painting 'Odysseus and the Sirens' by John William Waterhouse, 1891.

The main effects of music

In the context of sport and exercise, the extant literature has primarily explored the *psychological, psychophysical, psychophysiological* and *ergogenic* effects of music. *Psychological* effects entail the impact music has on mood, emotion, affect (feelings of pleasure/displeasure), cognition (thought processes) and behaviour. The *psychophysical* effects of music concern the psychological perception of one's physical state, a branch of psychology known as *psychophysics*. In the context of music and physical activity the measure that is most often used is that of ratings of perceived exertion (RPE; e.g. Szmedra and Bacharach, 1998; Nethery, 2002; Tenenbaum et al, 2004; Edworthy and Waring, 2006). *Psychophysiological* effects of music have to do with the impact of music on physiological functioning; typical dependent measures include heart rate, oxygen uptake and exercise lactate. Music has an *ergogenic* effect when it enhances work output or engenders higher than expected power output, endurance or productivity.

Music in sport and exercise – theoretical developments

Scientific studies into the effects of music in sport and exercise contexts have reported more modest reactions than those documented in history or mythology. Nonetheless, music has been shown to have the potential to make a meaningful difference to performance in the hotbed of competition where skills and abilities are often very closely matched. Moreover, music can have a profound effect on exercise performance and could play a major part in the solution to the nation's growing inactivity and obesity problem (Karageorghis et al, 2007).

Much of the early experimental work in this area was blighted by an atheoretical approach which yielded largely equivocal findings. The review of Karageorghis and Terry (1997) highlighted several methodological weaknesses that may have accounted for such findings and set the scene for future conceptual developments. The main weaknesses evident in past research were: a) the failure to consider the socio-cultural background of experimental participants; b) the imprecise approach to musical selection or failure to report the music played; c) inconsistencies regarding temporal factors such as the duration of music exposure and when it is played relative to the experimental task; d) inaccurate use of musical terminology by sports researchers; and e) the use of performance measures that were either inappropriate or difficult to control.

In the decade since the review of Karageorghis and Terry (1997), there has been a marked increase in the number of studies examining the effects of music in sport and exercise. This is evidenced by the small number of related studies (*k* = 13) cited in Karageorghis and Terry's review which covered research conducted over the 25-year period since the review of Lucaccini and Kreit (1972). In the subsequent decade, at least 42 related studies have been published. As well as an increase in the quantity of studies, there has also been a marked increase in quality; this is corroborated by the large number of music-related studies published in the foremost sports science and sports medicine journals. The present chapter will primarily consider theoretical advances and research conducted in the period since the 1997 review paper.

The first conceptual model (1999)

To address the paucity of theory, the author and his collaborators have published a number of conceptual frameworks over the last decade. The original conceptual framework for predicting psychophysical effects of **asynchronous music** in exercise and sport (Karageorghis et al, 1999) held that four factors contribute to the motivational qualities of a piece of music – rhythm response, musicality, cultural impact and association. These factors emerged from an earlier review (Karageorghis and Terry, 1997) and were subject to empirical examination using both exploratory and confirmatory factor analyses (Karageorghis et al, 1999). The term asynchronous music is used to describe the use of music as a background to exercise- or sport-related activities without any *conscious* attempt by the performer to synchronize their movements with musical tempo or rhythm.

Rhythm response relates to natural responses to musical rhythm, especially tempo which is the speed of music as measured in beats per minute (bpm). Musicality refers to pitch-related elements such as harmony (how notes are combined) and melody (the tune). Cultural impact concerns the pervasiveness of music within society or a particular sub-cultural group; exposure to music increases familiarity, which has an important role in terms of aesthetic response. Finally, association pertains to the extra-musical associations that music may evoke, such as *Eye of the Tiger* and the feats of Rocky Balboa in the Rocky film series. Such associations are built up by repetition and powerful images in which cinema, television, radio and the internet play an important role.

If the media promote an association between specific pieces of music and sporting activities this may work as a conditioned response that can *trigger* a particular mindset. In a similar way, music can just as easily trigger a relaxation response to relieve pre-competition anxiety. Its therapeutic, anxiety-relieving properties have been used for centuries. For example, think of Fleetwood Mac's classic track *Albatross* or go online to hear an excerpt on YouTube (www.youtube.com/watch?v=bSZHT2XvoLM). The piece is so slow, so simple and so beautifully structured that you immediately begin to feel more at ease, even by just imagining the music in your mind's ear.

Some aspects of music selection have to do with how music is composed and performed, whereas others have to do with how it is interpreted by the listener. Rhythm response and musicality, which determine the energy and mood of the music, are *internal factors*. This means they have to do with the way in which the music has been put together: the composition, the tempo, the instrumentation and so on. The cultural impact of the music and extra-musical associations are *external factors*, meaning that they are associated with the listener's interpretation of the music and their musical experiences.

Karageorghis et al (1999) showed that it is the internal factors which are more important in predicting how a person will respond to a piece of music and so the four factors that contribute to the motivational qualities of a piece of music are hierarchical in nature. The implication is that when selecting for a group with different musical experiences, it is possible to select music with motivational properties, as careful attention can be given to the internal factors. The relationship between internal and external factors, the motivation qualities of music and potential benefits can be seen in Figure 7.2.

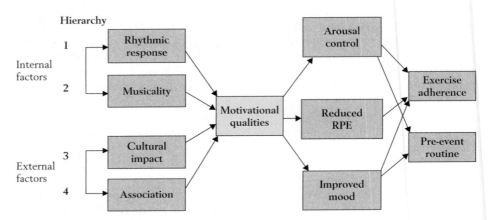

Figure 7.2 Conceptual framework for the prediction of responses to motivational asynchronous music in exercise and sport.

Source: Adapted with permission from Karageorghis et al, 1999, Journal of Sports Sciences, 17, 713–724.

The main benefits of listening to asynchronous (background) music are that it can act as a stimulant or sedative to influence arousal levels. In general terms, loud, upbeat music will function as a stimulant (increases arousal) while soft, slow music will function as a sedative (reduces arousal); music can reduce RPE, but only during sub-maximal work intensities because during high intensity activity physiological cues predominate attention and music has a negligible effect on RPE (Hernandez-Peon, 1961; Rejeski, 1985; Tenenbaum, 2001). Music can enhance the positive aspects of mood such as vigour and happiness, and reduce the negative aspects such as tension, depression, anger, fatigue and confusion (Karageorghis and Terry, 1999; Hewston et al, 2005; Edworthy and Waring, 2006; Terry et al, 2006). In turn, these benefits can impact upon adherence to exercise through making the exercise experience more pleasurable or be used as part of a pre-event routine in sport to engender an optimal mindset (arousal control and improved mood; cf. Chapter 1).

Motivational and oudeterous music

Alongside their conceptual model, Karageorghis et al (1999) developed an associated measure of the motivational qualities of music known as the Brunel Music Rating Inventory (BMRI). They indicated that the main characteristics of motivational music are that it has a fast tempo (>120 beats per minute [bpm]) and strong rhythm, while it increases energy and induces bodily action. They

Activity 7.1

The Brunel Music Rating Inventory-3

This questionnaire is designed to assess the extent to which the piece of music you are about to hear would motivate you during [insert activity here]. For our purposes, the word 'motivate' means music that would make you want to either pursue [insert activity here] with greater intensity or to stick at it for longer, or both. As you listen to the piece of music, indicate the extent of your agreement with the six statements listed below by circling one of the numbers to the right of each statement. You should provide an honest response to each statement. Give the response that best represents your opinion, and avoid dwelling for too long on any single statement.

		Strongly disagree	In-between					Strongly agree
1.	The rhythm of this music would motivate me during [insert activity here]	1	2	3	4	5	6	7
2.	The style of this music (i.e. rock, dance, jazz, hip hop, etc.) would motivate me during [insert activity here]	1	2	3	4	5	6	7
3.	The melody (tune) of this music would motivate me during [insert activity here].	1	2	3	4	5	6	7
4.	The tempo (speed) of this music would motivate me during [insert activity here].	1	2	3	4	5	6	7
5.	The sound of the instruments used (i.e. guitar, synthesizer, saxophone, etc.) would motivate me during [insert activity here]	1	2	3	4	5	6	7
6.	The beat of this music would motivate me during [insert activity here]	1	2	3	4	5	6	7

BMRI-3 Scoring instructions

Add the six items for a score between 6 and 42. A score in the range 36–42 indicates high motivational qualities in the piece of music, a score in the range 24–35 indicates moderate motivational qualities, while a score below 24 indicates that the rated track lacks motivational qualities or is oudeterous.

operationalized the term *oudeterous music* as music which is neither motivating nor demotivating. This was necessary owing to the confusion that may have ensued through using the term *neutral music*, which has connotations that transcend the motivational qualities of music (cf. neutral colours, neutral emotions, neutral point of view, etc.). Many subsequent studies used the BMRI and its derivatives to objectively rate the motivational qualities of music used in experimental conditions (e.g. Karageorghis and Lee, 2001; Atkinson et al, 2004; Elliott et al, 2004; Crust and Clough, 2006; Karageorghis et al, 2006a; Simpson and Karageorghis, 2006).

Through their research and application of the BMRI, Karageorghis and his collaborators found certain limitations in its psychometric properties and applicability in exercise and sport. This led them to radically redesign and revalidate the instrument (Karageorghis et al, 2006b). The process began with an extensive qualitative appraisal of the scale by exercise participants. The results of this contributed to a new item pool and each item was structured to refer to an *action*, a *time*, a *context* and a *target* at the same level of generality (cf. Azjen and Fishbein, 1977). The action concerned motivation, the time reference was *during* exercise, the context was exercise and the target was a property of the music such as melody or tempo. Hence, the generic form of each item was: 'The *property* [e.g. melody] of this music would motivate me during exercise'. For the purposes of this chapter, in Activity box 7.1 there is a slightly modified version of the BMRI-2 (the BMRI-3) included which can be used to rate the motivational qualities of music for both exercise and sport contexts.

A cautionary note on use of the BMRI-3

The authors of the BMRI-2 indicated that there are limitations in rating the multitudinous facets of the musical response using solely a psychometric-type approach. Some aspects of aesthetic experience transcend scientific evaluation; therefore, to elicit optimum selection of music in sport and exercise settings, it may be necessary to use the BMRI-3 in tandem with qualitative methods. The BMRI-3 can be used as a wide filter to identify music pieces that can then be considered on additional grounds such as extra-musical associations and lyrical content. Karageorghis et al (2006b: 907) presented a framework of criteria for music selection to which you may wish to refer.

The second conceptual model (2006)

Terry and Karageorghis (2006) later focused the conceptual framework primarily in a sport context (see Figure 7.3), postulating that the main benefits athletes would derive from listening to music would be: a) increased positive moods and reduced negative moods; b) pre-event activation or relaxation; c) dissociation from unpleasant feelings such as pain and fatigue; d) reduced RPE; e) increased work output through synchronization of musical tempo with movement; f) enhanced acquisition of motor skills when rhythm or association is matched with required movement patterns; g) increased likelihood of achieving flow state; and h) enhanced performance levels via combinations of the above mechanisms. The literature that is critically appraised in the second half of this chapter provides considerable support for these proposed benefits.

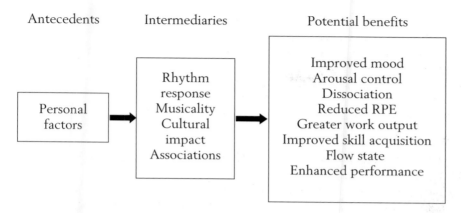

Figure 7.3 Conceptual framework for benefits of music in sport and exercise contexts.

Source: Reproduced with permission from Australian Psychological Society Ltd.

The grounded theory model (2007)

Most recently, Bishop, Karageorghis and Loizou (2007) developed a grounded theory of young tennis players' use of music to manipulate emotional state (see Figure 7.4). **Grounded theory** is a technique developed by Glaser and Strauss (1967) for developing theory from qualitative data through a form of content analysis. This is one of very few studies that take a qualitative approach to the application of music in sport. Bishop et al's data, which were derived from a music questionnaire, interviews, a two-week diary and observation of facial expressions (smiling, **piloerection** [hair standing on end] and increased liveliness), indicated that the tennis players consciously selected music to elicit various emotional states. The most frequently reported consequences of music listening included improved mood, increased arousal, and visual and auditory imagery. The grounded theory in tennis lent support to the generic sport benefits reported a year earlier by Terry and Karageorghis. A number of factors were found to mediate the choice of music tracks and the impact of music listening: these included extra-musical associations (cf. Karageorghis et al, 1999), inspirational lyrics, music properties (e.g. rhythm, melody and harmony) and desired emotional state.

Bishop et al's (2007) model can be used to inform psychological music-related interventions at the delivery stage. For example, increasing the tempo and/or intensity (volume) of a piece of music can increase an athlete's arousal or activation level. There are at least two reasons why music affects arousal levels. First, physiological processes tend to react sympathetically to the rhythmical components of music. Fast, upbeat music increases respiration rate, heart rate, sweat secretion and other indicators of physical activation. Second, arousal is increased through extra-musical association. In other words, the music promotes thoughts that inspire physical activity or superior sporting performance. Just as the association between a first love and 'your song' can be very strong, so is the relationship between certain pieces of music and sporting endeavour.

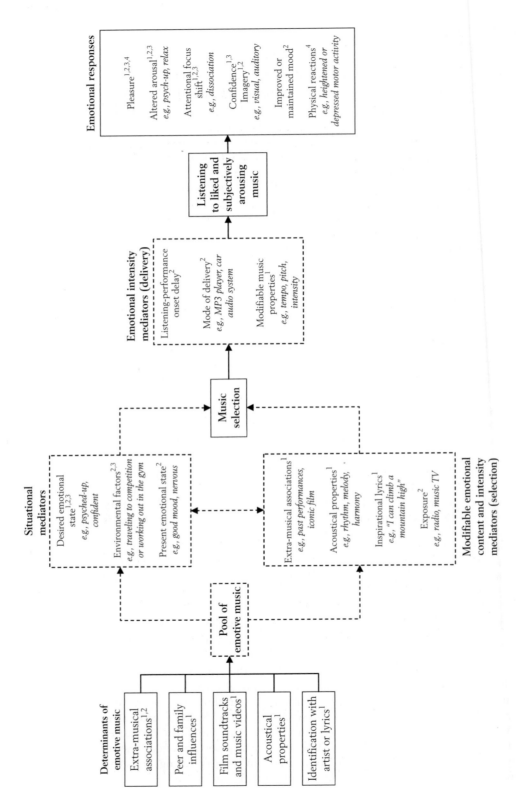

Figure 7.4 A model of young tennis players' use of music to manipulate emotional state. 1= Interview data, 2 = Diary data, 3 = Questionnaire data, 4 = Interview observation data.

Source: Reproduced with permission from Human Kinetics. Journal of Sport & Exercise Psychology, 2007, 29, 584–607.

Application 7.2

Football's Coming Home

When England football fans hear the chant 'It's coming home, football's coming home' from the song *Three Lions* performed by popular TV comedians Badiel and Skinner, they immediately think of the 1996 European Soccer Championships hosted by England and are reminded of the sense of optimism and expectation that surrounded this event. The lyrics alluded to the fact that England, the spiritual home of football, had not won a major championship since the World Cup they hosted in 1966. Unfortunately, it was not to be for England on this occasion, however, the catchy lyric served to bridge the gap between a mere soccer tournament and a stage for the nation's hopes and dreams.

Pre-task music

A small number of studies have investigated music as a pre-task stimulant or sedative. **Pre-task music** describes the introduction of music before, as opposed to during, a task. For example, Karageorghis et al (1996) examined the effects of fast tempo, energizing music and slow tempo, relaxing music on grip strength. Participants produced significantly higher hand-grip dynamometer scores after listening to stimulative music compared to sedative music or a **white noise** control. White noise is a random sound with equal power at all frequencies (flat power spectral density) which equates to featureless noise in the perception of the listener. White noise is analogous therefore to white light in that it blocks other frequencies and distracts the listener from other sounds in their environment. Sedative music yielded lower scores than white noise. The authors concluded that a simple motor task such as grip strength provides a sensitive proxy measure of the psychophysiological effects of music.

Karageorghis and Lee (2001) investigated the effects of pre-test motivational music and imagery on isometric muscular endurance. Participants were required to hold dumbbells weighing 15 per cent of their body mass in a crucifix position until they reached voluntary exhaustion. The researchers found that the combination of music and imagery, when compared to imagery only, enhanced muscular endurance performance, although it did not appear to enhance the potency of imagery. These findings were in contrast to the earlier findings of Gluch (1993) and might be explained, in part, by the motoric nature of the experimental task; imagery use has proven more effective in preparation for cognitive tasks (see Chapter 8).

Pates et al (2003) examined the effects of pre-task music on flow states and netball shooting performance using an idiographic, single subject, multiple-baselines, across-subjects design ($n = 3$). Two participants reported an increase in their perception of flow and all three dramatically improved their shooting performance. The netball players also reported that the intervention helped them to control the emotions and cognitions impacting upon their performance. Pates et al concluded that interventions including self-selected music and imagery could enhance athletic performance by triggering emotions and cognitions associated with flow.

In a similar vein, Lanzillo et al (2001) investigated the impact of pre-event music on competition anxiety and self-confidence among intercollegiate athletes from a wide variety of sports. One group of athletes listened to a three-minute selection of their preferred music prior to competition while a control group did not listen to any music. The experimental group reported higher state self-confidence than the control group although there were no differences reported in competition anxiety.

Application 7.3

Olympic double-trap shooting champion, Richard Faulds

Peter Terry worked as consultant psychologist to British trap shooter Richard Faulds at the 2000 Olympic Games in Sydney. As they approached the shooting range each day for training and on the day of competition, Terry would play a CD of Whitney Houston's *One Moment in Time* on the car stereo while Faulds would visualize how he would calmly and decisively seize the moment. On the final day of competition, that is exactly what he did, in a gripping contest in which he won gold by the narrowest of margins, edging out the hot favourite, Russell Mark of Australia.

Summary of findings relating to pre-task music

Collectively, research has shown that pre-task music can be used to: a) manipulate activation states through its arousal control qualities; b) facilitate task-relevant imagery; c) promote flow; and d) enhance perceptions of self-confidence. There is a paucity of research in this area creating considerable scope for examination of the role of music in eliciting optimal pre-performance states for sport and in priming individuals for bouts of exercise.

Asynchronous music

Most research has examined the impact of background music where it is used simply to change the environment during the performance of a sport- or exercise-related task. *Asynchronous* use of music, as this is known, occurs when there is no *conscious* synchronization between movement and music tempo. That is not to say that unintentional synchronous movement does not occur. For example, the Brazilian football team has a large contingent of percussion players among its supporters. Many observers have noted that the Brazilian style of play often appears to emulate the lilting swing of the samba, a rhythm synonymous with Brazilian culture. Indeed the national team are commonly referred to as the

'Samba Boys'. Researchers normally investigate psychophysical or psychophysiological effects of asynchronous music rather than ergogenic effects.

In the asynchronous application of music, tempo is postulated to be the most important determinant of the response to music (Brown, 1979; Karageorghis et al, 1999) and preference for different tempi may be affected by the physiological arousal of the listener and the context in which the music is heard (Berlyne, 1971; North and Hargreaves, 1997; Karageorghis et al, 2006a). This suggests there might be a stronger preference for fast tempo music during physical activity, although some research has indicated that slower tempi may increase physiological efficiency and thus prolong exercise performance (e.g. Copeland and Franks, 1991).

Application 7.4

Charlotte, the triathlete

Charlotte is an outstanding cyclist and runner, but a relatively weak swimmer. This 'chink in her armour' has prevented her from enjoying international success in her sport. She makes a concerted effort to improve by swimming at least 15 miles in training each week. This is often a lonely and physically challenging task with little variation. Her coach aims to make Charlotte a more competent swimmer. To achieve this, Charlotte needs to relax and avoid wasting energy through excessive muscular tension. To aid her improvement, she uses a specially designed waterproof MP3 player in her swimming cap – Soundwaves. Charlotte listens to soulful ballads and soft, relaxing music. In particular she enjoys listening to the slow, ambient dance track *Terrapin* by Bonobo. She associates this soft music with the graceful, submarine movements of these elegant reptiles. The harmonies within the music create a positive mood while the flowing rhythms and slow

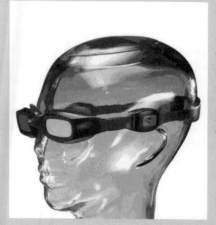

tempo help her to relax and maintain an efficient and regular stroke. The music also becomes a focus on long-distance swims and distracts her from the negative bodily sensations associated with fatigue. In fact, the effects of the music can be quite hypnotic and after a while, she feels as though she is gliding effortlessly through the water.

Figure 7.5 The Soundwaves underwater MP3 player.
Source: With permission from Sam James, Designer.

A body of work has investigated the relationship between working heart rate, usually during an exercise task, and preference for music tempo (e.g. Karageorghis et al, 2006a). Such work stems from the notion espoused by many exercise practitioners that music tempo should be allied to expected heart rate (see Gfeller, 1988). Also, work in the field of experimental aesthetics (e.g. Berlyne, 1971) indicates that the *arousal potential* of stimuli determines preference. By arousal potential, Berlyne meant the amount of activity that stimuli induce in areas of the brain such as the reticular activating system. Stimuli that have a moderate degree of arousal potential are liked most and the degree of liking decreases towards the extremes of arousal potential in a classic inverted-U relationship.

Early research tested the hypothesis that people prefer auditory stimuli with tempi within the range of normal heart rate patterning during everyday activity (e.g. 70–100 bpm). For example, Iwanaga (1995a) required participants to search for their favourite tempo through a process of self-regulation wherein they adjusted the frequency of a 440 Hz pure tone. As predicted, the preferred tempi were close to heart rate. Iwanaga (1995b) then sought to extend this line of investigation to a musical stimulus through examining the relationship between resting heart rate and music tempi preferences. Participants were able to control the tempo of the music using a computer and, as in the previous study, there was a significant positive relationship between heart rate and preferred tempo.

Iwanaga's (1995a,b) work was heavily criticised by the psychomusicologist LeBlanc (1995) who contended that the methodologies used were unrepresentative of those employed in traditional music research and generally lacking in external validity. In Iwanaga's defence, it is common practice in the early stages of scientific inquiry to explore a phenomenon in a controlled laboratory environment with a high level of internal validity, before extending investigation to more real-life or externally valid environments.

LeBlanc's (1995) main contention was that, in normal circumstances, listeners are seldom able to alter the tempo of a piece of music to which they are listening. The reality of the matter is that most judgements of tempo preference are made *post hoc*. With modern-day listening devices such as the iPod™ it is actually possible to alter tempo while listening; however, this was not possible when Iwanaga published his research in the mid 1990s. LeBlanc argued that in traditional music research (e.g. LeBlanc et al, 1988) it was evident that listeners preferred tempi slightly higher than their heart rate if at rest or performing normal activity (i.e. not vigorous physical activity). LeBlanc also highlighted that younger listeners generally prefer higher tempi (LeBlanc, 1982; LeBlanc et al, 1988) and this is a finding supported through a large-scale survey commissioned by David Lloyd Leisure Ltd. (Priest et al, 2004).

LeBlanc (1995) suggested that Iwanaga's findings could be validated through having the same group of participants select their preferred tempi at varying work intensities. If these participants preferred tempi close to their heart rates in a range of conditions at different work intensities, it would offer support to Iwanaga's (1995a,b) hypothesis and subsequent findings. This suggestion

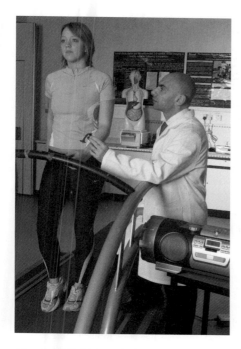

Figure 7.6 Assessing tempo preference at different exercise intensities.

Source: Photograph courtesy of Brunel University photographer, Sally Trussler.

prompted the present author's research group to initiate two experiments examining the heart rate–music tempo preference relationship in an exercise context (Karageorghis et al, 2006a; Karageorghis, Jones and Stuart, in press).

Karageorghis et al (2006a) examined the relationship between exercise heart rate and preferred tempo. Participants reported their preference for slow (80 bpm), medium (120 bpm), and fast (140 bpm) tempo music selections in each of three treadmill walking conditions at 40 per cent, 60 per cent and 75 per cent of maximal heart rate. A significant main effect for music tempo was found, wherein a general preference for fast and medium tempo music over slow music was evident ($\eta_p^2 = .78$). An exercise intensity by tempo interaction effect was also observed ($\eta_p^2 = .09$), with participants reporting a preference for either fast or medium tempo music during low and moderate exercise intensities, but for fast tempo music during high intensity exercise (see Figure 7.7). Interestingly, the most gratifying listening experience occurred while participants listened to fast tempo music at high work intensity (75 per cent maximal heart rate).

Karageorghis et al (in press) conducted a follow-up study to extend this line of investigation from listening to music excerpts to entire music programmes. The genesis of this study was a suggestion in the earlier study (Karageorghis et al, 2006a) that although fast tempo music was preferred at a high exercise intensity, continued exposure to such music during an exercise bout would result in negative psychological outcomes such as boredom and irritation. Accordingly, Karageorghis et al tested a medium tempi condition, a fast tempi condition, a

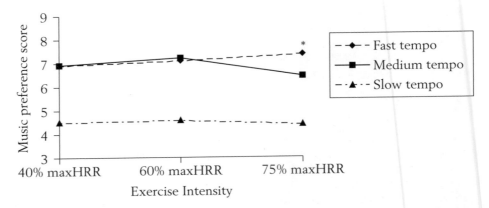

Figure 7.7 Significant two-way interaction for exercise intensity × music tempo.
Note. * p < .05.

Source: Karageorghis et al, Research Quarterly for Exercise and Sport, 26, 240–250. With permission.

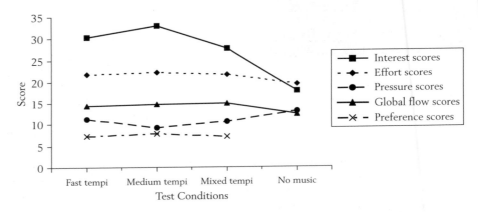

Figure 7.8 Combined male and female mean scores for Intrinsic Motivation
Inventory sub-scales, global flow and preference ratings.

Source: Karageorghis et al, International Journal of Sports Medicine. DOI: 10.1055/s–2007-989226, Georg Thieme Verlag.
With permission.

mixed tempi condition (tracks arranged in the order medium-fast-fast-medium-fast-fast) and a no-music control condition while participants walked on an inclined treadmill at 70 per cent maximal heart rate.

Dependent measures included music preference ratings, three Intrinsic Motivation Inventory sub-scales (interest-enjoyment, pressure-tension and effort-importance) and global flow. **Global flow** is a composite score of the nine dimensions of flow as operationalized within the Flow State Scale-2 (Jackson and Eklund, 2002). Flow is a holistic experience associated with total involvement in an activity and with peak performance in a sporting context. The authors expected the mixed tempi condition to yield the most positive motivation outcomes owing to the variety of medium and fast tempi. The results served to refute the experimental hypothesis (see Figure 7.8) given that it was the medium tempi condition which yielded the most positive outcomes. Karageorghis et al suggested that there may be a step change in preference between 70 and 75 per cent maximum heart rate in which participants express greater preference for fast tempi music. This is also the point at which they begin to rely more upon anaerobic pathways for energy production and become more acutely aware of physiological sensations (Rejeski, 1985).

If you wish to find out the tempo of any given piece of music, you can try searching on the internet. There are more and more websites in development dedicated to presenting various characteristics of music that include tempo. Examples of such websites include www.thebpmbook.com, www.ez-tracks.com or, in the case of dance and hip hop selections, www.jamglue.com. There are also various software packages such as *Tangerine* (www.potionfactory.com), which can assess the tempo of each track on your PC and automatically add this information to an iTunes™ library. Table 7.1 shows the tempi of a range of music selections that have proved popular in the domain of sport and exercise. Activity box 7.2 encourages you to create a music programme to accompany a typical training or exercise session. You might use the internet sites presented above to complete this exercise.

Szabo et al (1999) found that a switch from slow to fast tempo music yielded an ergogenic effect during cycle ergometry. The practical implication of this finding is that a change of music tempo from slow to fast may enhance participants' motivation and work output, especially when work level plateaus or in the latter stages of an exercise bout. Similarly, Atkinson et al (2004) indicated that the careful application of asynchronous music during a simulated 10 km cycle time-trial could be used to regulate work output. The music was particularly effective in the early stages of the trial when perceived exertion was relatively low. Using the BMRI to rate the motivational qualities of accompanying music, participants supported the prediction that rhythmical components of music contribute more to its motivational qualities than melodic or harmonic components (Karageorghis et al, 1999).

Karageorghis and Terry (1999) assessed affective and psychophysical responses to motivational and oudeterous music during treadmill running at 50 per cent $\dot{V}O_2$ max using RPE, affect, heart rate and post-exercise mood as dependent measures. Motivational music had the most positive influence on affect, RPE and the vigour component of mood. Differences were found primarily between the motivational and control conditions with no differences between the oudeterous and control conditions. In a similar study, Szmedra and Bacharach (1998) showed that asynchronous music was associated with reduced heart rate, systolic blood pressure, exercise lactate, norepinephrine production and RPE during treadmill running at 70 per cent $\dot{V}O_2$ max. The reduction in RPE for music versus control was approximately 10 per cent, a figure replicated in a subsequent study by Nethery (2002). Szmedra and Bacharach suggested that music allowed participants to relax, reducing muscle tension, and thereby increasing blood flow and lactate clearance while decreasing lactate production in working muscle.

It is evident that the beneficial effects of asynchronous music seem to disappear once exercise intensity approaches maximal levels. For example, a

Track title	Artist(s)	Tempo (bpm)	Style	Length (min)
We Are The Champions	Queen	64	Rock	03:00
Beautiful Girls	Sean Kingston	65	R 'n' B	03:45
Chariots Of Fire	Vangelis	68	Classical	03:26
Fix You	Coldplay	70	Pop/Rock	03:46
Gotta Get Thru This	Daniel Beddingfield	70	Pop/ R 'n' B	04:31
Milkshake	Kelis	75	R 'n' B	03:05
Umbrella	Rihanna ft. Jay-Zee	90	Hip Hop	04:11
Heads High	Mr Vegas	92	Reggae	03:31
Faith	George Michael	96	Pop	03:07
Like Glue	Sean Paul	98	Reggae	03:54
A Little Bit Of Ecstasy	Jocelyn Enriquez	100	Dance	03:48
Hippychick	Soho	102	Pop	03:46
Wake Me Up When September Ends	Greenday	105	Rock	04:45
Flap Your Wings	Nelly	106	Hip Hop	04:49
Gettin' Jiggy With It	Will Smith	108	Hip Hop	03:51
The Power	Snap	112	Dance/ Hip Hop	04:05
Crazy	Gnarls Barkley	112	R 'n' B	02:59
Everybody Dance Now (Gonna Make You Sweat)	C and C Music Factory	113	Dance	04:10
A Little Respect	Wheatus	115	Pop/Rock	03:19
Stacy's Mom	Fountains of Wayne	118	Rock/Pop	03:21
My Love	Justin Timberlake	120	R 'n' B/ Pop	04:36
Drop It Like It's Hot	Snoop Dogg ft. Pharrell Williams	123	Hip Hop	04:19
Let Me Entertain You	Robbie Williams	124	Pop/Rock	04:23
Sunset (Bird Of Prey)	Fatboy Slim ft. Jim Morrison	125	Dance	05:04
Get Ready For This	2 Unlimited	125	Dance	03:21
Porcelain	Moby	126	Dance	04:04
Brimful Of Asha (Norman Cook Remix)	Cornershop	126	Pop	03:56

Table 7.1 Widely-used music selections in sport and exercise contexts.

Track title	Artist(s)	Tempo (bpm)	Style	Length (min)
Hey Ya!	Outkast	127	R 'n' B/Pop	04:00
This Love	Maroon 5	127	Rock/Pop	03:21
Push The Button	Sugababes	128	Pop	03:33
Where's Your Head At	Basement Jaxx	128	Dance	03:53
Get Down	Groove Armada ft. Stush and Red Rat	129	Dance/UK Garage	03:28
Put Your Hands Up For Detroit	Fedde Le Grande	129	Dance	02:33
Discoteka	Starkillers	130	Dance	04:45
Jump Around	House of Pain	134	Hip Hop	03:22
Sandstorm	Da Rude	135	Dance	05:34
Firestarter	Prodigy	136	Dance	03:54
Ace Of Spades	Motörhead	142	Rock/Metal	03:45
Oh Yes (Mr Postman)	Juelz Santana	148	Hip Hop	03:45
Danger Zone (from Top Gun soundtrack)	Kenny Loggins	154	Rock/Pop	03:14
Burn Baby Burn	Ash	162	Rock	03:29

Table 7.1 (continued).

Activity 7.2

An example of how musical selections can be moulded around the components of a typical training session

Musical selections to accompany a workout

Workout component	Title	Artist(s)	Tempo (bpm)
Mental preparation	*Lose Yourself*	Eminem	86
Warm-up activity	*Superstar*	Jamelia	112
Stretching	*Hips Don't Lie*	Shakira	100
Strength component	*Push It*	Salt 'N' Pepa	124
Endurance component	*The Heat Is On*	Glenn Frey	152
Warm-down activity	*Boombastic*	Shaggy	84

Now prepare your own version of the above table and use the music programme to give your training sessions a boost.

Workout component	Title	Artist(s)	Tempo (bpm)
Mental preparation			
Warm-up activity			
Stretching			
Strength component			
Endurance component			
Warm-down activity			

study of anaerobic performance using the Wingate test (a maximal effort over 30 s) showed no benefit of music (Pujol and Langenfeld, 1999). It appears likely that the intensity of physiological feedback would overwhelm the effects of music at maximal and supramaximal intensities. This conclusion was corroborated in a subsequent study (Tenenbaum et al, 2004) using a hill-running task at 90 per cent VO_2 max which showed that although motivational asynchronous music did not influence perceptions of effort, it did shape participants' interpretations of fatigue symptoms.

Research has not always supported the benefits of motivational music. For example, Elliott et al (2004) showed that, compared to a control condition, motivational music enhanced affect during sub-maximal cycle ergometry, but showed no benefits over oudeterous music; and neither music condition influenced the distance cycled. However, the authors concede that the motivational music tracks scored relatively low on the BMRI ($M = 20.92$; BMRI max score $= 33.33$), which may explain the lack of support for theoretical propositions.

Summary of findings relating to asynchronous music

The main trends emanating from the body of work that has examined asynchronous music are: a) slow asynchronous music is inappropriate for exercise or training contexts unless used solely to limit effort exertion; b) fast tempo asynchronous music played for high intensity activity yields high preference scores and is likely to enhance **in-task affect** (the feeling of pleasure or displeasure experienced *during* an exercise task and often assessed on an 11-point bipolar scale known as *The Feeling Scale*); c) an increase in tempo from slow to fast might engender an ergogenic effect in aerobic endurance activities; d) asynchronous music played during sub-maximal exercise reduces RPE by approximately 10 per cent but the degree to which this effect is moderated by the motivational qualities of music remains unclear; e) the most sensitive marker of the psychophysical impact of asynchronous music appears to be in-task affect; f) asynchronous music is less influential on psychological, psychophysical and psychophysiological responses during very high intensity activities.

Figure 7.9 Assessing the motivational qualities of music.

Source: Photograph courtesy of Brunel University photographer, Sally Trussler.

Synchronous music

Synchronous music describes conscious synchronization between rhythmical aspects of music (e.g. tempo) and movement patterns during sport- or exercise-related tasks. People have a strong tendency to respond to the rhythmical qualities of music. This tendency sometimes results in synchronization between the tempo or speed of music and an athlete's or exercise participant's movements. When movement is consciously performed in time with music then the music is said to be used *synchronously*.

Synchronous music is used in sports such as figure skating, rhythmic gymnastics and dance aerobics contests. Reviewers have explained the synchronization between musical tempo and human movement in terms of the predisposition humans have to respond to the rhythmical qualities of music (Lucaccini and Kreit, 1972; Karageorghis and Terry, 1997). Ostensibly, musical rhythm can replicate natural movement-based rhythms. Despite this, relatively few studies have investigated the impact of synchronous music (e.g. Anshel and Marisi, 1978; Hayakawa et al, 2000; Simpson and Karageorghis, 2006; Bacon et al, under review).

Researchers have consistently shown that synchronous music yields significant ergogenic effects in non-highly-trained participants. Such effects have been

Application 7.5

Haile impressive

A classic example of synchronous music having an ergogenic effect came at an athletics invitation meeting at Birmingham's National Indoor Arena in February 1998. The meeting showcased the talents of legendary Ethiopian distance runner Haile Gebrselassie, who broke Eamonn Coughlan's world indoor record in the 2000 metres. Gebrselassie made the unusual request to the meeting organizers for his favourite pop song – *Scatman* – to be played during the race. He took off from the gun at a furious pace and the pacemakers were soon left trailing in his wake. The Ethiopian contingent in the crowd went wild, their passions fuelled by the pulsating beat of the music. Gebrselassie took more than a second off the existing record, finishing in a time of 4 minutes 52.86 seconds. When interviewed by *Athletics Weekly* about the race and his unusual request, he said 'The music gives me a rhythm that fits in with my record pace'. Gebrselassie had consciously synchronized his stride rate with the music tempo to achieve a world record.

demonstrated in bench stepping (Hayakawa et al, 2000), cycle ergometry (Anshel and Marisi, 1978), callisthenic-type exercises (Uppal and Datta, 1990), 400-metre running (Simpson and Karageorghis, 2006) and in a multi-activity circuit task (Michel and Wanner, 1973). Independent of such research, there has been a wave of commercial activity focused on the development and promotion of walking programmes that use synchronous music either to enhance fitness (e.g. www.run2r.com) or as part of a cardiac rehabilitation programme (e.g. www.positiveworkouts.com).

One of the earliest and arguably best-designed studies (Anshel and Marisi, 1978) compared synchronous and asynchronous music using a cycle ergometer endurance task. The researchers found that endurance was prolonged by the use of synchronous music relative to asynchronous music and a no-music control condition. In both the non-synchronous conditions, a blinking light was provided for participants to synchronize their pedal rate to, thus isolating the effect of the music.

Synchronous music yielded longer endurance than either asynchronous music or a no-music control (Cohen's $d = 0.6$ for synchronous versus control). However, the music was chosen somewhat arbitrarily from the 'popular rock category' (Anshel and Marisi, 1978: 111) without due consideration of the musical preferences and socio-cultural background of the participants. A further limitation that the authors themselves acknowledged was that a male experimenter tested female participants. This might explain why female participants underperformed when compared to their male counterparts, despite the fact that both sexes worked at relative workloads (75 per cent $\dot{V}O_2$ max).

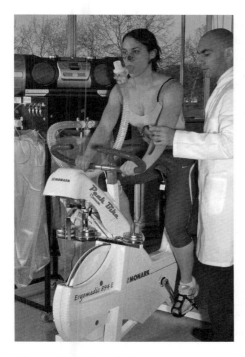

Figure 7.10 Assessing oxygen uptake in response to synchronous music.

Source: Photograph courtesy of Brunel University photographer, Sally Trussler.

Hayakawa et al (2000) compared the effects of synchronous and asynchronous music on mood during step aerobics classes. Participants reported more positive moods when classes were conducted with synchronous music versus asynchronous music and a no-music control. However, it remains unclear whether the purported benefits of synchronous music were associated with the music itself or the physiological demands of the class (e.g. thermoregulation or oxygen uptake).

In addition to the benefits associated with asynchronous music detailed within the conceptual framework of Karageorghis et al (1999), it has been proposed that the synchronous use of music elicits a reduction in the metabolic cost of exercise by promoting greater neuromuscular or metabolic efficiency (Smoll and Schultz, 1978). This proposition was the subject of a very recent study by Bacon et al (under review). Participants performing a sub-maximal cycle ergometry task were able to maintain a set intensity (60 per cent of their maximal heart rate) using 7.4 per cent less oxygen when listening to a selection of synchronous music as opposed to music that was asynchronous (slightly slower than the movement tempo).

Another recent study (Karageorghis et al, 2007) examined the effects of two experimental conditions, motivational synchronous music and oudeterous synchronous music, and a no-music control on four dependent measures during treadmill walking at 75 per cent maximal heart rate: time to exhaustion, RPE, in-task affect and exercise-induced feelings states. The authors hypothesized that

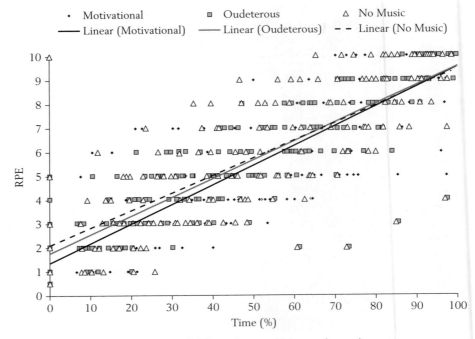

Figure 7.11a Scattergraph for RPE under conditions of synchronous motivational music, synchronous oudeterous music and a no-music control.

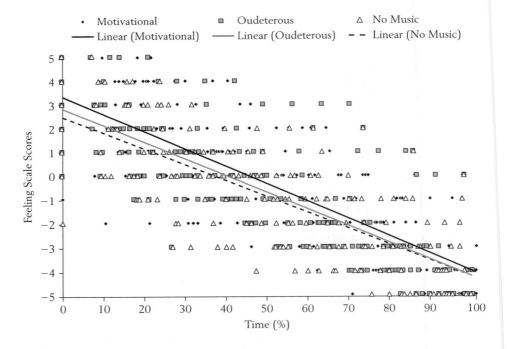

Figure 7.11b Scattergraph for in-task affect under conditions of synchronous motivational music, synchronous oudeterous music and a no-music control.

the motivational synchronous music condition would yield the most positive outcomes followed by the oudeterous music condition. It was also expected that RPE during the early stages of the task would be lower in the motivational music condition when compared to the oudeterous and control conditions. The results indicated that RPE was lowered, and in-task affect was enhanced at moderate work intensity (first half of the exercise bout) during the motivational synchronous music condition (see Figure 7.11). This condition also yielded a 14 per cent increase in endurance over a no-music control. Both experimental conditions consistently yielded more positive outcomes than the no-music control.

Until recently, there had been no research into the effects of synchronous music on anaerobic endurance performance. Simpson and Karageorghis (2006) sought to address this gap in the knowledge by testing the effects of synchronous music during 400-metre track running. Their findings indicated that both motivational and oudeterous music elicited faster times than a no-music control ($\eta_p^2 = .24$; see Figure 7.12), however times associated with the two experimental conditions did not differ. This would suggest that the motivational qualities of music are not of critical importance when it is used synchronously for an anaerobic endurance task.

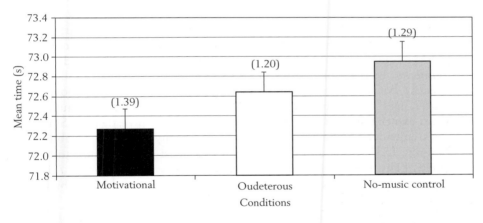

Figure 7.12 Mean 400-metre times for synchronous motivational music, synchronous oudeterous music and a no-music control.

Summary of findings relating to synchronous music

It appears that synchronous music can be applied to aerobic and anaerobic endurance performance among non-elite athletes and exercise participants with positive psychological, psychophysical and psychophysiological effects; it also yields a meaningful ergogenic effect. Very recent findings indicate that synchronous music applied to sub-maximal repetitive activity can result in an approximate 7 per cent decrease in oxygen uptake. However, there is limited research and specific theory underlying the use of synchronous music, rendering this a particularly fruitful area for additional investigation.

Directions for future research

With regard to pre-task music, an important area for future investigation is the use of music in the attainment of individual zones of optimal functioning (cf. Hanin, 1997). Much of the pre-task work to date has been nomothetic in nature and it appears that idiographic, qualitative work such as the grounded theory approach adopted by Bishop et al (2007) has the potential to shed considerable light on the antecedents, intermediaries and consequences of music use. Grounded theory is a complete methodology that could be extended to music use in other sports and to the exercise and health domain.

Some specific issues that need to be addressed by future researchers include the mechanisms through which music can be used to *trigger* specific mindsets, and also how music can be combined with visualization or hypnosis to increase the potency of these interventions. Such approaches are espoused by practitioners but have a very limited empirical basis. There is a need for a sister instrument for the BMRI-2 that will assess the sedative qualities of music to aid its use as an anxiety-control technique. More research is needed into the interactive effects of music, video and priming, and this suggestion is prompted by the prevalence of motivational video use in elite and professional sports teams (e.g. Riley, 1994).

The body of work into asynchronous music has yielded some fairly robust findings – particularly when used as an adjunct for sub-maximal exercise – and it is perhaps time for the work to be extended to more externally valid, real-life environments. In particular, interventions designed to enhance public health could easily be structured around music programmes that correspond with different ranges of expected heart rate. The health benefits and motivation outcomes associated with such programmes should be investigated. Similarly, there is tremendous scope for the use of music in physiotherapy rehabilitation programmes. Indeed, the author is engaged in a quasi-experimental study with the NHS (The Music in Rehab Project: www.westfocus.org.uk/Health/ p18_Music_in_Rehab.aspx) using an array of psychological and psychobiological outcome measures.

The experimental work into exercise heart rate and preferred music tempo should be extended to examine whether there is a step change somewhere between 70 per cent and 75 per cent maximal heart rate at which fast tempi are more likely to be preferred. Also, the music variable of intensity (volume) needs to be examined in addition to tempo as this can be easily manipulated by the listener. Moreover, the BMRI-2 requires further testing of its validity and reliability; in particular, criterion validity and test-retest reliability which were not examined as part of the initial validation process.

A conceptual framework specific to synchronous music is needed to direct future research efforts and to present researchers with a series of testable hypotheses. Using an existing framework (i.e. Karageorghis et al, 1999) it is unclear whether the motivational qualities of music are salient when it is used synchronously, particularly during anaerobic tasks. All of the work into the effects of synchronous music has been conducted with non-elite or recreational sports participants. It would be useful to examine whether the large effect sizes discovered with such participants could be replicated with elite athletes; the likelihood is that far smaller effect sizes would be found. There is also a dearth of research examining the physiological mechanisms that underlie the synchronization effect (e.g. heart rate, oxygen uptake, blood lactate concentration, etc.). The moderating influence of gender in terms of reactivity to synchronous music should be re-examined. Although gender has, for the most part, not moderated the synchronization effect when simple repetitive tasks have been used, it is likely that future research conducted in a choreographic context would reveal gender differences in musical response.

Conclusions

There are now three complementary conceptual approaches underlying the study and application of music in sport and exercise contexts (Karageorghis et al, 1999; Terry and Karageorghis, 2006; Bishop et al, 2007). Music can be applied to exercise, sports training and competition in many different ways. One of the main benefits of music use is that it enhances psychological state, which has implications for optimizing pre-competition mental state and increasing the enjoyment of exercise. Used synchronously, music can boost work output and makes repetitive tasks such as cycling or running more energy efficient. It is hoped that through judicious application of the principles outlined in this chapter, you will be able to harness the psychological, psychophysical, psychophysiological and ergogenic effects of music with greater precision. The author anticipates that in the next decade, music-related exercise interventions will play a significant role in the battle against obesity and inactivity throughout the developed world.

I put together a playlist and listen to it during the run-in. It helps psych me up and reminds me of times in the build-up when I've worked really hard, or felt good. With the right music, I do a much harder workout. (Paula Radcliffe, marathon world record holder)

Acknowledgements

Much of the Brunel-based work presented in this chapter would not have been possible were it not for the author's longstanding collaboration with Professor Peter Terry (University of Southern Queensland, Australia) and Professor Andrew Lane (University of Wolverhampton, UK). He is most grateful for their wise counsel, kindness and patience. The author would also like to thank his graduate students from whom he has drawn, and continues to draw, much inspiration: Dr David-Lee Priest, Dr Kelly Ashford, Dr Ruth Hewston, Dr Daniel Bishop, Dr Georgios Loizou, Leighton Jones, Massimo Vencato, Roberto Forzoni, Michael Kouzaris and Harry Lim.

Key concepts and terms

Asynchronous music
Global flow
Grounded theory
In-task affect

Piloerection
Pre-task music
Synchronous music
White noise

Sample essay titles

- What evidence is there to suggest that structured music use might contribute to exercise adherence?
- Discuss the conceptual approaches that have been advanced to explain the effects of music in the domain of sport and exercise.
- How can sport psychologists harness the power of music to enhance the potency of psychological interventions?
- 'Music is a totally ineffective auditory stimulus at high exercise intensities.' Discuss with reference to relevant empirical evidence.

Further reading

Books

Juslin, P.N., and Sloboda, J.A. (2001). *Music and Emotion: Theory and Research.* Oxford: Oxford University Press.

Levitin, D. (2007). *This is Your Brain on Music: Understanding a Human Obsession.* London: Atlantic Books.

Lucaccini, L.F., and Kreit, L.H. (1972). 'Music.' In: W.P. Morgan (Ed.), *Ergogenic Aids and Muscular Performance.* New York: Academic Press, 240–245.

North, A.C., and Hargreaves, D.J. (Eds) (2008). *The Social and Applied Psychology of Music.* Oxford: Oxford University Press.

Terry, P.C. (2004). 'Mood and emotions in sport.' In: T. Morris and J. Summers (Eds), *Sport Psychology: Theory, Applications and Issues,* (2nd Ed.). Brisbane: Wiley, 31–57.

Journal articles

Anshel, M.H., and Marisi, D.Q. (1978). Effects of music and rhythm on physical performance. *Research Quarterly,* 49, 109–113.

Bishop, D.T., Karageorghis, C.I., and Loizou, G. (2007). A grounded theory of young tennis players' use of music to manipulate emotional state. *Journal of Sport & Exercise Psychology,* 29, 584–607.

Gluch, P. (1993). The use of music in preparing for sport performance. *Contemporary Thought*, 2, 33–53.

Elliott, D., Carr, S., and Savage, D. (2003). Effects of motivational music on work output and affective responses during sub-maximal cycling of a standardized perceived intensity. *Journal of Sport Behavior*, 27, 134–147.

Karageorghis, C.I., and Terry, P.C. (1997). The psychophysical effects of music in sport and exercise: A review. *Journal of Sport Behavior*, 20, 54–68.

Karageorghis, C.I., Terry, P.C., and Lane, A.M. (1999). Development and validation of an instrument to assess the motivational qualities of music in exercise and sport: The Brunel Music Rating Inventory. *Journal of Sports Sciences*, 17, 713–724.

Karageorghis, C.I., Jones, L., and Low, D.C. (2006a). Relationship between exercise heart rate and music tempo preference. *Research Quarterly for Exercise and Sport*, 77, 240–250.

Karageorghis, C.I., Priest, D.L., Terry, P.C., Chatzisarantis, N.L.D., and Lane, A.M. (2006b). Redesign and initial validation of an instrument to assess the motivational qualities of music in exercise: The Brunel Music Rating Inventory-2. *Journal of Sports Sciences*, 24, 899–909.

Priest, D.L., Karageorghis, C.I., and Sharp, N.C.C. (2004). The characteristics and effects of motivational music in exercise settings: The possible influence of gender, age, frequency of attendance, and time of attendance. *Journal of Sports Medicine and Physical Fitness*, 44, 77–86.

Simpson, S.D., and Karageorghis, C.I. (2006). The effects of synchronous music on 400-m sprint performance. *Journal of Sports Sciences*, 24, 1095–1102.

8 Imagery and sport performance

Dave Smith and Caroline Wright

Imagery is one of the hottest topics in sport psychology. This chapter explains what imagery is and how it is commonly used by athletes to enhance performance. We explain why imagery is such a potent tool for enhancing sports performance, and provide guidelines based on sport psychology and neuroscience research aimed at making imagery the most effective it can be.

Learning outcomes

When you have completed this chapter you should be able to:

1. Define imagery and explain how it is commonly used by athletes.
2. Identify the different imagery types and understand how these may be used in different situations to improve sports performance.
3. Explain the key mechanisms and processes that increase the effectiveness of imagery.
4. Name and describe the elements of the PETTLEP (physical, environment, task, timing, learning, emotion and perspective) model and explain how these could be integrated into an imagery intervention.

What is imagery?

Imagery can be defined as 'using all the senses to recreate or create an experience in the mind' (Vealey and Walter, 1993: 201). One of the first reported references to imagery was by Virgil in 20 BC. In his poem he explains that 'possunt quia posse videntur' which translates as 'they can because they see themselves as being able'. More recently, many studies have focused on imagery, the ways in which it can improve performance, the target population that would benefit most from imagery, and different types of imagery that can be used.

A study by Vandell, Davis and Clugston in 1943 on free-throw shooting and dart throwing found that mental practice was beneficial in improving performance, and almost as effective as physical practice. Many other studies have shown that mental practice produces higher scores than controls, but lower ones than physical practice (Mendoza and Wichman, 1978; MacBride and

Rothstein, 1979). However, many studies found that combinations of physical and mental practice can be as effective as physical practice alone (Oxendine, 1969).

In order to clarify the effect of imagery on performance, several authors have completed meta-analytic studies on the topic. Richardson (1967a,b) reported on 25 mental practice studies and concluded that this technique was effective in improving motor performance. In 1983, a meta-analysis of 60 studies carried out by Feltz and Landers found an average effect size of .48 (indicating a large effect on performance) and another meta-analysis (Hinshaw, 1991) revealed an average effect size of .68. A further meta-analysis within this area compared 35 studies, using strict selection criteria (Driskell et al, 1994). This concluded that mental practice is an effective way to enhance performance, and found that the effects of mental practice were stronger when cognitive elements were contained within the task.

Focus 8.1

A meta-analysis is a study which accumulates previous research on a topic and draws general conclusions about the effectiveness of an intervention from a number of different studies.

It appears, therefore, that imagery is effective in improving sports performance; however, the mechanisms behind imagery and how this effect on performance can be optimized are still unclear.

How is imagery used by athletes?

Imagery training is commonly used by elite and aspiring athletes in order to improve performance. This is due to the number of benefits that can be gained from its use. Imagery training can increase self-awareness, facilitate skill acquisition and maintenance, build self-confidence, control emotions, relieve pain, regulate emotional states believed to be associated with performance, and enhance preparation strategies (Murphy and Jowdy, 1992).

Currently, imagery is used with the specific aim of improving athletic performance. It is arguably the most widely practised psychological skill used in sport (Gould et al, 1989; Jowdy et al, 1989). For example, Jowdy et al (1989) found that imagery techniques were used regularly by 100 per cent of consultants, 90 per cent of athletes and 94 per cent of coaches sampled. Athletes, especially elite athletes, use imagery extensively and believe that it benefits performance (Hall et al, 1998).

Imagery is traditionally practised by athletes in the training phases of sports performance to aid with competition. However, it can also be used during the competition phase.

Activity 8.1

Jonny Wilkinson describes his imagery as a:

sort of clarified daydream with snippets of the atmosphere from past matches included to enhance the sense of reality. It lasts about twenty minutes and by the end of it I feel I know what is coming. The game will throw up many different scenarios but I am as prepared in my own head for them as I can be. If you have realistically imagined situations, you feel better prepared and less fearful of the unexpected. (Wilkinson, 2004: 49).

Reflect on your own experiences in sport and exercise and describe situations when you engaged in imagery and recall how this imagery affected how you felt. Jonny Wilkinson recalls imagery having a positive effect; this might not always be the case.

Imagery types

As noted above, imagery can be used to obtain various outcomes. Hall et al (1998), in developing a questionnaire to measure imagery use, the Sport Imagery Questionnaire, noted that there are five basic types of imagery that athletes can perform. These are as follows:

■ Cognitive specific (CS): imagery of specific sport skills (e.g. taking a basketball free throw).

■ Cognitive general (CG): imagery of strategies and routines (e.g. a golfer's pre-putt routine, a football team's defensive strategy).

■ Motivational specific (MS): imagery of specific goals and goal-orientated behaviour (e.g. a weightlifter lifting a record weight, holding up the winner's trophy).

■ Motivational general arousal (MGA): imagery of emotions associated with performance (e.g. excitement felt when competing in front of a large crowd).

■ Motivational general mastery (MGM): imagery of mastering sport situations (e.g. a footballer keeping focused while being barracked by opposition fans).

Research has shown that all five types of imagery are used by athletes, but motivational imagery is used more than cognitive imagery. However, Hall et al (1998) never claimed that their five imagery types represented all the imagery used by athletes. Indeed researchers have uncovered other types of imagery used in sport that do not fall easily into one of the above categories. For example, Nordin and Cumming (2005) found that competitive dancers often use imagery of body posture. Also, dancers reported imaging characters and roles related to their dance pieces. Metaphorical imagery, where athletes image movements, sensations or pictorial images that are not necessarily possible, is also commonly used by aesthetic sport athletes such as dancers and bodybuilders. According to a study by Dreidiger et al (2006), injured athletes use physiological images of their injuries healing.

Given the evidence presented, depending on the particular aim of the athlete, various types of imagery can be used. Not surprisingly, CS imagery can enhance performance of the specific skill being imaged, as per the studies mentioned in the 'What is imagery?' section. However, as mentioned previously, there can be other benefits too. For example, studies have shown that CS imagery can lead to greater motivation to practise, and increase confidence. CG, MS and MGA imagery can also be effective in enhancing confidence, and MGA imagery can be very useful in psyching up or calming down athletes, and getting their arousal to an optimal level so they can perform at their best. Athletes should, therefore, use a combination of imagery types depending upon their specific preferences and goals. However, if improved skill is the aim, CS imagery is usually the most appropriate to focus on initially.

How imagery works

The positive effect that imagery has on performance has been investigated in the neuroscience literature. Through a number of different research methods, discussed below, several authors have concluded that a 'functional equivalence' exists between imagery and actual performance. That is, the process that occurs in the brain during motor imagery mimics the process that occurs during actual performance of a skill.

Focus 8.2

Neuroscience is a field in which concepts of neurobiology and cognitive psychology are combined (Decety, 1996).

Different areas of the brain contribute towards movement. If a 'functional equivalence' exists, the areas of the brain working during imagery would be expected to be similar to those working during actual performance. Scientists have developed a number of methods to discover whether this is the case.

One way in which this can be tested is to measure cerebral activity. When areas of the brain are being specifically used, the blood flow to these areas will increase. This can then be mapped during imagery and actual performance to assess whether the same areas are being activated. In a study by Decety, Philippon and Ingvar (1988), the authors asked participants to image themselves completing a writing task. They found that the equivalent areas of the brain were active when imaging and actually completing the writing task. The only difference was that the primary motor cortex was not active during imagery, but this is responsible for the final execution of movements, so this finding was expected. This indicates that the same areas of the brain are functioning during real and imagined movements, suggesting that improvements gained from imagery are occurring centrally within the brain structure.

Focus 8.3

Whatever type of imagery is being used, it appears that athletes with a greater imagery ability (i.e. who find it easier to image clearly) will benefit most from imagery use. However, using structured and theoretically based imagery techniques (such as those described in the section on PETTLEP imagery below) will help athletes achieve vivid imagery.

Another technique used is mental chronometry. This technique is based on the comparison of time taken to complete an activity and the time taken to imagine it. Decety and Michel (1989) compared the times needed to complete actual and imagined movements on two tasks: drawing a cube and writing a sentence. Participants were required to do both of these tasks twice, once using their dominant hand and once using their non-dominant hand. Results showed that participants were slower when completing the tasks with their non-dominant hand, but that this was also reflected in the length of time needed to imagine the tasks.

Within the sports setting, Moran and MacIntyre (1998) completed a study focusing on the kinaesthetic imagery experiences of elite canoe-slalom athletes. As part of this study, the athletes were required to image themselves completing a recent race. The time taken to image the race was then compared to the actual race completion time with results showing a positive correlation between the two. These studies indicate that a central mechanism is responsible for the timing of motor imagery.

A further technique used to establish the relationship between imagery and actual performance focuses on the autonomic system. If actual movement and imagery use the same neural mechanisms, this should also be apparent within the body's responses. Involuntary responses such as heart rate and respiration have been found to increase without delay during the onset of actual or imagined exercise (Decety et al, 1991, 1993; Wuyam et al, 1995).

Finally, other techniques such as electroencephalography (EEG) and positron emission tomography (PET) scanning have been used to highlight the relationship that exists between actual performance of a skill and imagery of the same skill. Both of these techniques have found very similar movement-related neural activity in the brain prior to and during actual and imagined movements (Fox et al, 1987; Naito and Matsumura, 1994; Stephan and Frackowiak, 1996).

Focus 8.4

Electroencephalography (EEG) involves measuring the level and location of electrical currents within the brain by placing electrodes on the skull and measuring the trace of this current.

Focus 8.5

Positron emission tomography (PET) involves injecting the participant with radioactive molecules which, when broken down, can be detected by a PET camera.

Research using all of the techniques described above supports the idea that a functional equivalence exists between imagery and overt movement. There is evidence that imagery shares a common mechanism (mental chronometry), utilizes the same areas of the brain (EEG and cerebral blood flow), and produces similar physiological responses (autonomic system). However, to date, this research has not been considered fully within the sports setting and, as a result of this, many athletes may not be completing imagery capable of having an optimal effect on performance.

How should imagery be performed?

Many sport psychology publications promote imagery as an important psychological intervention and give advice on how it should be implemented to provide the most effective results. However, such advice is often provided with nothing in the way of theoretical justification or empirical support. One reason for this may because the field is relatively narrow, and sport psychology has often ignored theories from other fields (Murphy, 1990). In an attempt to rectify this, Holmes and Collins (2001) developed a model based on the cognitive neuroscience research findings noted above, aiming to produce functionally equivalent mental simulation: **the PETTLEP model**. PETTLEP is an acronym, with each letter standing for an important practical issue to consider when implementing imagery interventions: physical, environment, task, timing, learning, emotion and perspective.

PETTLEP aims to closely replicate the sporting situation through imagery, including physical sensations associated with performance and the emotional impact that the performance has on the athlete. The PETTLEP model is comprised of seven key elements and each one of these needs to be considered and implemented as fully as possible for the imagery to be most effective.

The *physical* component of the model is related to the athlete's physical responses in the sporting situation. Some authors claim that athletes are able to most vividly imagine a skill or movement if they are in a completely relaxed and undisturbed state. However, research has not found any significant benefits from combining imagery and relaxation and it seems unlikely that this approach would be beneficial. Holmes and Collins (2002) point out that the physical effect of relaxation is in complete contrast to the physical state of the athlete during performance.

Smith and Collins (2004) agree that imagery is more effective when it includes all of the senses and kinaesthetic sensations experienced when

Focus 8.6

PETTLEP stands for:

- Physical
- Emotion
- Task
- Timing
- Learning
- Emotion
- Perspective

performing the task. The inclusion of these sensations will lead to the imagery being more individualized and may increase the functional equivalence between imagery and actual movement. Holmes and Collins (2002) describe various practical ideas that can be used to enhance the physical dimension of an athlete's imagery. These include using the correct stance, holding any implements that would usually be held, and wearing the correct clothing.

The *environment* component of the model refers to the environment in which imagery is performed. In order to access the same motor representation, the environment when imagining the performance should be as similar as possible to the actual performing environment. If a similar environment is not possible, photographs of the venue or audio tapes of crowd noise can be used. Hecker and Kaczor (1988) conducted a study and reported that physiological responses to imagery occurred consistently when the scene was familiar. By using photographs or video tapes of venues, athletes can become more familiar prior to the competition and therefore the imagery will be more effective.

The *task* component is an important factor as the imagined task needs to be closely matched to the actual one. According to Holmes and Collins (2002), if functional equivalence conditions are to be achieved, the content of the imagery should be different for elite and non-elite performers. This is primarily because the skill level, and therefore the specific skills being imaged, will be different. When the non-elite performers improve, and begin to display characteristics of the elite, it is then necessary for the imagery script to be altered in accordance with this change. The task should be closely related and specific to the performer, focusing on individual emotions.

The *timing* component refers to the pace at which the imagery is completed. Some researchers advocate using imagery in slow motion to experience the action fully (Whetstone, 1995). However, precise timing is often very important in actual game situations and in the execution of specific skills. It would, therefore, be more functionally equivalent if the imagery was completed at the same pace at which the action would be completed.

The *learning* component of the model refers to the adaptation of the imagery content in relation to the rate of learning. As the performer becomes more skilled at a movement, the imagery script should be altered in order to reflect this. Perry and Morris (1995) explain how the complexity of imagery may change as the athlete improves their performance of a skill. Holmes and Collins (2001) suggest that regularly reviewing the content of the imagery is essential to retain functional equivalence.

The *emotion* component refers to the emotions included within the imagery, which should be closely related to those experienced during actual performance. During the imagery the athlete should try to experience all of the emotion and arousal associated with the performance. Weinberg and Gould (1999) point out that athletes should remain focused on the sensations associated with performing well, and the PETTLEP model advocates the inclusion of any emotion associated with performance to aid the athlete in dealing with the emotions prior to competition.

Finally, the *perspective* component refers to the way imagery is viewed. Imagery can be internal (first person) or external (third person). Internal perspective refers to the view that an athlete would have when he was actually performing, whereas external perspective would be like watching yourself performing on a video tape. From a functional equivalence perspective, internal imagery would appear preferable as it more closely approximates the athlete's view when performing. However, some studies have shown external imagery to be beneficial (White and Hardy, 1995; Hardy and Callow, 1999). Research indicates that the more advanced performers will be able to switch from one perspective to another (cf. Smith et al, 1998) and, in doing this, gain advantages from both perspectives, optimizing the imagery experience and enhancing performance.

Although research has previously been completed on the different elements of the PETTLEP model, little research has been conducted since the model was developed to explicitly test it. A recent study completed by Smith et al (2007) compared the use of PETTLEP imagery and more traditional, primarily visual, imagery of a full turning gymnastics jump. They found that, over six weeks performing the interventions, the PETTLEP imagery group improved, but the traditional imagery group did not. Also, the PETTLEP imagery group improved by a similar amount as a group who physically practised the skill. This supports the use of an individually tailored PETTLEP approach when producing an imagery intervention. The PETTLEP imagery group also completed their imagery while standing on the beam in their gymnastics clothing, which may have led to an increased functional equivalence and subsequent performance benefit.

In a follow-up study by the same authors, PETTLEP interventions were employed with a hockey penalty flick task. The study compared a sport-specific group (incorporating the physical and environment components of the PETTLEP model, wearing their hockey strip and doing their imagery on the hockey pitch) with a clothing-only group (who also wore their hockey strip while doing their imagery but did their imagery at home) and a traditional imagery group (who did their imagery sitting at home in their everyday clothing). They found that the sport-specific group improved by the largest amount, followed by the clothing-only group, and then the traditional imagery group. This supports the PETTLEP model as, when adding components of the PETTLEP model to the intervention, a greater improvement in performance was apparent.

Although these studies have examined components of the PETTLEP model, these have generally been in isolation. Weinberg and Gould (2003) point out that the model has not yet been systematically tested as a whole, and Holmes and Collins (2001) believe that the model will benefit from comprehensive testing in a variety of settings. Research into this area of imagery is currently being undertaken.

Example imagery study

Traditionally, studies into imagery and mental practice consist of a pre-test in a specific motor skill, followed by an intervention period, a post-test in the same skill, and possibly a follow-up retention test after a period of time when the intervention has been withdrawn. Groups typically include a physical practice group, an imagery group, a control group, and often a group that combines physical practice with the imagery intervention. This allows each intervention to be tested to establish its effectiveness.

A study was completed by Smith and Collins (2004) to assess the effect of including stimulus and response propositions in imagery on the performance of two tasks. Stimulus propositions are units of information relating to the content of a scene, whereas response propositions are units of information relating to the individual's response to being in that situation. For example, if a footballer was imaging performing in an important match, stimulus propositions would include the sight of the other players and the sound of the crowd, and response propositions would include increased heart rate, sweating and feelings of butterflies in the stomach. Smith and Collins compared groups using physical practice, stimulus and response proposition and stimulus-only proposition interventions. The task used was a contraction of the abductor digiti minimi (the muscle responsible for moving the little finger away from the hand). They also measured the late contingent negative variation (CNV) (which is a negative shift that occurs in the brain prior to movement) to assess any differences between the groups during the movement. They found that the physical practice group, stimulus and response proposition group and the stimulus proposition only group all improved significantly from pre-test to post-test. However, there was no significant difference in the magnitude of their improvement. The CNV waves were also apparent in all conditions.

The second of this series of studies compared similar groups on a barrier knock-down task. They found that the stimulus and response imagery group and physical practice group improved significantly from pre-test to post-test, whereas the stimulus-only group did not. Additionally, the late CNV was observed preceding real or imagined movement in the physical practice and stimulus and response imagery groups, but not in the stimulus-only group. This has strong implications for imagery interventions, as it appears that physical practice is more accurately mimicked by the inclusion of response propositions. The inclusion of these propositions may also enhance the functional equivalence of the intervention, which would explain the larger increase in performance by the stimulus and response group.

Ethics

There are ethical issues to consider when administering any intervention. Participants must give informed consent, and be free to withdraw from the studies at any time without repercussions. Additionally, if the intervention used can benefit the participant (from exam preparation to stroke rehabilitation) then the intervention should be offered to all of the other participants after the study has finished. This ensures that the group allocation does not lead to a useful intervention being withheld from some of the participants.

Conclusions

Imagery can be a very effective means of enhancing sports performance. Although it is very commonly used by athletes, often they may not get the most out of it as it is frequently performed in an unstructured and unrealistic (non-functionally equivalent) way. There are several different types of imagery that can be used by athletes, all of which may have different effects on performance and self-confidence. To make the most of the various kinds of imagery that can be performed, imagery needs to be practised consistently in a purposeful and structured way, and also needs to be as realistic as possible. Using the guidelines of the PETTLEP model can be very helpful in achieving these goals for imagery training.

Key concepts and terms

Imagery   The PETTLEP model

Sample essay titles

- There are many different positive effects that imagery can have on performance. Choose one imagery type and describe how implementing it may benefit performance.
- Describe how functionally equivalent imagery could be achieved, using the example of a golf tee shot.
- Explain how a study could be organized to compare different interventions, and the benefits of including each of the interventions.

Further reading

Journal articles

Decety, J. (1996). Do imagined and executed actions share the same neural substrate? *Cognitive Brain Research*, 3, 87–93.

Driskell, J.E., Copper, C., and Moran, A. (1994). Does mental practice improve performance? *Journal of Applied Psychology*, 79, 481–492.

Hall, C., Mack, D., Paivio, A., and Hausenblas, H. (1998). Imagery use by athletes: Development of the sport imagery questionnaire. *International Journal of Sport Psychology*, 29, 73–89.

Holmes, P.S., and Collins, D.J. (2001). The PETTLEP approach to motor imagery: a functional equivalence model for sport psychologists. *Journal of Applied Sport Psychology*, 13, 60–83.

Smith, D., and Collins, D. (2004). Mental practice, Motor performance, and the late CNV. *Journal of Sport & Exercise Psychology*, 26, 412–426.

Smith, D., Wright, C.J., Allsopp, A., and Westhead, H. (2007). It's all in the mind: PETTLEP-based imagery and sports performance. *Journal of Applied Sport Psychology*, 19, 80–92.

3 | Leadership

9 Leadership development in athletes and coaches

Adrian Schonfeld

The sporting world places significant emphasis on leaders. The success and failure of a team is often attributed to the good or poor coach or manager, charged with the responsibility of leading the team. Martin Johnson, the captain of the Rugby World Cup winning team of 2003, is often praised and revered for his **leadership**. Indeed, his leadership, along with that of Clive Woodward, is often claimed as a critical factor in that tournament victory.

This chapter presents analysis of some of the research that has been conducted into leadership in sport. It begins with a summary of some of the theoretical approaches to leadership that have been applied to sport. Most research in sport leadership has been conducted with the coach in mind and consequently the evaluation of the theories presented relies heavily on coach-based evidence. The second section presents a summary of some of the recent interesting research occurring into leadership from the athlete role. The third section investigates **leadership development** in coaches and athletes. Finally, ethical issues related to leadership are presented through an examination of coaching dilemmas.

Learning outcomes

When you have completed this chapter you should be able to:

1. Describe the major theoretical perspectives underpinning leadership research in sport.
2. Critique research that attempts to understand the development of leadership in athletes and coaches.
3. Understand the principles behind ethical decision-making for leaders in sport.

Leadership theories based on individuals

Trait theories are premised on the basis that leadership is a characteristic inherent to a person (Northouse, 2007). The consequence of this approach is that a leader, once identified, should be able to lead in all situations and that someone who is not a leader will never be able to lead in any situation. Possible

Figure 9.1 Leadership is key to success in sports.

Source: Steve Cuff/EMPICS Sport/PA Photos.

Focus 9.1

Leadership definitions often include four components: a) a process;
b) influence; c) a group of people; d) taking action to a common goal
(Northouse, 2007). Research within sport has focused mainly on trying
to understand the structure of leadership, antecedents of leadership and
the consequences of leadership. A number of different theories have
been investigated in sport, mostly originating in other psychology
disciplines, particularly social psychology and organizational psychology.

traits for leadership in sport may be extraversion and conscientiousness. Trait-
based leadership research in sport has not consistently identified one set of
leadership traits (Horn, 2002). Research of this style lost favour and has
consequently been overtaken by the development of differing theoretical
approaches.

Activity 9.1

Characteristics of leaders

Take a moment to think of one famous leader from sport. It could be a
great player or coach or manager who you believe was also a wonderful
leader. Write their name down on a piece of paper. Then list the factors
that you think made them a great leader.

On a separate sheet, write down the name of someone who is/was the best leader you have known personally, i.e. the person you wanted to follow the most. Again write down what it was about that person that made them the leader they were.

Now working as a group, pool your sheets with famous leaders and look for the common elements. Likewise, pool your pages of personal leaders and look for the similarities between them. What do you notice? Are there any differences between the famous and the personal leader qualities? What does this tell us about popular portrayals of famous people?

Behavioural approaches to leadership infer that leadership is still based on an individual (as with trait theory), however the factors that set them apart are behaviours or skills (Horn, 2002). The skills of leadership are consistent across situations and the person/people who choose to use them will be the leader/s. Leadership behaviour is rarely distinguished from coach behaviour, and instruments such as the Coach Behaviour Assessment System (CBAS; Smith et al, 1977) provide tools for measuring coach behaviour. Mallett and Côté (2006) suggest that systematic observation studies, where measures such as the CBAS are used to record coach behaviour, have offered information about coaching environments and specific strategies effective coaches use. The CBAS measures coaches on reactive behaviours and spontaneous behaviours. Within the reactive behaviours class, distinction is made between responses to desirable behaviours, responses to mistakes and responses to misbehaviour. Spontaneous behaviours include categories for game-related actions and game-irrelevant actions.

Activity 9.2

Observation of coaches

One category of behaviours on the CBAS is 'Responses to mistakes' (Smoll and Smith, 1980). It has the following dimensions:

- *Mistake contingent encouragement* – encouragement given to a player following a mistake.
- *Mistake contingent technical instruction* – instructing or demonstrating to a player how to correct a mistake they have made.
- *Punishment* – a negative reaction, verbal or non-verbal, following a mistake.
- *Punitive technical instruction* – technical instruction following a mistake which is given in a punitive or hostile manner.
- *Ignoring mistakes* – failure to respond to a player mistake.

Watch two different coaches for 20 minutes each and record how often they respond to mistakes according to the classifications above.

Continued . . .

. . . Continued

Reflect on the two coaches and ask yourself the following questions:

1. Which coach would I prefer to be coached by? Why?
2. Which coach would get the better performances from their athletes? Why?
3. What are the situational factors surrounding this coach that impact upon their work?
4. If the coach came to you after your observations and asked you what you would suggest they do differently, what would you tell them?

Leadership theories based on the person and on the environment

The interaction theories are based on the idea that a certain leadership style or set of behaviours will be more successful in some environments that others. They are theories that suggest that for leadership to be effective there must be a match between the leader and the situation. One of the more commonly cited theories is Fiedler's contingency theory (1967). In Fiedler's theory, he proposes that leaders can be either task oriented or relationship oriented. Situations vary along a continuum of favourableness. The degree of favourableness is said to relate to leader–member relations, task structure and the position power of the leader. The contingency component of the model suggests that when the situation is highly favourable or not favourable then a task leader will be more effective than a relationship-oriented leader. Conversely, when the situation is only moderately favourable, a relationship-oriented leader will be more effective. The implications of this theory are twofold: first, for a given context, identify the correct leader style required and insert the person who has it; and second, for any given leader, the right context will allow them to be effective. No published studies were located that found support for Fielder's model within the sport literature. Danielson (1976) suggested that it may not be appropriate for use in sport. Fiedler's theory has been criticised heavily based on a perceived lack of validity in the major measurement tool, the Least Preferred Co-worker Scale (Northouse, 2007). This, along with its limited utility for solving leadership problems in organizations, means that it has fallen from favour with researchers and practitioners. However, the model does provide a basic model for understanding how the leader and the environment may both contribute to the success of the leadership in place. It lays a foundation for establishing more complex interaction models.

The **multidimensional model of leadership in sport** (MMLS; Chelladurai, 1990, 2001) is a sport-specific interaction theory. The dominant theory in sport leadership research to date, it proposes that performance and satisfaction consequences are dependent on the interaction of actual leadership, preferred leadership and required leadership. It also proposes that leadership is contingent upon the situation, the team members and the leader. Working from right to left in Figure 9.2, it is proposed how the three leader behaviours are prefaced by the leader's characteristics, the team member's characteristics and the situational characteristics. The MMLS has been the guiding theory underpinning much of the leadership research in sport since its proposal (Riemer, 2007). Unfortunately only certain areas of the model have been tested and the evidence gathered only lends partial support to the model. Many of the problems associated with building the evidence base supporting the model stem from measurement issues concerning leadership and the other constructs in the model (e.g. performance), simplistic and primarily observational (as opposed to experimental) designs. Riemer (2007) suggests that a priority for future research into the MMLS should be refining measurement and the consideration of leadership, satisfaction and performance as dynamic constructs. In much the same way as team cohesion research progressed to consider reciprocal relationships between cohesion and performance, leadership research may benefit from considering a temporal dimension within methodological designs.

A significant amount of research has investigated the preferences of athletes and how these relate to some of the antecedent factors. For instance, Riemer and Toon (2001) found an interaction between the gender (measured as biological sex) of the athlete, the gender of the coach and the preferred leadership style. Specifically, female athletes with female coaches request less social support than female athletes with male coaches. In situations with a male coach, both female and male athletes had similar preferences for leadership behaviour. To address situational characteristics that may influence leader behaviour preferences, Chelladurai et al (1987) tested the leader behaviour preferences across different cultures and different types of sport within cultures to demonstrate that both of these factors may contribute to the leadership preferences of athletes. They found that Japanese athletes had different leadership preferences depending on whether they were engaged in a western sport (e.g. basketball) or eastern sport (e.g. kendo). Other factors found to influence preference are ability (e.g. Riemer and Toon, 2001), gender, task dependence and task variability (Beam et al, 2004). Overall, research in this vein has supported the MMLS by identifying some of the characteristics of the situation, leader and team that influence preferences.

Research has looked to evaluate the level of congruence between the leader behaviours (specifically preference and actual) to determine if they influence performance and satisfaction. Generally, research in this domain is limited and shows contradictory results (Riemer and Chelladurai, 1995; Riemer and Toon, 2001). Riemer and Toon (2001) hypothesize that many factors may contribute to the inconsistency, including: a) that research has usually considered only the head coach to provide leadership, yet in reality a number of sources of leadership may exist in a team; b) that differences in situational characteristics (sport type, team size) may affect the relationship between leadership and outcome to a greater extent than previously thought; and c) there are different measures of satisfaction.

To complement the development of the MMLS, Chelladurai and Saleh (1980) developed a measure of leadership with which they could start to evaluate the accuracy of their model. They developed the questionnaire by taking 99 items adapted from various non-sport leadership scales and, using a

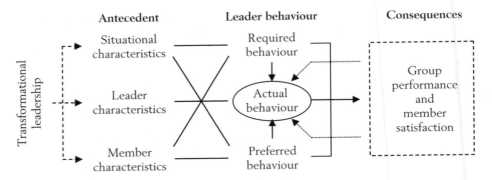

Figure 9.2 The multidimensional model of leadership in sport.

Source: A adapted from Chelladurai, 2007.

factor analytic procedure based on a sample of 160 physical education students, were able to create a refined version. This version was then administered to two further samples of physical education students and male university athletes, resulting in a 40-item measure. This has been assessed for reliability and validity through assessment of internal consistency and test-retest procedures. Using Cronbach's alpha, the internal reliability of the measure has been demonstrated to be consistently adequate for four of the five sub-scales, however the autocratic behaviours scale is often found to be less than satisfactory (<0.7).

The Leadership Scale for Sport (LSS) measures five types of leader behaviours split into three dimensions. There is one direct task factor (training and instruction), two decision-making styles (autocratic and democratic) and two motivational factors (social support and positive feedback). In contrast to the CBAS, the LSS is a more traditional style 'pencil and paper' measure. Horn (2002) suggests that observational field studies are needed to determine if behavioural correlates can be identified for the sub-scales of the LSS. If these could be demonstrated, it would enhance the credibility of the LSS as a measure of sport leadership. Chelladurai and Riemer (1998) commented that the LSS has limited scope as a true measure of coach leadership as the MMLS has undergone further development since the measure was developed (to incorporate concepts of transformational leadership theory; Chelladurai, 2001, 2007) and also the LSS may not capture all relevant behaviours. Zhang, Jensen and Mann (1997) attempted to expand the LSS to include two new scales, situation consideration behaviours and group maintenance behaviours. The resultant statistical analysis as part of the development process did not support the inclusion of the group maintenance factor, and Chelladurai's (2007) questioning of the development process advocates continued use of the original five-factor LSS until a better credentialed scale is developed.

There are a range of theories of leadership, widely espoused in organizational research, that have not yet been investigated significantly in sport psychology research. Transformational and transactional leadership (e.g. Bass, 1990), leader member exchange theory (e.g. Graen and Uhl-Bien, 1995) and path-goal theory (e.g. Evans, 1970) are all well developed and have been applied to business settings (Northouse, 2007) but are yet to make a substantive impact in sport. Vallée and Bloom (2005) use transformational leadership theory to understand their results in exploring coaches of successful university sport programmes. They identify four components of transformational leadership (inspirational motivation, idealized influence, intellectual stimulation and individualized consideration) as being closely aligned to the four common elements of the coaches that they identified through the analysis of semi-structured interviews (coaches' attributes, individual growth, organizational skills and vision). These results should lead to further exploration of transformational leadership in sport.

Chelladurai's (2007) most recent version of the MMLS includes the influence of transformational leadership on the leader, member and situational characteristics. He provides substantial analysis of how transformational leadership concepts may be integrated into the MMLS, and readers are directed to Chelladurai for further information.

Leadership in the athlete role

A new theme of research has developed over the past four years with the consideration that leadership does not only come from the coach but also from players on teams. Loughhead and colleagues (Loughhead and Hardy, 2005; Loughhead et al, 2006; Eys, Loughhead and Hardy, 2007) have begun to understand what role peer leaders like Martin Johnson fulfil. Their research builds on earlier work by Glenn and Horn (1993) who investigated psychological and personal predictors of athlete leadership. Glenn and Horn asked captains, their peers and their coaches to rate the captain's leadership behaviours. Using simple correlational analyses they found that peer and coach ratings were moderately correlated, peer and self ratings were moderately correlated and coach and self ratings were only minimally correlated. This means that depending on who rates the leader heavily influences what characteristics are associated with leadership. Unfortunately there is no way of knowing which is correct, and consequently if you want to measure peer leadership you may need to consider more than one perspective.

The recent proliferation of peer leadership research has focused on describing the roles that peer leaders fulfil. Peer leadership is typically discussed as team members occupying formal roles (i.e. the captain/s) or informal roles (i.e. facilitating social outings). Loughead et al (2006) also attempt to distinguish between team members who are leaders to the majority of the team (called 'team leaders') and those who are nominated by only a few members of the team (called 'peer leaders'). Using Kogler Hill's (2001) framework that identifies team leaders as having three functions (task, social and external), Loughead et al demonstrated that leadership is a widely distributed role. Task functions relate to the performance elements of the team, and social functions relate to the interpersonal processes within the team. External functions relate to the outward-facing roles of the team such as dealing with other organizations or the community. Approximately half of the team members served some sort of task leadership role either as a team leader (15 per cent) or as a peer leader (35 per cent). For social leadership roles, nearly 60 per cent of members had a role with 11 per cent acting as team leaders and 47 per cent as peer leaders. External leadership roles were carried by fewer people with only 8 per cent as team leaders and 31 per cent as peer leaders. This research demonstrates the diversity of team members that provide leadership in some form to other members on a team. It contradicts methodologies that measure an individual, e.g. the coach, as the only source of leadership.

In comparing the roles of peer leaders' with coach leaders' behaviours, Loughead and Hardy (2005) discovered that the roles these two types of leaders fill for team members is different. Using an adapted Leadership Scale for Sport (LSS; Chelladurai and Saleh, 1980) to make it suitable for measuring peer leadership, the researchers were able to identify that coaches supply more autocratic behaviours, and training and instruction behaviours whereas peer leaders supplied more social support, positive feedback and democratic behaviours. Dupuis, Bloom and Loughead (2006) conducted interviews with team captains identified as among the best their coaches had worked with. Using Chelladurai's (1980) multidimensional model, the research was able to identify three categories of leader behaviours: interpersonal characteristics and experiences, verbal interactions and task behaviours. Interpersonal characteristics and experiences contained a number of skills or attributes (e.g. controlling emotions, communication skills, positive attitude) the captains thought necessary to have along with elements of their development in ice hockey and specifically about captaining in hockey (e.g. playing from a young age, early leadership roles). The verbal interactions category related heavily to the position the captains had as intermediary between coach and team members. The verbal communications in both directions were considered important for success in the role and for the team. For the task dimensions category, the authors identified a number of tasks the players completed that were aimed at improving the team's functioning, climate and norms. These involved off-court duties such as administrative tasks or representing the team at functions. They were also involved in organizing team meetings, whether they were formal to deal with team issues or social to enhance morale. The most important role that captains identified as critical to their position was to set the right example, whether that be on court or off court.

The three studies detailed above represent a new theme to leadership research in sport. They are not without methodological issues. For instance, if the LSS has been criticised for being a limited measure of leadership for coaches (Chelladurai and Riemer, 1998) then it is unlikely to be an adequate measure of leadership when adapted to athletes. In fact, given the range of personal, interpersonal and task factors identified by Dupuis et al (2006) as representative of good leadership, the adapted LSS used by Loughead and Hardy (2005) would not capture the essence of peer leadership. The small sample size (six participants) in Dupuis et al and limited range (all Canadian university ice hockey players) brings into question the generalizability of these findings. Further, while Dupuis et al raise interesting questions, confirmatory research is needed to test their suggestions on a broader range of leaders.

Overall, the research presented above demonstrates the existence and importance (though not quantifiably) of peer leadership. The evidence base under construction may also explain why research into leadership that only considers the coach in the measurement of leadership does not consistently show strong relationships to outcomes. As a whole, studies into peer leadership and coach leadership may suggest that leadership is something that is a property of a group rather than the property of an individual.

Activity 9.3

Reconsidering the definition of leadership

At the start of this chapter, it was suggested that definitions of leadership contained four components. In this box, we borrow from Keith Grint's (2005) analysis of leadership in various domains and individuals to re-conceptualize what leadership is.

Grint (2005) chooses to look at leadership from four different perspectives:

1. Leadership as a person.
2. Leadership as a process.
3. Leadership as a result.
4. Leadership as position.

To understand leadership as a person is to consider that leadership is inherent to an individual. It is something that a leader has that makes others willing to follow in that person's path. Leadership theories that are trait based or charisma based can easily be conceptualized under this framework.

Grint's (2005) referral to leadership as results is based on a premise that without results there must not have been any leadership. In sport, it would be to say that the coach has led the team to a championship. It is not something about the coach that makes you believe they are a leader, nor something about the way they did it; it is the reference to the result that infers leadership.

Process-based leadership suggests a premise that leaders *do* something differently to non-leaders. There is a considerable amount of research that concerns the behaviours of leaders, particularly coaches, which give them success or popularity in their role. Conceptualizing leadership in this way allows us to entertain the idea that leadership can be prescriptive. However, it is difficult to accept that distinguishing between the behaviours of leaders and non-leaders in one context will allow us to infer that those differences will remain constant in new contexts.

The final conceptualization of Grint (2005) is that leadership is position based. Traditional hierarchical structures which exist in sport, such as the

Continued . . .

. . . Continued

coach and captain, are position based. The coach and captain are leaders because they are put in that position and it is because they are in that position that people will follow them.

A key question for researchers and practitioners alike is 'how could these conceptualizations affect the way research into leadership and leadership development could be advanced in sport?'. How would you approach the selection and training of leaders differently under each view of leadership? Do any seem to resonate with your own experience more than others? If so, why?

Leadership development in coaches

Leadership development is the process by which a person learns to improve their capacity for leading people or projects. As previously identified, there is very little distinction made in coaching research between leadership and coaching. Examining leadership development can only occur by looking at how coaches develop more broadly. There are two styles of research that have investigated this area. The first is recall-type studies where coaches are asked to recall their developmental experiences that they believe contributed to their current position. A recent example of this is Erickson, Côté and Fraser-Thomas' (2007) recent exploration of 19 Canadian inter-university coaches. Erickson et al identified that experience in the sport and some formal coach education or mentoring were consistently found in performance sport coaches. They also identified that for team sport coaches, experiences in team sports other than the one they were currently involved and leadership roles as an athlete were likely contributing factors to the coaches' development. This was not matched for individual sport coaches, possibly due to fewer leadership opportunities. Erickson et al suggest a model for coach development that includes maximizing opportunities for athletes to take leadership roles during their competitive careers.

A consistent finding in studies of coach development is the lack of time spent in formal coaching programmes (e.g. Gilbert and Trudel, 2006). Erickson et al's (2007) stages of development of high-performance coaches include descriptive categories for each stage. They identify that most of the coaching development occurs through assisting other coaches, coaching developmental teams while still playing at a high level, and being mentored by other coaches. Nelson, Cushion and Potrac (2006) also note that several studies have identified that most coach learning occurs in informal ways. Nelson et al suggest that reflection (Gilbert and Trudel, 2006), mentoring (Cushion, 2006, see Jones, 2006) and experience within a community of practice (Culver and Trudel, 2006) are the facilitating factors in coach development.

The second style of research that contributes to our knowledge of coach/leadership development is intervention studies. Smith, Smoll and colleagues' original studies (e.g. Smith et al, 1979; Smoll and Smith, 1980) using the CBAS were part of a larger programme of coach development. Smith et al provided cognitive behavioural training programmes to coaches, influencing and evaluating change with behavioural analysis. The programmes being conducted were grounded in a belief that development of children as people was paramount rather than winning in children's sporting environments. Their research identified (among other things) that coach training can be effective in increasing children's self-esteem and promoting in-team attraction when compared to untrained coaches, though without necessarily making a difference to win/loss records.

For researchers and practitioners interested in elite sport environments, Mallet and Côté (2006) advocate a process for evaluating high-performance coaches that extends beyond winning and losing. They contend that, even in the high-performance context, there are so many extraneous factors that influence win/loss analyses that they become inefficient as a sole arbitrator of coach performance. In Mallett and Côté's paper they utilize the Coaching Behaviour Scale for Sport (CBS-S; Côté et al, 1999) to measure coach behaviours based on factors determined as relevant to high-performance coaches. The seven factors assessed are: physical training and planning, goal-setting, mental preparation, technical skills, personal rapport, negative personal rapport and competition strategies. The system they report for evaluation is a three-step process. First, data are gathered using the CBS-S. This is followed by writing a summary report including qualitative and quantitative data. The third stage in their model is to feed back the results from the evaluation to the coach under scrutiny, to inform their individual development. A key aspect of research in this area is the notion that accurate measurement and feedback are critical for the success of interventions to enhance coaching.

Leadership development in athletes

Few research articles have been published that shed light on how athlete leaders develop. Wright and Côté (2003) conducted small-scale research to investigate the development of acknowledged team leaders. Using a three-part interview-based method, they explored the factors in the development of six athletes who were acknowledged by their team members as the leaders in their team. In parts one and two of the interview process, participants identified the types of activities they were involved in throughout their development (e.g. organized sport, activities with parents) and provided details about the social context of the activities (i.e. hours spent, leadership roles held, age compared to peers). In the third part of the interview, participants added another layer of description, this time focusing on their behaviour, the three major socializing influences of peers, coaches and parents, and relationships. Wright and Côté identified a number of factors that appeared in each person's developmental pathway.

The results of the study indicated that three groups of influencing components could be identified: a) peers, b) coaches, and c) parents. Within each component

Component	Categories
Peers	Characteristics of peers
	Leader–athlete demonstrates strong work ethic
	Rapport with peers
	Roles in play activities
	Roles in organized sport
Coaches	Are nice people
	Develop skills
	Are stimulating figures
	Designate leader roles
	Engage in mature conversations
Parents	Introduction to sport
	Support
	Coaching role
	Mentoring role

Table 9.1 Components and categories of factors influencing leader development.

Source: From Wright and Côté (2003).

there was a further distinction between influences which were labelled as categories. These are shown in Table 9.1.

Throughout the methodology the researchers also looked to make distinctions between what happened at different chronological age stages. These were designated according to schooling such that stage 1 corresponded to primary school, stage 2 with middle school and stage 3 with high school. This allowed the researchers to understand how different activities at different times may influence leader development.

Within the peer component Wright and Côté (2003) identified that the athletes were involved in competition as much with older athletes as they were their own age group. They indicated that this competition might not always be in a formal setting. As the athletes got older they were often given opportunities with older athletes to develop the playing and tactical skills which would then allow them to appear to be advanced within their own age group. This also appeared to have an effect on leadership in that while no leadership roles were thrust upon the child when playing with the advanced group, when they returned to their own age group they assumed leadership roles. Wright and Côté (2003: 282) also suggest that there appeared a pattern of 'non-threatening' sport environments early in the process followed by 'increasingly challenging competition'.

Athletes also revealed that their work ethic was important in establishing the respect of their team-mates. It is also likely that a strong work ethic contributed to the advanced development of their sporting skills (Gould et al, 2002a; Smith, 2003; Wright and Côté, 2003). The athletes' advanced skills also contributed to other factors such as being offered or appointed to formal leadership roles in organized sport, and attention from parents and coaches that in turn contributed to conversations and opportunities to develop tactical knowledge and sport skills.

The authors concluded that there were four main areas that came to light in categorizing the pathway to leadership. Athletes all had high levels of skill compared to their age peers, a strong work ethic, advanced tactical sport knowledge and good rapport with team-mates. Consider the following hypothetical example: A child plays a variety of different sports and games with the local children from the neighbourhood. When they commence primary school, they show advanced skills within their peer group. This comes to the attention of their parents and coaches and allows opportunities for them to train or play with older age groups. During these experiences they learn a strong work ethic and through the environment are challenged to keep pace with older peers. Consequently when they return to their own peers their sport skills are further advanced. It becomes clear through recognition from coaches and other officials that the player is better at the sport and receives respect from their team-mates, and consequently the player is invited to assume a formal leadership role. This requires them to interact with the coach about tactics and the player acts as a communicator between the coach and the other players. Both the coach and the parents engage with the developing athlete in a mature way, which gives the player opportunities to consider tactical concepts and team issues in a way that other players are not. The person who is the product of this developmental pathway is now recognized by peers as a team leader.

Wright and Côté (2003) acknowledge that the limited sample used in their study may restrict the generalizability of their conclusions. However, they also suggest that there is little reason to believe that, with further research, they will not be supported. Wright and Côté suggest that while the pathways of development may vary, the four elements of leadership are not likely to. While there are many studies in sport that look to explore the pathway to the development of expertise, Wright and Côté's research is the only one to look specifically at the development of leadership. Further research in this area is required to establish if the findings are consistent across cultures. Another possibility is to see if environments can be constructed to give more young athletes opportunities to engage in the situations that lead to leadership development.

Future directions

A research question that has received scant attention is the hypothesis that leaders' behaviours (coaches and/or athletes) predict performance. Given that team performance is how leaders are judged, it is surprising that few studies have attempted to address this question. Methodological issues have plagued leadership research both in terms of measurement of leadership issues and the effects of leadership on performance. Recent research by Eys et al (2007) explored leader dispersion in teams in relation to athlete satisfaction. They identified that sport teams which have equal numbers of team members contributing to the three leadership functions (task, social, external) are likely to report higher levels of satisfaction with team performance and satisfaction with team integration. The authors acknowledge that while this represents a step forward in tying leadership beyond the dimensions of the LSS to consequences, leader dispersion is still an incomplete measure of leadership as it estimates quantity but does not deal with the quality of the leadership supplied.

Other researchers have begun to consider variables that may mediate the impact of leadership on performance. Trail (2004) identified an effect of leadership on cohesion and cohesion on performance, thereby questioning the MMLS. Chelladurai (2007) identifies motivation and self-efficacy as two examples of potentially mediating variables, though others such as collective efficacy could hold potential for future research.

There are many aspects of leadership in sport that are ready to be researched. The MMLS has many areas which still need further exploration, particularly with different conceptualizations of who or what leadership is. Also, other leadership models and theories, particularly relating to transformational leadership, have enough promise to warrant further exploration.

Ethics and leadership

Most codes of ethics are based on a set of principles that should lead a person to display ethical behaviour in any given situation. In sport, the ethics of leadership are most noticeable in the codes of conduct that national governing bodies, sports clubs and other organizations commit to uphold. The ethics of leadership have long been discussed from a philosophical standpoint rather than a research-informed perspective. Northouse (2007) suggests five principles of ethical leadership:

- Respects others.

- Serves others.

- Shows justice.

- Manifests honesty.

- Builds community.

In sporting domains, codes of conduct designed to ensure ethical behaviour can be found for coaches, parents, volunteers, administrators, athletes and spectators. Of particular interest for leadership are the codes of conduct/ethics for coaches. Websites for organizations such as Clubmark, the Australian Sports Commission (ASC), and the Coaches of Canada all have readily available information to help coaches behave in an ethical manner. Specific research into coaching ethics at a principle level is hard to identify, though research into issues with an ethical theme such as sexual abuse by coaches or spectator behaviour at children's sport events is more readily available. A report prepared for the ASC (Colmar Brunton Social Research, 2003) identified that inappropriate coach behaviour was the fourth highest ethical issue perceived to have the most impact across all levels of sport. Dodge and Robertson (2004) advocate the role coaches can play in teaching and reinforcing ethical behaviour and sanctioning unethical behaviour in sport. Their research identified that the coaches' influence was a justification for athletes to engage in specific types of unethical behaviour. This was more pronounced in males than females.

Activity 9.4

Ethics

Consider each of the following situations and identify which of Northouse's (2007) ethical principles are being questioned. Identify a more ethical behaviour for each situation.

1. The coach's own child is selected to open the batting and bowling in every match of a cricket season.
2. The coach wants an under-15 player to play an important match with a pain-killing injection.
3. The coach tells players that they should be caught breaking the rules at least once in a match as it is likely that, for every time they are caught, they will have managed to get an advantage four times without being caught.
4. The coach works with players to analyse opposition players to identify which ones might be most susceptible to 'sledging'.
5. The coach tells a player what they think they need to hear rather than what they actually believe.
6. Early in a season, two players break a team rule and are suspended for a game. Before the final, the team's best player is caught breaking the same rule but the coach lets him play.
7. A player is known for having a bad temper and using abusive language at opposition players and officials. The coach believes the player plays best when they are 'fired up' and so does not do anything to help the player gain control of their emotions.

Key concepts and terms

Leadership
Leadership development

Multidimensional model of
leadership in sport (MMLS)

Sample essay titles

- Using research evidence, critically evaluate the common perception that involvement in sport develops leadership in individuals.
- Discuss the utility of the multidimensional model of leadership in sport for enhancing performance and satisfaction in teams. Use empirical evidence to support your arguments.
- Discuss the relative advantages and disadvantages of different ways of measuring leadership in coaches.

Further reading

Books

Grint, K. (2005). *Leadership: Limits and Possibilities*. Hampshire: Palgrave Macmillan.

Jones, R.L. (2006). *The Sports Coach as Educator: Re-conceptualising Sports Coaching*. London: Routledge.

Riemer, H.A. (2007). 'Multidimensional model of coach leadership.' In: S. Jowett and D. Lavallee (Eds), *Social Psychology of Sport*. Leeds: Human Kinetics, 57–74.

Journal articles

Dupuis, M., Bloom, G.A., and Loughead, T.M. (2006). Team captains' perceptions of athlete leadership. *Journal of Sport Behavior*, 29, 60–78.

Erickson, K., Côté, J., and Fraser-Thomas, J. (2007). Sport experiences, milestones and educational activities associated with high-performance coaches' development. *The Sport Psychologist*, 21, 302–316.

Eys, M.A., Loughead, T.M., and Hardy, J. (2007) Athlete leadership dispersion and satisfaction in interactive sport teams. *Psychology of Sport and Exercise*, 8, 281–296.

Loughead, T.M., and Hardy, J. (2005). An examination of coach and peer leader behaviours in sport. *Psychology of Sport and Exercise*, 6, 303–312.

Wright, A., and Côté, J. (2003). A retrospective analysis of leadership development through sport. *The Sport Psychologist*, 17, 268–291.

Useful websites

www.ausport.gov.au/ethics/coachofficial.asp
www.coachesofcanada.com/Professionals/
www.clubmark.org.uk

4 | The effects of exercise on psychological states

10 Physical activity and self-esteem

Michael J. Duncan

The way we feel about ourselves is important in every domain of life and we can almost certainly identify when we feel on top of the world about something. In this case we are enjoying the benefits of high **self-esteem**, a concept that has been branded a 'social vaccine' that can empower individuals and make them more productive and confident in their own abilities. Historically, both the academic literature and the popular media presuppose that every person has a sense of self and the self is a social phenomenon (Cooley, 1902; Mead, 1934; James, 1950).

Self-esteem is often seen to be one of the most important indicators of psychological well-being. In many instances, enhanced self-esteem resulting from physical activity is one of the main benefits put forward by those individuals or agencies promoting regular exercise and those concerned with physical education in schools. This chapter provides an overview of the literature pertaining to the link between physical activity and self-esteem. Alongside this, conceptual models of this relationship are discussed together with applied case studies that illustrate the theoretical constructs related to the assessment of self-esteem in the physical activity domain. The aims of this chapter are threefold. The first aim is to describe relationships between physical activity and self-esteem reported in the literature as evidence varies between studies. A second aim is to evaluate the **conceptual exercise self-esteem model of Sonstroem and Morgan** (1989) and evidence that has examined this model. The third aim is to develop an understanding of the methods available to assess self-esteem in relation to physical activity.

Learning outcomes

When you have completed this chapter you should be able to:

1. Evaluate relationships between physical activity and self-esteem reported in the literature and be aware of methodological factors influencing this relationship.
2. Evaluate the conceptual exercise self-esteem model of Sonstroem and Morgan (1989) and evidence that has examined this model.
3. Understand and evaluate the methods available to assess self-esteem in relation to physical activity.

Focus 10.1

Physical activity and self-esteem: Starting point

- Self-esteem influences psychological well-being.
- Physical activity influences physical self-perceptions.
- Physical self-perceptions shape physical self-esteem.
- Physical activity can enhance self-esteem.

Activity 10.1

Think about a physical activity or related situation that you have recently found yourself in. What made you feel that you were able to complete your chosen physical activity? Did you feel positive about what you were doing? Did you feel that you were able to complete the activity as well as anyone else could?

Write down all the factors that you think contribute to the psychological changes that are associated with regular participation in physical activity. Try not to confuse this with mood (see Chapter 2 for information regarding the impact of mood on sport performance).

Examine Fox's physical self-perception model presented in Figure 10.1 and compare your list with this model. I suspect at least some of the factors you have noted down could fit in the subdomains within this model.

Read Fox (2000) and compare his description of how these subdomains contribute to the development of self-esteem through physical activity to the list of factors that make you feel that you could complete your chosen physical activity example.

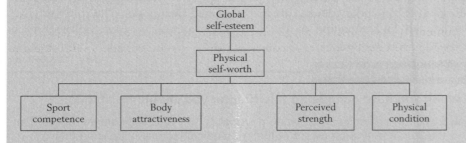

Figure 10.1 The physical self-perception model.

Source: Fox, K.R. (2000) Self-esteem, self-perceptions and exercise. International Journal of Sport psychology, 31, 228–240.

The relationships between physical activity and self-esteem reported in the literature

Physical activity and self-esteem: The evidence

Self-esteem refers to the value placed on aspects of the self, such as academic and social domains. (Biddle and Mutrie, 2007: 181)

Rosenberg (1965) also proposed that self-esteem was a positive or negative orientation towards oneself or an overall evaluation of one's worth or value.

Although a range of studies have examined the relationship between physical activity and self-esteem, it is only recently that methodological factors in the measurement of self-esteem have been addressed. In most cases exercise psychologists have employed a global measure of self-esteem. Global self-esteem comprises differentiations of the self including physical, social and academic self-perceptions. In the exercise and physical activity arena, physical self-perceptions are underpinned by subdomains best illustrated by **Fox's physical self-perception model** (see Figure 10.1). Fox and Corbin (1989) suggested that the subdomains of sport competence, body attractiveness, perceived strength and physical condition positively influence our feelings of physical self-worth. Therefore, physical self-worth mediates the influence of physical activity on global self-esteem.

Meta-analyses

A plethora of research studies and meta-analytic studies have reported that physical activity can enhance self-esteem or physical self-worth. However, the magnitude of any enhancement in self-esteem still remains to be fully elucidated. Meta-analysis results reported by Spence, McGannon and Poon (2005) found that physical activity positively enhanced global self-esteem, although the overall effect size (0.23) was moderate. Spence tested a number of potentially moderating factors. Interestingly, they found the type of exercise programme (i.e. intensity, frequency, duration or mode), fitness levels of participants did not influence the effect of exercise on self-esteem and did not appear to moderate the physical activity–self-esteem relationship. However, larger effect sizes were documented for lifestyle programmes that incorporated nutritional advice alongside exercise. Spence et al concluded that exercise enhances self-esteem in adults but that this effect is smaller than previously thought. However, it should be noted that Spence et al included both published and unpublished studies. While meta-analysis research should seek to include the full number of studies, including unpublished studies can compromise findings as they have not been scrutinized by going through the peer review process.

The meta-analysis results reported by Spence et al were in contrast to an earlier meta-analysis conducted by McDonald and Hodgdon (1991) that examined the effect of aerobic training on self-concept (this included measures of self-esteem and body image). McDonald and Hodgdon (1991) reported an effect size of 0.56 and concluded that fitness training is associated with improvements in ratings of the 'self'. However, the breadth of measures employed by studies included in this meta-analysis may cloud the true effect of exercise on global self-esteem. Additionally, Gruber (1986) reported an effect size of 0.41 for self-esteem based on a meta-analysis of 27 studies of play and physical education programmes in children.

Randomized controlled trials

Fox (2000) reviewed 36 randomized controlled trials (RCTs) completed since 1970 that examined the efficacy of physical activity to promote self-esteem. Seventy-six per cent of all RCTs reported positive changes in physical self-perceptions or self-esteem as a result of physical activity. Fox (2000) concluded that exercise can be used to promote physical self-perceptions/self-esteem but that the mechanisms that underpin this are not clear. More recently, Ekeland, Heian and Hagan (2005) asked the question: 'Can exercise improve self-esteem in children and young people?'. They completed a systematic review of 23 RCTs and concluded that exercise can improve self-esteem in children. However, they stressed caution when examining this issue in younger populations as different types of intervention have been used in studies of this nature. For example, some studies used physical activity only, some used physical activity plus skills training and counselling. Furthermore, although most of the studies included in their review used valid and reliable measures of self-esteem, there was a high risk of bias in most of the studies. Further, no study had included a long-term follow up to determine the time course of any enhancement in self-esteem due to physical activity. Ekeland et al (2005) concluded that there is a need for rigorous, well-designed research that investigates the impact of physical activity on self-esteem in young people before scientists can answer the question they posed in the title of their review.

Overall, the research evidence related to the relationship between physical activity and self-esteem indicates that, for both adults and children, physical activity and exercise is associated with higher self-esteem. However, the effect sizes reported in studies on this topic are generally small to moderate due to methodological reasons. Furthermore, there is still a need for research to clarify the mechanisms that facilitate the association between physical activity and self-esteem. A researcher should ask the question 'why should exercise raise self-esteem?', rather than 'how much has exercise raised self-esteem?'.

The conceptual exercise–self-esteem model of Sonstroem and Morgan (1989)

Numerous researchers have examined behavioural influences on self-esteem, and physical activity has been considered to be an important component in self-evaluations. Reviews of the literature have concluded that testing the relationship between physical activity and self-esteem has been hindered due to two issues: a) the measurement of self-esteem, and b) a lack of clarity regarding conceptual models of the physical activity–self-esteem relationship. The second part of this chapter will consider one conceptual model of the exercise/physical activity–self-esteem relationship that has shown promise in explaining the interaction between these two variables.

Approaches to the physical activity–self-esteem relationship

Biddle and Mutrie (2007) summarized the two main approaches used to study the physical activity–self-esteem relationship. The first approach put forward by Sonstroem (1997), termed the 'motivational approach' or 'personal development hypothesis', posits that self-esteem is a determinant of physical activity. That is, individuals high in self-esteem are more likely to engage in physical activity behaviours as this is an area where their self-worth can be enhanced. Second, the 'skill development hypothesis' (Sonstroem, 1997) suggests that self-esteem is modified through experience and that self-esteem enhancement (or reduction) is a product of our experiences in physical activity or exercise. Biddle and Mutrie (2007) go on to highlight that these two approaches are not mutually exclusive and that initial participation in physical activity may be externally motivated but can lead to enhanced self-esteem/self-worth which, in turn, becomes a motivator for any subsequent physical activity.

The Sonstroem and Morgan exercise–self-esteem model

Sonstroem and Morgan (1989) proposed a model to explain how the effects of physical activity generalize to global self-esteem (see Figure 10.2). This model is based on the dimensions of perceived physical competence and perceived physical acceptance as these elements were postulated to be the two foundations of global self-esteem. Self-efficacy describes confidence-estimates to how well an individual can perform a particular task (Bandura, 1997). In the case of the exercise–self-esteem model, self-efficacy perceptions relate to perceived physical competence (i.e. an individual's evaluation of their overall level of ability). It is hypothesized that increases in physical self-efficacy lead to increases in perceived physical competence, which in turn increase in global self-esteem (Sonstroem, 1997). This model has also been termed the skill development hypothesis.

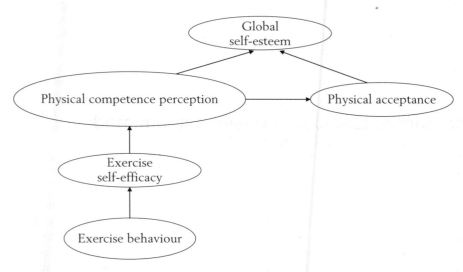

Figure 10.2 The exercise and self-esteem model.

Source: Sonstroem and Morgan, 1989. Exercise and self-esteem: Rationale and Model. Medicine and Science in Sports and Exercise, 21, 329–337.

Activity 10.2

Think about the exercise and self-esteem model of Sonstroem and Morgan (1989) and write down how you think the two elements of physical competence perception and physical acceptance influence global self-esteem.

Read Levy and Ebbeck (2005) and compare your notes to their assertions regarding the Sonstroem and Morgan model. How do your thoughts compare to their comments regarding this self-esteem model? In particular, did your considerations of the importance of physical acceptance match theirs?

Physical activity and self-esteem: The importance of physical acceptance

Although the Sonstroem and Morgan model suggests that exercise behaviour is associated with self-esteem through perception of self-efficacy, physical competence and physical acceptance, the majority of research employing this model has primarily examined the role of physical competence perceptions on global self-esteem. Overwhelmingly, individuals who perceive that they are more competent in the physical domain report higher self-esteem (Sonstroem et al, 1992, 1993, 1994; Van de Vliet et al, 2002). However, while the role of physical competence in mediating self-esteem appears to have been well researched, the influence of physical acceptance on self-esteem has been less well examined. As physical acceptance is purported to mediate the relationship between physical competence perceptions and global self-esteem (see Figure 10.2), this may be a particularly important area for physical activity practitioners to study if they are to fully understand the physical activity–self-esteem relationship. Despite this, the relationship between measures of body image and body satisfaction (often used as a proxy for physical acceptance) and global self-esteem has been supported, particularly in females (Furnham et al, 2002; Mendelson et al, 2002; Stice, 2002; Palladino-Green and Pritchard, 2003). These relationships have also been noted in children. For example, Mendelson and White (1982) found body esteem to be significantly related to self-esteem in both normal and obese children. These findings have also been supported by Cohane and Pope (2001), Guinn et al (1997) and Tiggemann and Wilson-Barratt (1998). Mendelson and White (1985) reported significant relationships between self-esteem and body esteem in children aged 8–17 years. Overweight children in this study were also found to have lower body esteem than normal weight children.

More recently, Levy and Ebbeck (2005) examined the importance of physical acceptance in mediating the physical competence perception–global self-esteem relationship in adult women who completed measures of exercise behaviour, exercise self-efficacy, perceptions of physical competence, perceptions of physical acceptance and global self-esteem. Using multiple regression analysis their model components explained 22 per cent of the variability in global self-esteem. More significantly, perceptions of physical acceptance made a unique contribution to the model, explaining 12.6 per cent of the variability in global self-esteem. They concluded that, for females, physical acceptance plays a vital role in the physical self-perception and self-esteem relationship. Physical acceptance made the largest and only significant contribution to global self-esteem in their study. Despite the clear indication of physical acceptance as a strong predictor of global self-esteem in their study, Levy and Ebbeck (2005) stress the need for future research to examine the role of physical acceptance on global self-esteem in a variety of populations and activity settings. Indeed, this may be an important future research avenue as considerable research exists that indicates children suffer from considerable body dissatisfaction (and thus lower physical acceptance) and that body dissatisfaction is related to physical activity behaviour (Duncan et al, 2006).

A modified exercise–self-esteem model

The development of Fox's physical self-perception model, and later the physical self-perception profile by Fox and Corbin (1989), led to a re-conceptualization of the original Sonstroem and Morgan (1989) exercise self-esteem model. This revised model, or **EXSEM** as it is currently termed, combined the original Sonstroem and Morgan (1989) model with Fox's physical self-perception model (see Figure 10.3). Within the revised model, changes in physical activity and associated physical parameters (e.g. fitness, weight) that are brought about by exercise or physical activity are proposed to have indirect effects on changes in global self-esteem. Changes in self-efficacy as a result of changes in physical activity are proposed to influence subdomains of physical

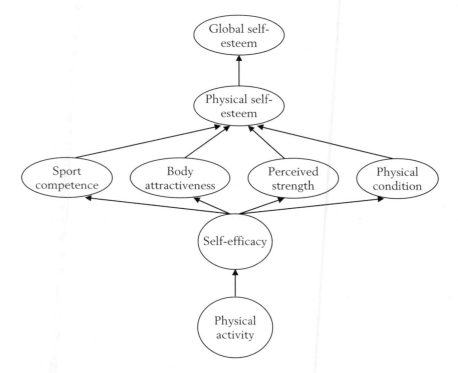

Figure 10.3. The EXSEM model.

Source: Sonstroem et al, 1994. Exercise and self-esteem: Validity of model expansion and exercise associations.
Journal of Sport and Exercise Psychology, 16, 29–42.

esteem, notably self-perceptions of physical conditioning, body attractiveness, sport competence and strength. These changes are theorized to be associated with changes in physical self-worth which then influence global self-esteem.

The EXSEM has been supported by a number of empirical studies although the majority of studies have used a cross-sectional design. Sonstroem et al (1994) assessed 214 females who had enrolled on an aerobic dance programme. Participants completed the global self-worth scale (to assess self-esteem), the physical self-perception profiles (to assess the physical self-perceptions in Fox's model) and self-efficacy measures for jogging, sit-ups and dance. Standardized regression coefficients were used to explain the amount of variance within the model. The overall model was able to explain 32.8 per cent of global self-esteem variance and 88.6 per cent of the variance in physical self-worth scores. Sonstroem et al (1994) concluded that the EXSEM was a valid model of the association between exercise and self-esteem.

More recently, several studies have been published that have added weight to the EXSEM model. These have supported the EXSEM in a range of populations and both cross-sectional and longitudinal study designs. For example, McAuley et al (2000) reported strong support for the EXSEM model over a six-month exercise intervention in older adults. These data have also been supported by research based on a six-month randomized controlled study of Tai-Chi in older adults by Li et al (2002). However, these studies have also postulated that physical activity and self-efficacy both directly influence the subdomain levels of self-esteem (as opposed to physical activity indirectly influencing self-esteem through its effect on self-efficacy). In an attempt to examine this issue, McAuley et al (2005) reported longitudinal data on the relationships between physical activity, self-efficacy and self-esteem in older adults. They examined a group of 174 older adults (aged 60–75 years of age) at one and five years after entry onto a structured physical activity/exercise programme. Physical activity was determined using a population-specific, self-report questionnaire, global self-esteem was assessed using the Rosenberg self-esteem scale (Rosenberg, 1965), and the physical self-perception profile (Fox and Corbin, 1989) was used to assess the subdomain levels of the EXSEM (both measures will be discussed in greater depth later on in this chapter). Using covariance modelling they found consistent relationships between the subdomain levels of self-esteem and physical activity and the subdomain levels of self-esteem and global self-esteem. These were also consistent over the four-year period of measurement. Furthermore, those adults reporting greater reductions in physical activity also reported greater reductions in subdomain levels of self-esteem and global self-esteem. The authors also support previous assertions that physical activity and self-efficacy both directly influenced the subdomain levels of self-esteem. This study represents one of the most comprehensive tests of the EXSEM model. Based on their longitudinal data, 69 per cent of the variance in physical self-worth was accounted for, as was 51 per cent of the variance in global self-esteem. This is important as, if the researcher is interested in the relation between physical activity and self-esteem, the focus should be on physical self-worth (i.e. physical self-esteem) rather than global measures. Certainly in this case the EXSEM appears to do a good job of accounting for the variance in physical self-esteem but also underlines how important physical activity and physical self-worth may be in an individual's global self-esteem. Despite this, the study by McAuley et al (2005) was based on a predominantly white population and the research design used in their study (i.e. a two-point time model) precludes any inference of causality in the physical activity–self-esteem relationship. Further research is clearly needed to address these issues.

Understand and evaluate the methods available to assess self-esteem in relation to physical activity

There are a variety of methods available to assess self-esteem. The aim of this section is to consider some of the issues related to the assessment of self-esteem in physical activity research. One of the main questions the researcher or practitioner needs to begin with is how to assess global self-esteem. The key question is whether to use a global self-esteem or whether to use subdomains of the physical self that are predictive of global self-esteem.

Activity 10.3

Consider how you feel generally about yourself. Fill in the Rosenberg self-esteem scale presented in Figure 10.4 as directed and calculate your self-esteem score. The higher the score, the higher the self-esteem. Once finished, consider the questionnaire you have just completed. The Rosenberg self-esteem scale is a well-used measure of global self-esteem. Would you consider this to be a good measure of self-esteem that could be used in the activity domain? If not, why not? By considering this issue you will start to learn more about the measurement of self-esteem and issues surrounding the conceptualization of self-esteem.

1. On the whole, I am satisfied with myself.	SA	A	D	SD
2. At times, I think I am no good at all.	SA	A	D	SD
3. I feel that I have a number of good qualities.	SA	A	D	SD
4. I am able to do things as well as most other people.	SA	A	D	SD
5. I feel I do not have much to be proud of.	SA	A	D	SD
6. I certainly feel useless at times.	SA	A	D	SD
7. I feel that I'm a person of worth, at least on an equal plane with others.	SA	A	D	SD
8. I wish I could have more respect for myself.	SA	A	D	SD
9. All in all, I am more inclined to feel that I am a failure.	SA	A	D	SD
10. I take a positive attitude toward myself.	SA	A	D	SD

Scoring: SA = 3, A = 2, D = 1, SD = 0. Items 2, 5, 6, 8 and 9 are reversed scored. Sum the scores for the 10 items. The higher the score, the higher the self-esteem.

Figure 10.4 The Rosenberg self-esteem scale.

Source: Rosenberg, 1965.

Should we measure self-esteem or physical self-perceptions?

Often researchers have employed a global measure of self-esteem such as the Rosenberg self-esteem scale (see Figure 10.4). This measure has shown good reliability and concurrent validity with measures of self-perceptions (Hagborg, 1993; Robins et al, 2001). However, although self-esteem is a global construct it is influenced by a number of domains. Thus, self-esteem is multidimensional and is composed of differentiated perceptions of the self which relate to areas such as academic, physical and social self-perceptions. Within the area of physical activity and exercise, physical self-perceptions appear to be important variables that underpin an individual's global self-esteem. As a result, the use of the Rosenberg self-esteem scale only provides an overall measure of self-esteem. It is argued that using an overall measure of self-esteem might lead to a substantial loss of information. If the goal of the researcher, student or scientist is to examine how physical activity relates to one's overall sense of self-worth, then physical self-esteem may be the most important concern relative to physical activity and/or exercise (McAuley et al, 2005). Fox's physical self-perception model presented earlier in this chapter (Figure 10.1) attempts to explain how global self-esteem is influenced by the physical self and has subsequently led to the development of psychometric measures of physical self-worth and the four subdomains within this construct.

Measurement of physical self-perceptions

Considerable research has documented a number of different measures of physical self-perceptions and physical self-concept. These include the physical self-perception profile (PSPP) (Fox and Corbin, 1989) and the physical self-description questionnaire (Marsh et al, 1994). Of these questionnaires, the PSPP has probably been the most widely used method to assess physical self-perceptions and self-esteem. Fox and Corbin (1989) developed the PSPP as a means to examine physical self-worth and the four subdomains of sport competence, body attractiveness, perceived strength and physical condition, based on the work of Harter (1985) into self-concept. The PSPP is a 30-item inventory which consists of four sub-scales that correspond to the four subdomains of physical self-perception as outlined in Fox's model. The PSPP also features one general scale to assess physical self-worth. Each sub-scale consists of six items in which participants are presented two contrasting descriptions (e.g. those with unattractive bodies and those with attractive bodies) and are asked which description is most like themselves and whether the description they select is 'sort of true' or 'really true' for them. Item scores can range from 1 to 4 and sub-scale scores can range from 6 to 24 (as each sub-scale consists of six items). The use of the PSPP allows exercise psychologists to examine how physical activity influences different aspects of our self-perceptions and, in turn, how these might influence self-esteem. For example, participation in physical activity may enhance an individual's feelings of body attractiveness and physical condition. This change may lead to enhancement of physical self-worth and increases in self-esteem. The PSPP was originally validated with American college students (Fox and Corbin, 1989) but subsequent research has demonstrated its utility and validity in older and younger people and cross culturally (Welk and Eklund, 2005). A range of studies have measured physical self-perceptions related to sport and exercise participation (McAuley et al, 2000, 2005) and the PSPP is a reliable and valid measure of the construct it purports to examine.

More recently the utility of the PSPP as a measure of physical self-perceptions and self-esteem in the physical domain has been undertaken with wording modifications being made to the original PSPP. Factor analysis has shown that, in younger populations, the four-factor structure of the original PSPP is supported. This scale was subsequently renamed the 'children and youth physical self perception profile' (CY-PSPP) (Whitehead, 1995; Eklund et al, 1997). Welk and Eklund (2005) have also examined the utility of the CY-SPP for the measurement of physical self-perceptions in a large sample of 8–12-year-old children. In their study, confirmatory factor analysis supported the utility of the PSPP model in young children. In addition to significant relationships between physical activity scores and physical-self perceptions, physical self-perceptions of children in this study were also significantly related to a range of fitness measures including measures of aerobic fitness and percentage body fat. Physical activity was also significantly related to each of the domains within the CY-PSPP. Welk and Eklund (2005) stress the importance of these relationships by suggesting that significant correlations between objective indicators of fitness and scores on the CY-PSPP indicate that the children in their study were able to make accurate self-perceptions.

Extracurricular physical activity and global self-esteem in children (Binsinger et al, 2006)

Physical activity is often suggested or prescribed as an effective tool to enhance young people's self-esteem as, compared to sedentary individuals, young athletes tend to show higher self-esteem (Strauss et al, 2001; Crews et al, 2004). However, the research base supporting this assertion in young people in general is not conclusive. As a result, Binsinger et al (2006) investigated the impact of regular, extracurricular sports/physical activity participation on self-esteem in a large sample ($n =1791$) of French adolescents who were tracked over a three-year period. A secondary aim of this study was to examine any protective effect of physical activity participation in fluctuations in global self-esteem. Self-esteem in this study was assessed using the Rosenberg self-esteem scale. Results for half-yearly variations in global self-esteem for children who participated in extracurricular sport (ECS) and those that did not (NECS) in their study are presented in Table 10.1. Binsinger et al (2006) reported that, over the three-year period, adolescents who engaged in extracurricular sports activities had significantly higher self-esteem than those who did not participate in extracurricular sport or physical activity. The novel finding of this study was that the incidence of severe decreases in self-esteem was lower in girls who participated in extracurricular sports or physical activity compared to boys. However, the authors of this paper acknowledged that the use of a global measure of self-esteem may have inhibited their ability to fully understand the impact that sports participation and physical activity may have on the subdomains that comprise global self-esteem.

	Nov 01	May 02	Nov 02	May 03	Nov 03	May 04
ECS	31.5	32.5	31.1	32.8	32.8	32.2
NECS	29.5	30.8	29.4	30.8	31.0	30.8

Table 10.1 Half-yearly variations in global self-esteem for children who did (ECS) and did not (NECS) participate in extracurricular sport over a two and a half year period.

Source: Binsinger et al, 2006.

Activity 10.4

Consider the Rosenberg self-esteem questionnaire you filled out as part of Activity 10.2 and then consider the exercise and self-esteem model as portrayed in Figure 10.3. Do you think the questionnaire links to the exercise and self-esteem model? Take this issue in the context of the applied case study of Binsinger et al (2006) and note down what this research paper tells the practitioner about self-esteem and its link with participation in after-school sports.

I suspect your notes may highlight that all that can be inferred from the work of Binsinger et al (2006) is that extracurricular sports participation is linked to higher global self-esteem scores. You may also have highlighted that this research does not actually tell us about the construct or constructs that might be responsible for the findings reported by Binsinger et al (2006). This highlights an important issue when considering research that has examined the physical activity–self-esteem relationship. If we are interested purely in global self-esteem, the Rosenberg questionnaire can provide this information. However, if we are interested in assessing what constructs influence the physical activity–self-esteem relationship then we need to look beyond a simple measure of global self-esteem. Instead we would need to fully examine physical self-worth and the subdomains of physical condition, sport competence, body attractiveness and physical strength as depicted in Fox's hierarchical model of self-esteem in the physical domain (see Figure 10.1).

Physical self-perceptions and physical activity in boys and girls (Crocker et al, 2000)

Crocker et al (2000) completed a study which evidences the importance of assessing physical self-perceptions when examining the physical activity–self-esteem relationship. In this study, 220 boys and 246 girls completed a self-report measure of physical activity and the physical self-perception profile. This was an important research topic for a number of reasons. Crocker et al (2000) noted that few data are available that assess the physical activity–self-esteem relationship in younger populations and even fewer studies have examined the impact of gender on this relationship. The results of their study indicated that there were significant relationships between all four domains within the PSPP and physical activity scores. Moreover, boys were more physically active than girls and had more positive perceptions of physical strength, sport competence and physical self-worth compared to girls. Mean scores by subdomain on the PSPP for boys and girls in this study are presented in Table 10.2. Using structural equation modelling, 27–29 per cent of the variance in physical activity scores was predicted from scores on the PSPP. There was also no evidence that gender moderated the relationship between physical self-perceptions and physical activity.

	Boys	**Girls**
Physical condition	3.09	3.08
Sport competence	3.15	2.88
Body attractiveness	2.72	2.58
Strength competence	2.93	2.74

Table 10.2 Mean scores by subdomain on the PSPP for boys and girls.

Source: Crocker et al, 2000.

Activity 10.5

Consider the study mentioned above and examine the mean scores on each subdomain of the PSPP reported by Crocker et al (2000). Scores on all four sub-scales were significantly related to physical activity in this study. Can you provide a theoretical explanation as to why each of the subdomains might be related to physical activity and why, in the case of both boys and girls, subdomain scores for physical condition and sport competence were higher than those for body attractiveness and strength competence?

Crocker et al (2000) suggested that the higher scores for physical condition and sport competence and the stronger relationship with physical activity reported in their study were not unusual as a number of studies have suggested that physical self-perceptions of physical condition are related to actual physical activity. Second, the higher scores in sport competence are likely to be related to physical activity due to children's involvement in school sport and extracurricular physical activity as all children experience some form of school sport/physical education. Although causality cannot be determined from this study, the suggestion by Crocker et al (2000) is that participation in physical activity strengthens children's self-perceptions of their sport competence more than their perceptions of body attractiveness and strength competence.

Ethics

Ethical considerations when examining the physical activity–self-esteem relationship

Consider the variety of research studies that have been outlined within this chapter. Do you think there are any ethical issues related to the examination of the impact that physical activity has on self-esteem? If so, what are they, and what should sport and exercise psychologists consider when investigating this topic?

The consideration of ethics within the physical activity –self-esteem domain is not always explicitly considered within research studies. However, we have a duty to consider the ethical issues surrounding psychological research with any population we work with. When you considered the research presented in this chapter, did you consider that self-esteem is a dynamic construct that can change? As practitioners we need to consider that our intervention could change the way a person feels about themselves. In some instances we need to be prepared that a physical activity programme that we prescribe could result in an individual or individuals feeling worse about themselves. We also need to consider the ethical issues associated with such an occurrence and our responsibility to deal with this should it happen to any research participant we are working with.

Conclusions

Self-esteem is often considered a central component in psychological well-being and a range of research studies have reported that physical activity can enhance self-esteem. Meta-analytical research and studies of randomized controlled trials conclude that physical activity can be used to promote increases in self-esteem and physical self-perceptions although the mechanisms that underpin this change are still unclear. Sonstroem and Morgan's (1989) conceptual model and subsequent modifications encompassing Fox's physical self-perception model are presented. Fox's model appears to be the most robust, and scientifically supported. Despite this, the examination of the impact of physical activity on self-esteem has been clouded by use of different measures to assess self-esteem. In some cases these measures assess different constructs within the physical activity–self-esteem model but have inferred self-esteem from them. Some research has used a general measure of global self-esteem, while others have used measures of physical self-perceptions. I would argue that the use of a global measure of self-esteem in studies of the impact of physical activity on self-esteem only provides the researcher with limited information. Instead, the assessment of physical self-perceptions can provide practitioners and scientists with a more comprehensive understanding of the ways in which physical activity influences self-perceptions and subsequently global self-esteem. The final part of this chapter presented case studies to illustrate the limitations of using a global measure of self-esteem and the differing contribution that the subdomains of the physical self-perception model can make if a measure such as the physical self-perception profile is used to examine the impact of physical activity on self-esteem.

Key concepts and terms

EXSEM model
Fox's physical self-perception
  model

Self-esteem
Sonstroem and Morgan
  conceptual model

Sample essay titles

- The conceptual model of Sonstroem and Morgan (1989) provides the most robust explanation of the physical activity–self-esteem relationship to date. With reference to empirical evidence, discuss the validity of this model in the context of physical activity and exercise behaviour.
- The physical self-perception profile offers the scientist the most comprehensive tool to assess the impact of physical activity on self-esteem. Discuss this statement with reference to the measures available to assess self-esteem and the theoretical models that attempt to explain the relationship between physical activity and self-esteem.
- Critically evaluate research evidence on the relationship between physical activity/exercise and self-esteem. Outline how empirical research on this topic supports the conceptual models of the physical activity–self-esteem relationship reported in the literature.

Further reading

Books

Biddle, S.J.H., and Mutrie, N. (2007). *Psychology of Physical Activity*. London: Routledge.

Fox, K.R. (1997). The physical self and processes in self-esteem development. In: K.R. Fox (Ed.), *The Physical Self*. Champaign, IL: Human Kinetics, 111–140.

Sonstroem, R.J. (1997). The physical self-system: A mediator of exercise and self-esteem. In: K.R. Fox (Ed.), *The Physical Self*. Champaign, IL: Human Kinetics, 3–26.

Journal articles

Binsinger, C., Laure, P., and Ambard, M-F. (2006). Regular extra curricular sports practice does not prevent moderate or severe variations in self-esteem or trait anxiety in early adolescents. *Journal of Sports Science and Medicine*, 5, 123–129.

Crocker, P.R.E., Eklund, R.C., and Kowalski, K.C. (2000). Children's physical activity and self-perceptions. *Journal of Sports Sciences*, 18, 383–394.

Duncan, M., Al-Nakeeb, Y., Jones, M., and Nevill, A. (2006). Body dissatisfaction, body fat and physical activity in British children. *International Journal of Pediatric Obesity*, 1, 89–95.

Ekeland, E., Heian, F., and Hagen, K.B. (2005). Can exercise improve self-esteem in children and young people? A systematic review of randomised control trials. *British Journal of Sports Medicine*, 39, 792–798.

Fox, K.R. (2000). Self-esteem, self-perceptions and exercise. *International Journal of Sport Psychology*, 31, 228–240.

Sonstroem, R.J., Harlow, L.L., and Josephs, L. (1994). Exercise and self-esteem: Validity of model expansion and exercise associations. *Journal of Sport & Exercise Psychology*, 16, 29–42.

Spence, J.C., McGannon, K.R., and Poon, P. (2005). The effect of exercise on global self-esteem: A quantitative review. *Journal of Sport & Exercise Psychology*, 27, 311–334.

Welk, G.J., and Eklund, B. (2005). Validation of the children and youth physical self perceptions profile for young children. *Psychology of Sport & Exercise*, 6, 51–65.

11 Exercise addiction

Attila Szabo and Mária Rendi

This chapter presents a psychological dysfunction in which obsessive and compulsive exercise is a means of coping with life stress or other psychological problems. The motivational incentives in exercise addiction are discussed from a behaviouristic perspective. Subsequently, a physiological and a psychological model for the aetiology of exercise addiction are presented. Six common symptoms of exercise addiction, on the basis of which a brief questionnaire aimed at screening of the dysfunction was developed, are illustrated with examples. It is suggested that symptom-based identification of exercise addiction is incomplete as it represents only a surface screening shedding light merely on the tip of the iceberg. The chapter concludes with a succinct discussion of actions to be taken by addicted exercisers, health professionals and researchers.

Learning outcomes

When you have completed this chapter you should be able to:

1. Define the concept of exercise addiction.
2. Differentiate between high levels of commitment to exercise and exercise addiction.
3. Understand the motivational incentives in exercise addiction from the behaviouristic viewpoint.
4. Present and explain a physiological and a psychological model for exercise addiction.
5. Know the common symptoms and means of assessment of exercise addiction.

Introduction and definition of exercise addiction

In sport and recreational physical activity, the frequency, duration, and intensity (effort) of the activity jointly comprise the **dose of exercise**. Moderation of the dose of exercise in sport and physical activity is important to prevent overtraining that could result in physical and psychological damage. Even when training for world-class competition, athletes and, in particular, their coaches must plan carefully the training sessions to avoid injury and **staleness** (mental fatigue and loss of enthusiasm, often associated with overtraining or unimaginative, repetitive training sessions) before the crucial event. Nevertheless, innocent or careless miscalculations occur and the athlete pays the price in such circumstances. Overtraining is a serious issue in sport as well as general psychology, but the scope of this chapter is to present, discuss and evaluate exercise addiction, a condition in which the dose of exercise is *self-selected* or self-imposed by the exerciser. Those who wish to learn more about overtraining in competitive sports should refer to Kreider, Fry and O'Toole (1998).

Overdoing an adopted recreational physical activity may lead to severe physical injuries as well as to the neglect of other personal responsibilities. Indeed, in some rare cases, exercisers may lose control over their exercise and walk on the 'path of self-destruction' (Morgan, 1979). The psychological condition associated with over-exercising is referred to as **exercise addiction** (Griffiths, 1997; Thaxton, 1982). Another term frequently adopted by some scholars is **exercise dependence** (Cockerill and Riddington, 1996; Hausenblas and Symons Downs, 2002). Further, some describe the condition as **obligatory exercising** (Pasman and Thompson, 1988); in the media the condition is often described as **compulsive exercise** (Eberle, 2004) and the term **exercise abuse** (Davis, 2000) is also used. It is important to note that all these synonymous labels describe the same psychological condition. However, in light of some arguments, as elaborated below, alternating the terminology may be incorrect.

While the term 'dependence' is used as a synonym for addiction, the latter includes the former and also includes 'compulsion' (Goodman, 1990). Accordingly, a formula for addiction may be: *addiction = dependence + compulsion*. Goodman specifies that not all dependencies and compulsions may be classified as addiction. Therefore, in this chapter the term *addiction* is deemed the most appropriate because it incorporates both dependence and compulsion. Addiction is defined as a behavioural process that could provide either pleasure or relief from internal discomfort (stress, anxiety, etc.) and it is characterized by repeated failure to control the behaviour (state of powerlessness) and maintenance of the behaviour in spite of major negative consequences (Goodman, 1990). This definition is complemented by six symptoms of addiction (discussed in detail herein) as criteria for identifying the condition: salience, mood modification, tolerance, withdrawal symptoms, personal conflict and relapse (Brown, 1993).

Exercise addiction has been classified as *primary exercise addiction* when it manifests itself as a behavioural addiction and as *secondary exercise addiction* when it is present as a co-symptom to eating disorders (De Coverley Veale, 1987). In the former, the motive for exercise abuse is often unknown even to the affected person. In the latter, however, exercise is used as a means of weight loss (in addition to strict dieting). Therefore, secondary exercise addiction has a different route than primary exercise addiction. Nonetheless, many symptoms of exercise addiction are common between primary and secondary addictions. A key (and distinguishing) difference between the two is that in primary exercise addiction *exercise is the objective*, whereas in secondary exercise addiction *the objective is weight loss*. This chapter is limited to the discussion of primary exercise addiction.

Over-commitment or addiction?

Glasser (1976) introduced the term **positive addiction** to highlight the personally and socially beneficial aspects of regular exercise in contrast to self-destructive behaviour like drug or alcohol abuse. The 'positive' perception and adoption of the terminology led to its widespread and 'weightless' use within both athletic and scientific circles. For example, many runners claimed that they were *addicted* to their running while they referred to their high level of commitment and dedication to their chosen exercise. Morgan (1979) long ago recognized this dilemma. Therefore, to discuss the negative aspects of exaggerated exercise behaviour, he introduced the term *negative addiction* as an antonym to Glasser's positive addiction. The fact is, however, that all addicted behaviours represent a dysfunction and, therefore, they are *always* negative (Rozin and Stoess, 1993).

Glasser's (1976) 'positive' notion referred to the benefits of *commitment* to physical exercise (a healthy behaviour) in contrast to the negative effects of 'unhealthy' addictions. In fact, positive addiction is a synonym for **commitment to exercise** (Carmack and Martens, 1979; Pierce, 1994). However, when commitment to exercise is used as a synonym for *addiction* or *dependence* (Conboy, 1994; Sachs, 1981; Thornton and Scott, 1995) a major conceptual error is emerging. For example, Thornton and Scott (1995) reported that they could classify 77 per cent of a sample of 40 runners as moderately or highly addicted to running. Such a figure is enormous if one considers that among 20,000 runners in a marathon race, for example, more than three quarters of the participants may be addicted! The figure is obviously exaggerated (Szabo, 2000). Therefore, some scholars have recognized this problem and have attempted to draw a line between commitment and addiction to exercise (Summers and Hinton, 1986; Chapman and De Castro, 1990; Szabo et al, 1997; Szabo, 2000).

Commitment to exercise is a measure of how devoted a person is to their activity. It is an index of the strength of adherence to an adopted, healthy or beneficial activity that is a part of the daily life of the individual. For committed people, satisfaction, enjoyment and achievement derived from their activity are the incentives that motivate them to stick to their sport or exercise (Chapman and De Castro, 1990). Sachs (1981) believed that commitment to exercise results from the intellectual analysis of the rewards, including social relationships, health, status, prestige or even monetary advantages, gained from the activity. Committed exercisers, in Sachs' view: 1) exercise for extrinsic rewards; 2) view their exercise as an important, but not the central part of their lives; and 3) may not experience major withdrawal symptoms when they cannot exercise for some reason (Summers and Hinton, 1986). Perhaps the key point is that committed exercisers *control* their activity (Johnson, 1995) rather than being controlled by the activity. In contrast to committed exercisers, addicted exercisers: 1) are more likely to exercises for intrinsic rewards; 2) are aware that exercise is the central part of their lives; and 3) experience severe deprivation feelings when they are prevented from exercising (Sachs, 1981; Summers and Hinton, 1986). Items on two psychometrically validated questionnaires assessing commitment and addiction to exercise are illustrated in Tables 11.1 and 11.2.

Please note the difference between the items or the individual statements on the two questionnaires while keeping in mind that half of the 12 items on Table 11.1 are reversely rated. These items present the statement in the 'opposite' or negative direction and the smaller number on the scale, like a rating of '1', is reversed and is counted as '5'. On some scales, or questionnaires, such items are embedded to ascertain valid responses from those who complete the questionnaires. For example, a statement like 'I do not enjoy running/exercising' (statement 4) would be rated with the lowest number (i.e. 1) by the highly committed runner or exerciser and would be consistent with a rating of 5 on the opposite, positively formulated, statement 'Running (or exercising) is pleasant' (statement 5). Should such opposite statements disagree in ratings, deception, whether careless or voluntary, on the part of the respondent may be suspected and the answers could be considered unreliable.

1.	I look forward to my exercise/sport.
2.	I wish there were a more enjoyable way to stay fit.
3.	My exercise/sport is drudgery (unpleasant hard work).
4.	I do not enjoy my sport/exercise.
5.	My exercise/sport is vitally important to me.
6.	Life is so much richer as a result of my exercise/sport.
7.	My exercise/sport is pleasant.
8.	I dread the thought of exercising or performing my sport.
9.	I would arrange or change my schedule to meet the need to exercise or perform my sport.
10.	I have to force myself to exercise or do my sport.
11.	To miss a day's exercise/sport is sheer relief.
12.	Exercising (doing my sport) is the high point of my day.

Table 11.1 Commitment to running (exercise) scale (Carmack and Martens, 1979). The statements are rated on a five-point Likert scale anchored by 1 (strongly disagree) and 5 (strongly agree). The negative statements (2, 3, 4, 8, 10, 11) are inversely rated (i.e. 1 = 5, 2 = 4, 3 remains 3, 4 = 2, 5 = 1). The sum of all items (after the inverse rating has been performed on six items) is the index of commitment to exercise. The maximum score is 60 (12 × 5) and, usually, respondents scoring above 50 are considered to be highly committed to their exercise.

1.	Exercise is the most important thing in my life.
2.	Conflicts have arisen between me and my family and/or my partner about the amount of exercise I do.
3.	I use exercise as a way of changing my mood (e.g. to get a buzz, to escape, etc.).
4.	Over time I have increased the amount of exercise I do in a day.
5.	If I have to miss an exercise session I feel moody and irritable.
6.	If I cut down the amount of exercise I do, and then start again, I always end up exercising as often as I did before.

Table 11.2 The exercise addiction inventory (EAI; Terry et al, 2004). The statements are rated on a five-point scale, similar to the commitment to running (exercise) scale (Carmack and Martens, 1979). There are no negative items on this questionnaire. The total ratings (maximum $6 \times 5 = 30$) are summed and where the cut-off point of 24 is reached or exceeded, the likelihood of exercise addiction is established. Please note the EAI is a *not* a diagnostic tool but simply a surface screening brief questionnaire that helps in the identification of the symptoms of exercise addiction. The dysfunction itself needs to be diagnosed via interviews by mental health professionals or other qualified health or medical personnel.

Activity 11.1

The following quote illustrates the path of addiction of an exercise addict:

I moved to a new town and decided to join a health club as a way of meeting people. Soon, exercise began to become a focal part of my life and I became more determined to keep fit and improve my physique. Gradually, the 3 hours a day I was doing increased to 6 hours and I started to become totally obsessive about exercise. I wouldn't miss a day at the gym. I just lost sight of my body really – I just had to do my workout, come what may, and get my fix. (*Evening Standard* 1 August, 2000).

From the quote, on how many items of the EAI would you predict an almost certain score of 5?

Motivational incentives in addiction

Motivation for exercise is another distinguishing characteristic between commitment and addiction to exercise. People exercise for a reason. The reason is often an intangible reward like being in shape, looking good, being with friends, staying healthy, building muscles, maintaining body weight, etc. The subjective experience of the reward reinforces or strengthens the exercise behaviour. Scholars known as *behaviourists*, adhering to one of the most influential schools of thought in the field of psychology, postulate that behaviour can be understood and explained through reinforcement and punishment. Accordingly, the **operant conditioning theory** suggests that there are three principles of behaviour: **positive reinforcement, negative reinforcement** and **punishment** (Bozarth, 1994). Positive reinforcement is a motivational incentive for doing something to *gain* a reward that is something pleasant or desirable (e.g. increased muscle tone). The reward then becomes a motivational incentive, which increases the likelihood of that behaviour to reoccur. In contrast, negative reinforcement is a motivational incentive for doing something to *avoid* a noxious or unpleasant (e.g. feeling sluggish) event. The avoidance or reduction of the noxious stimulus is the reward, which then increases the probability of that behaviour to reoccur. It should be noted that both positive and negative reinforcers increase the likelihood of the behaviour (Bozarth, 1994), but their mechanism is different because in positive reinforcement there is a *gain following the action* (e.g. feeling revitalized), whereas in behaviours motivated by negative reinforcement one *avoids something bad or unpleasant before happening* that otherwise could occur without the behaviour (e.g. feeling guilty or fat if one misses a planned exercise session).

Punishment refers to situations in which the imposition of some noxious or unpleasant stimulus or event or alternately the removal of a pleasant or desired stimulus or event reduces the probability of a given behaviour to reoccur. In contrast to reinforcers, punishers suppress the behaviour and, therefore, exercise or physical activity should never be used (by teachers, parents or coaches) as punishment.

People addicted to exercise may be motivated by negative reinforcement (e.g. to avoid withdrawal symptoms) as well as positive reinforcement (Pierce, 1994; Szabo, 1995) (e.g. **'runners' high'** which is a pleasant feeling associated with positive self-image, sense of vitality, control and a sense of fulfilment reported by exercisers after a certain amount and intensity of exercise. This feeling has been associated with increased levels of endogenous opioids and catecholamines resulting from exercise). However, negative reinforcement, or avoidance behaviour, is not a characteristic of committed exercisers (Szabo, 1995). Indeed, committed exercisers maintain their exercise regimen for benefiting from the activity. On the other hand, addicted exercisers *have to do it* or else something will happen to them. Their exercise may be an 'obligation' (also reflected by the popular term 'obligatory exercise') that needs to be fulfilled or otherwise an unwanted life event could occur like the inability to cope with stress, or gaining weight, becoming moody, etc. Every time a person undertakes behaviour to avoid something negative, bad or unpleasant, the motive behind that behaviour may be classified as negative reinforcement. In these situations, the person involved *has to do it* in contrast to *wants to do it*. There are many examples in other sport areas where a behaviour initially driven by positive reinforcement may turn into negatively reinforced or motivated behaviour. For example, an outstanding football player who starts playing the game for fun, after being discovered as a talent and being offered a service contract in a team, becomes a professional player who upon signing the contract *is expected* to perform.

Although the player may still enjoy playing (especially when all goes well), the pressure or expectation to perform is the 'has to do' new facet of football playing and the negatively reinforcing component of his (or her) sporting behaviour. Activity box 11.2 illustrates the major differences between the underlying motives in behaviours guided by negative and positive reinforcement.

Activity 11.2

Behaviours driven by positive and negative reinforcement

Provide several examples in which the behaviour or action is motivated by positive and negative reinforcement.

Positive reinforcement	Negative reinforcement
Origin: Behaviouristic school of thought *Definition*: Positive reinforcement strengthens a behaviour because a tangible or intangible gain is secured as a result of the behaviour	*Origin*: Behaviouristic school of thought *Definition*: Negative reinforcement strengthens a behaviour because a negative condition is stopped and/or avoided as a consequence of the behaviour
Examples: 'I like the fresh and energizing feeling after exercise' (*gains* good feeling) 'I like running shorter and shorter times on the same distance' (*gains* skill and confidence) 'I run to be in good shape' (*gains* physical benefits, good shape)	*Examples*: 'I run *to avoid* circulatory problems that my parents had' 'I go to gym *to avoid* getting fat' 'I have to run my 10 miles every day, or else I feel guilty and irritated' (*avoids* feeling of guilt and irritation)

Although positive reinforcement like the runners' high and brain reward systems have been implicated in the explanation of exercise addiction, the motivational incentive in addiction may be more closely connected to prevention, escape or avoidance of something unwanted as in some recent models of addiction (Baker et al, 2004). Accordingly, the process of addiction is more likely motivated by negative reinforcement in which the affected individual has to exercise to avoid an unwanted consequence. Two models trying to account for the path of addiction to exercise are presented below.

Two models of addiction

A physiological model suggesting how adaptation of the organism to habitual exercise may lead to addiction is based on Thompson and Blanton's (1987) work. From most exercise physiology textbooks it is known that regular exercise, especially aerobic exercise like running, if performed for a sustained period, results in decreased heart rate at rest. While heart rate is only a crude measure of the body's sympathetic activity (which is directed by the autonomic nervous system), it is nevertheless a sensitive measure and it is often used to mirror sympathetic activity. A lower resting heart rate after training results from the adaptation of the organism to exercise. Figure 11.1 illustrates a hypothetical case in which the exerciser's initial basal heart rate on the average is about 62 beats per minute (bpm). Every single session of exercise raises the heart rate to well above 100 bpm (depending on exercise intensity of course) that upon recovery following exercise returns to lower than the pre-exercise or basal heart rate. With repeated exercise challenge, resulting from aerobic training and a concomitantly more efficient cardiovascular system, the basal heart rate, partially reflecting sympathetic activity, decreases. Lower sympathetic activity at rest means a lower level of arousal. This new arousal state may be experienced as a lethargic or energy-lacking state, which according to Thompson and Blanton's hypothesis urges the exerciser to do something about it, or to increase the level of arousal. The obvious means to do that is exercise. However, the effects of exercise in increasing arousal are only temporary and, therefore, more and more bouts of exercise may be needed to achieve an optimal state of arousal. Further, not only the frequency but also the intensity of exercise sessions may need to increase due to training effect. Such an increase accounts for the tolerance aspect of the addiction process.

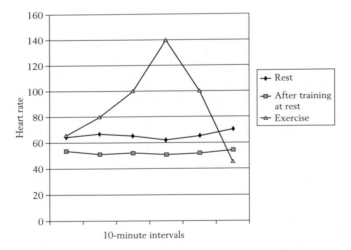

Figure 11.1 A hypothetical illustration of how one's basal (resting) heart rate may decrease after prolonged aerobic training. Note that the dashed line illustrates the change in heart rate during one exercise session only. The adaptation, reflected by the difference between the lines with squares and triangles, may require several months and in some cases even longer.

Uncomfortable sensations of 'non-optimal' level of arousal are a form of withdrawal feelings or symptoms that prompt the exerciser to get moving and engage in a workout. As the frequency of workouts and the reliance on exercise to regulate arousal increase, the behaviour progressively assumes a central part in the exerciser's life, which is known as salience. When the need to exercise is not fulfilled, the addicted person will feel lethargic, lacking energy, guilty, irritated, etc. (see Figure 11.2). They have to exercise, as mentioned above, to avoid a constellation of uncomfortable feelings. At this point the exerciser loses control over their exercise, which is no longer performed for fun or pleasure but it becomes a negatively reinforced obligation.

Figure 11.2 The sympathetic arousal hypothesis.

Source: Thompson and Blanton, 1987.

There is a psychological explanation for exercise addiction as well. Some exercisers try to escape from their psychological problems (Morris, 1989). They are very few in number and use exercise as a means of coping with stress. Like others, who turn to drugs and alcohol in difficult life situations, exercisers may abuse their exercise so that behavioural addiction becomes evident (Griffiths, 1997). However, because exercise, in contrast to alcohol or drugs, involves significant physical effort (Cockerill and Riddington, 1996), it is an inconvenient coping method that requires strong self-determination, self-discipline and possibly a bit of masochistic attitude. Therefore, the incidence of exercise addiction is very rare in contrast to other forms of escape behaviours.

Szabo (1995) proposed a cognitive appraisal hypothesis for better understanding of the psychological path in exercise addiction, as summarized in Figure 11.3. Accordingly, once the exerciser uses exercise as a method of coping with stress, the affected individual starts to depend on exercise to function well. They believe that exercise is a healthy means of coping with stress based on information from scholastic and public media sources. Therefore, they use rationalization to explain the exaggerated amount of exercise that progressively takes a toll on other obligations and daily activities. However, when the interference of exercise with other duties and tasks obliges the exerciser to reduce the amount of daily exercise, a psychological hardship emerges, which is manifested through a set of negative feelings like irritability, guilt, anxiousness, sluggishness, etc. These feelings collectively represent the withdrawal symptoms experienced because of less or zero exercise. When exercise is used to cope with stress, apart from the collection of negative psychological feeling states there is also a loss in the coping mechanism (exercise). Concomitantly, the exerciser loses control over the stressful situations that they used to deal with by resorting to exercise. The loss of the coping mechanism, followed by the loss of control over stress, generates an increased perception of vulnerability to stress, therefore further amplifying the negative psychological feelings associated with the lack of exercise. This problem can be resolved only through resuming the previous pattern of exercise at the expense of other obligations of daily life. Obviously, while exercise provides an instant reduction in the negative psychological feelings, the neglect or superficial treatment of other social and work obligations results in conflict with people, possibly losses at work or school, or even loss of

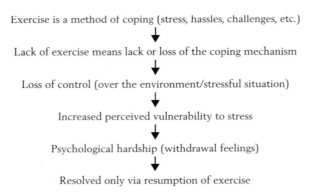

Figure 11.3 The cognitive appraisal hypothesis.

Source: Szabo, 1995.

Activity 11.3

In groups of three to five, discuss whether the two models (the sympathetic arousal hypothesis and the cognitive appraisal hypothesis) may mutually apply or exclude each other in the aetiology of exercise addiction. Think about how these models differ from the beta-endorphin hypothesis in which addiction may be caused by the desire to re-experience the exercise-induced release of beta-endorphins binding to the so-called **opioid receptors** (a group of G-protein coupled receptors with opioids as ligands: dynorphins, enkephalins, endorphins, endomorphins and nociceptin/orphanin FQ) in the brain and providing a positive feeling of 'high' (i.e. runners' high).

job, together causing further stress. The addicted exerciser is then trapped in a vicious circle needing more exercise to deal with the consistently increasing life stress, part of which is caused by exercise itself.

Withdrawal symptoms

Sachs (1981: 118) described addiction to running as 'addiction of a psychological and/or physiological nature, upon a regular regimen of running, characterized by withdrawal symptoms after 24 to 36 hours without participation'. This definition is popular in the literature (Sachs and Pargman, 1984; Morris, 1989; Furst and Germone, 1993). However, there is a problem with this definition because withdrawal symptoms, although most characteristic, are only one of several symptoms of addictive behaviours (Brown, 1993; Griffiths, 1997). Incorrectly, many studies have simply assessed the mere presence, rather than the type, frequency and intensity of withdrawal symptoms (Szabo, 1995; Szabo et al, 1997). Yet negative psychological symptoms are reported by almost all habitual exercisers (or hobby makers) for the times when exercise or a hobby-activity is prevented for an unexpected reason (Szabo et al, 1997; Szabo, Frenkl, and Caputo, 1996). Indeed, Szabo et al (1996), conducting survey research on the Internet, have shown that even participants in physically 'light effort' types of exercise such as bowling report withdrawal symptoms when the activity (in this case bowling) is prevented. However, the intensity of the symptoms reported by this group was less than that reported by aerobic dancers, weight-trainers, cross-trainers or fencers (Szabo et al, 1996).

Consequently, it must be appreciated that the presence of withdrawal symptoms alone is insufficient for the diagnosis of exercise addiction. The intensity of these symptoms is a crucial factor in separating committed from addicted exercisers. Cockerill and Riddington (1996) do not even mention withdrawal symptoms in their list of symptoms associated with exercise addiction. In fact, the presence of withdrawal symptoms in many forms of physical activity suggests that exercise has a positive effect on people's psychological well-being. This positive effect is then, obviously, missed when an interruption in the habitual activity is necessary for some reason.

Six common symptoms of exercise addiction

Six common symptoms of behavioural addiction were identified through the systematic observation of several behaviours such as exercise, sex, gambling, video games and also use of the Internet. Based on Brown's (1993) general components of addictions, Griffiths (1996, 1997, 2002) has reiterated them into the following six components:

Salience

This symptom is present when the physical activity or exercise becomes the most important activity in the person's life and dominates their thinking (preoccupation and cognitive distortions), feelings (cravings) and behaviour (deterioration of social behaviours). For instance, even if the person is not actually engaged in exercise, they will be thinking about the next time they will be. The mind of the addicted individual wanders off to exercise during driving, meals, meetings, and even between conversations with friends. The closer the planned time for exercise, the greater is the urge and even anxiety or fear of not starting on time. The addicted exerciser is literally obsessed with exercise and regardless of the time of the day, place or activity performed their mind is directed towards exercise during the majority of their waking hours.

Mood modification

This symptom refers to the subjective experiences that people report as a consequence of engaging in a particular activity and could be seen as a coping strategy (i.e. they experience an arousing 'buzz' or a 'high', or paradoxically tranquilizing feel of 'escape' or 'numbing'). Most exercisers report a positive feeling state and pleasant exhaustion after a session of exercise. However, the person addicted to exercise would seek mood modification not necessarily for the gain or the positive mental effect of exercise, but rather for the modification or avoidance of the negative psychological feeling states that they would experience if the exercise session were missed.

Tolerance

Tolerance is the process whereby increasing amounts of the particular activity are required to achieve the former effects. For instance, a gambler may have to gradually increase the size of the bet to experience the euphoric or satisfying effect that was initially obtained by a much smaller bet. The runner needs to run longer distances to experience the 'runners' high' (Stoll, 1997). Similarly, the addicted exerciser needs larger and larger doses of exercise to derive the effects experienced previously with lower amounts of exercise. Tolerance is the main reason why individuals addicted to exercise progressively and continuously increase the frequency and duration of the workouts. (Read Activity box 11.1 again in this context.)

Withdrawal symptoms

These symptoms are the unpleasant psychological and physical feeling states that occur when exercise is discontinued or significantly reduced. The most commonly reported symptoms are guilt, irritability, anxiety, sluggishness, feeling fat, lacking energy, and being in a bad mood or depressed. The intensity of these states is severe in people affected by exercise addiction to the extent that they really feel miserable when the need for exercise is not fulfilled. The manifestation of these withdrawal symptoms in addicted individuals is clearly different from those experienced by committed exercisers who simply feel a void, or that something is missing, when exercising is not possible for a reason. Addicted exercisers have to exercise to overcome withdrawal symptoms even at the expense of other more important life obligations. In contrast, committed exercisers look forward to the next opportunity while prioritizing their obligations.

Conflict

This symptom represents the conflicts between the exercise addict and others around them (interpersonal conflict), conflicts with other daily activities (job, social life, hobbies and interests) or from within the individual themselves (intra-psychic conflict) which are concerned with the particular activity. Interpersonal conflict usually results from neglect of the relationship with friends or family because of the exaggerated time devoted to exercise. Conflict in daily activities arises because of the abnormally high priority given to exercise in contrast to even some of the survival activities like cleaning, taking care of bills, working or studying for exams. Intra-psychic conflict occurs when the addicted person has realized that fulfilling the need to exercise takes a toll on other life endeavours, but is unable to cut down or to control the exercise behaviour.

Relapse

Relapse is the tendency for repeated reversions to earlier patterns of exercise after a break, whether voluntary or involuntary. Relapse can be observed after injury (which is involuntary) or after a planned reduction in exercise volume as a consequence of a personal decision to put a halt to the unhealthy pattern of exercise behaviour or as a consequence of professional advice. Upon resumption of the activity, addicted individuals may soon end up exercising as much as or even more than before the reduction in their volume of exercise. This is similar to other substance and behavioural addictions: for example, the smoker who smokes a pack of cigarettes per day may quit smoking for several weeks, months, or even years and then start over again by smoking a pack or more cigarettes per day.

Activity 11.4

Provide several (at least two) examples of interpersonal conflict, conflict in daily activities and intra-psychic conflict that you or a friend of yours have experienced in the past. If you have never encountered such conflicts and are unaware of others who did, think of real-life situations in which the three forms of conflict may occur. Write down and also elaborate on the examples.

Activity 11.5

Log on to the Internet and using an appropriate browser find literature or documentation on withdrawal symptoms. Differentiate between physical and psychological withdrawal symptoms and then differentiate between withdrawal symptoms associated with substance (drugs, alcohol, tobacco) addiction and behavioural (gambling, sex, exercise, TV watching, video game playing) addictions. Try to rank the severity of withdrawal symptoms by considering the form (substance or behaviour) and history (experience) of addiction.

Activity 11.6

Match each statement on the exercise addiction inventory (EAI – left column) with one of the common symptoms of behavioural addictions listed in the middle column, by writing the corresponding question's number to the right of the symptom in the right-hand column. (The first – tolerance – is done for you as an example.)

1. Exercise is the most important thing in my life	Tolerance	4
2. Conflicts have arisen between me and my family and/or my partner about the amount of exercise I do	Withdrawal symptoms	
3. I use exercise as a way of changing my mood (e.g. to get a buzz, to escape, etc.)	Relapse	
4. Over time I have increased the amount of exercise I do in a day	Salience	
5. If I have to miss an exercise session I feel moody and irritable	Conflict	
6. If I cut down the amount of exercise I do, and then start again, I always end up exercising as often as I did before	Mood modification	

Assessment of exercise addiction

As seen in the previous section, exercise addiction cannot be positively assessed simply on the basis of the presence of withdrawal symptoms. Currently, there are more than a dozen so-called 'addiction' scales (for more information, please read Hausenblas and Symons Downs, 2002). However, like most quantitative scales or questionnaires they were developed to gauge a *degree of addiction*, rather than to positively diagnose exercise addiction. A sample scale, the EAI, is presented in Table 11.1. This scale is by no means better or superior to the questionnaires, however its brevity and structure around the six common symptoms of addiction (Brown, 1993; Griffiths, 1996, 1997, 2002) render it suitable for discussing the appropriateness of employing inventories or questionnaires in the assessment of exercise addiction.

All exercise addiction questionnaires, including the EAI, can only be used for surface screening. This method estimates the *likelihood of addiction* in the respondent. Even individuals scoring above average may not necessarily be addicted to exercise. Nevertheless, a score that is close to the maximum suggests that the possibility is there. A score of 24 on the EAI needs to be considered a potential warning sign. Still, the proper and unambiguous assessment of exercise addiction can only be established after a deep interview with a qualified professional. Exercise addiction scales or questionnaires serve the purpose of directing the individual, or those who are concerned, in the right direction. In schools, sport and leisure facilities, they are quite useful for screening, but many addicted exercisers perform their activity in an informal setting, by simply going out for a run on their own. In fact, it is likely that most exercise addicts are loners in some sense because no structured physical activity classes or exercising friends could keep up with the massive amount of exercise in which they engage on a daily basis. Assuming that only about one to three per cent of the exercising population may be affected by exercise addiction (Szabo, 2000) and that the majority of exercise addicts are 'lone wolfs', the use of the questionnaires may have further limited value in assessment.

The assessment of exercise addiction is based on some common symptoms of addiction that are also listed in the *Diagnostic and Statistical Manual of the American Psychiatric Association* (DSM IV; American Psychiatric Association, 1995) in the context of substance and behavioural addictions such as gambling. In spite of related or even common symptomology with most of the listed addictive behaviours, the DSM IV does not list exercise addiction as a separate category of dysfunction. There may be several reasons for the omission of exercise addiction from the DSM IV. First, the incidence of exercise addiction is very rare based on the number of case studies that are occasionally reported (Szabo, 2000). Therefore, there is perhaps insufficient medical or scientific evidence on which the DSM IV could draw solid conclusions. Second, in contrast to a passive and *let go/let down* attitude common to many self-destructive addictive behaviours, exercise addiction requires effort, determination and self-discipline. These characteristics are positive and in conflict with the *quick fix* aspects of other addictions. A third reason, that may also be true in other addictions, is that exercise addiction identified on the basis of certain symptoms may only be a *symptom in itself* of an underlying psychological or mental dysfunction in which exercise abuse is the escape vehicle from the problem rather than the root of the problem. In light of this conjecture, a closer analysis of the switch from healthy to unhealthy exercise habits needs to be examined.

Correlates of exercise addiction

Researchers have looked at the correlates of exercise addiction, but have been unable to identify when, how or why a transition takes place from healthy to unhealthy exercise behaviour (Johnson, 1995). Exercise addiction appears to be positively related to anxiety (Morgan, 1979; Rudy and Estok, 1989) and negatively correlated with self-esteem (Estok and Rudy, 1986; Rudy and Estok, 1989). Further, the length of experience with a particular physical activity appears to be positively correlated with exercise addiction scores (Hailey and Bailey, 1982; Thaxton, 1982; Furst and Germone, 1993). If experience is related to exercise addiction, it is reasonable to suspect that a stressful life event may trigger addiction that is manifested through 'revolutionary' rather than 'evolutionary' changes in the habitual physical activity pattern of the individual. The affected person may see this form of coping as healthy on the basis of popular knowledge and the media-spread information about the positive aspects of exercise.

It is well known that the media play an important role in what people think and believe about regular physical activity. Their beliefs influence their expectation from their exercise. The media-propagated positive image of the habitual exerciser provides a mental defence, known as rationalization, behind which a few exercisers with severe emotional problems may hide. Thus, the media-projected positive image about regular exercise may be used to deny the existence of the problem (a characteristic defence in most addictive behaviours) and to delay the detection of the problem to the advanced stages when all symptoms of addiction are vividly present. Because of denial, only few case studies reported in the literature may reflect genuine cases of exercise addiction. Their number and case-specificity delay the accumulation of scientific knowledge about this dysfunction. In a random sample of habitual exercisers only a few cases, if any (!), of exercise addicts may be identified (Morris, 1989). As such, the nomothetic (group) approach to studying exercise addiction is inappropriate. The idiographic (case-specific) approach may be more fruitful in enhancing knowledge about exercise addiction. In general, if exercise addiction is believed to be a constructive coping method with a deep psychological problem, it should be treated as a symptom of that problem. The psychological problem itself needs to diagnosed and treated by qualified mental health professionals, which are tasks beyond the scholastic mission of sport scientists.

What can the affected individual do?

Physically active people should keep their exercise in perspective. The person who feels that they are at risk may wish to evaluate the statements in Table 11.2. The statements are based on the most common symptoms of behavioural addiction. If one scores 24 or above on the scale, then there is likely to be a problem. To avoid negative consequences, the exercise behaviour needs to be discussed with an independent health professional familiar with exercise addiction. Denial of the problem is a meaningless delay allowing for the actual augmentation of the problem. At this stage it is important to remember that too much exercise may have detrimental and irreversible effects. If independent opinions suggest that there is a problem, the root of the problem (i.e. the reason/s for over-exercise) should be identified. The mere self-acknowledgement of the problem is already a significant step towards coming back on to a healthy exercise track.

What can health professionals do?

Individuals affected by exercise addiction frequently visit orthopaedic and physiotherapy clinics with injuries caused by sustained exercise in spite of contrary medical advice (Wichmann and Martin, 1992). These injuries become more severe with time and force the individual to seek medical help. Therefore, general practitioners, orthopaedic specialists or surgeons, occupational therapists and physiotherapists should be familiar with the main symptoms of exercise addiction. The EAI, which can be completed by patients in less than a minute, could be a reinforcing aid in the detection of addiction. Upon recognizing the symptoms in a patient, medical and health professionals should attempt to convince the affected individual that talking over the problem with an impartial specialist may be in their interest. Subsequently, they should refer the patient to their psychologist or psychiatrist colleague who is specialized in the area of behavioural addictions. Exercise addiction, like other behavioural addictions, should be considered a serious dysfunction. Therefore, its identification must be positive. Once a positive diagnosis has emerged, the principal concern should be to find the source or the root of addiction. Then the treatment should be geared towards the cause, not the symptom, of exercise addiction (Szabo, 2000).

How research in exercise addiction could be more productive

Research should treat exercise addiction as a symptom of a serious psychological disorder. Because it is estimated that a small fraction of the exercising population is affected by exercise addiction (Morris, 1989; Pierce, 1994; Szabo, 2000), clinical case studies should be accepted to be the framework of research on exercise addiction. Excessive exercise, whether conceptualized in terms of high frequency, intensity, duration or history, is insufficient for the diagnosis of exercise addiction. If the physically active individual has not experienced major negative life-events directly related to their exercise behaviour and they are not jeopardizing personal health and social relationships, then the person is a committed avid exerciser without signs of exercise addiction. Further, because existing tools for gauging exercise addiction are mostly questionnaires aiming at the quantification of exercise addiction, they always yield a score of addiction ranging from low to high. Graded scales are certainly effective in the evaluation of tendencies for exercise addiction, which represents a useful surface screening of the problem, but not in the diagnosis of the latter. People scoring in the upper end of these scales should be followed up by qualified mental health professionals who are able to diagnose exercise addiction and then also identify the psychological problem at its root. This method could also allow researchers to identify the life-event(s) that trigger exercise addiction.

Szabo (2001) proposed a 'pyramid approach' for the advancement of knowledge about exercise addiction (Figure 11.4). Accordingly, scholars with research training could do the surface screening ('population' on Figure 11.4). Professionals with clinical training may then follow up the surface screening with in-depth interviews and separate those who exercise a lot but maintain control over their exercise from those who lose control over their exercise behaviour ('group' on Figure 11.4). The reason for exercise with special attention to 'wants to do it' and 'has to do it' should be kept in perspective. Once separation at group level has taken place, professionals with clinical training should engage in the treatment of the positively identified individuals while, with patients' consent, maintaining a confidential record of the causes and consequences of their addiction ('person' on Figure 11.4). Data from several case studies, then, could be compiled and analyzed with qualitative methods to promote the understanding of exercise addiction.

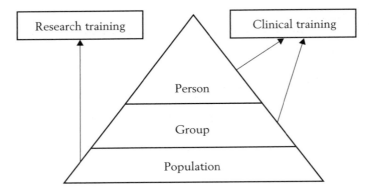

Figure 11.4 The interdisciplinary and collaboration-requiring 'pyramid approach' for the understanding of exercise addiction.

Source: Szabo, 2001.

Conclusions

Exercise addiction is a relatively rare dysfunction within the exercising population that is manifested through obsessive, compulsive and excessive exercise behaviour. It results in negative consequences to the affected individual and their social environment. The maintenance of the behaviour is probably driven by negative reinforcement, an incentive through which the exerciser tries to avoid an unpleasant event by regularly engaging in exaggerated amounts of exercise. Several symptoms characteristic of other behavioural addictions are present in exercise addiction as well. Scales or questionnaires developed around the common symptoms are useful in the screening but not the diagnosis of exercise addiction. Only case studies are promising in advancing knowledge about this exercise-related dysfunction. The detection of more cases could be expedited through population-wide surface screening conducted by researchers who need to share the data with clinically trained professionals for the isolation of positively diagnosed cases.

Key concepts and terms

Commitment to exercise
Compulsive exercise
Dose of exercise
Exercise abuse
Exercise addiction
Exercise dependence
Negative reinforcement
Obligatory exercising

Operant conditioning theory
Opioid receptors
Positive addiction
Positive reinforcement
Punishment
Runners' high
Staleness

Sample essay titles

- With reference to theory and research, define and distinguish the concept of exercise addiction from commitment.
- Outline the common symptoms of exercise addiction and evaluate how exercise psychologists identify these in their clients.
- Critically evaluate a physiological and a psychological model for exercise addiction.
- Evaluate motivational incentives in exercise addiction from the behaviouristic viewpoint.

Further reading

Books

Bozarth, M.A. (1994). 'Pleasure systems in the brain.' In: D.M. Warburton (Ed.), *Pleasure: The Politics and the Reality*. New York: John Wiley and Sons, 5–14.

Brown, R.I.F. (1993). 'Some contributions of the study of gambling to the study of other addictions.' In: W.R. Eadington and J.A. Cornelius (Eds), *Gambling Behavior and Problem Gambling*. Reno: University of Nevada Press, 241–272.

Glasser, W. (1976). *Positive Addiction*. New York, NY: Harper and Row.

Kreider, R.B., Fry, A.C., and O'Toole, M.L. (1998). *Overtraining in Sport*. Champaign, IL: Human Kinetics.

Journal articles

Chapman, C.L., and De Castro, J.M. (1990). Running addiction: Measurement and associated psychological characteristics. *The Journal of Sports Medicine and Physical Fitness*, 30, 283–290.

Cockerill, I.M., and Riddington, M.E. (1996). Exercise dependence and associated disorders: a review. *Counselling Psychology Quarterly*, 9, 119–129.

De Coverley Veale, D.M.W. (1987). Exercise dependence. *British Journal of Addiction*, 82, 735–740.

Goodman, A. (1990). Addiction: definition and implications. *British Journal of Addiction*, 85, 1403–1408.

Hausenblas, H.A., and Symons Downs, D. (2002). How much is too much? The development and validation of the exercise dependence scale. *Psychology and Health*, 17, 387–404.

Terry, A., Szabo, A., and Griffiths, M.D. (2004). The exercise addiction inventory: A new brief screening tool. *Addiction Research and Theory*, 12, 489–499.

Thompson, J.K., and Blanton, P. (1987). Energy conservation and exercise dependence: A sympathetic arousal hypothesis. *Medicine and Science in Sports and Exercise,* 19, 91–97.

Useful websites

Titles and web addresses all functional in October 2007

www.acefitness.org/fitfacts/pdfs/fitfacts/itemid_353.pdf (Too much of a good thing.)

www.addictions.co.uk/addiction.asp?ID=exercise (Exercise addiction.)

www.eatingproblems.org/epsexer.html (Exercise addiction.)

www.jsonline.com/alive/fit/jun02/49920.asp (Endorphins' role in addiction to exercise unclear.)

www.mclean.harvard.edu/pdf/news/fitnessmanage0704.pdf (Exercise addiction and eating disorders.)

www.nbc10.com/dietandfitness/1572502/detail.html (Could you be getting too much exercise?)

www.nodependence.com/addictions/exercising-addiction/exercise-addiction.html (Exercise addiction.)

www.nurseminerva.co.uk/exercise.htm (Can I have some information on exercise addiction?)

www.salon.com/it/col/guest/1999/01/04guest.html (Confessions of a stair mistress.)

www.shs.uwo.ca/publications/fitness/exercise.htm (Exercise mania.)

www.spiritofrecovery.com/exercise.html (Exercise: The 'good' addiction.)

www.springerlink.com/content/x8460707wj28kp71/fulltext.pdf (Exercise addiction in British sport science students.)

www.thefifthspace.com/12_13_exercise_add.pdf (Exercise addiction.)

www.utmem.edu/campusrec/exaddiction.htm (Exercise addiction and overtraining syndrome.)

5 | The placebo effect

12 Beliefs versus reality, or beliefs as reality? The placebo effect in sport and exercise

Chris Beedie and Abby Foad

The **placebo effect** is a positive outcome arising from the belief that a beneficial treatment has been received (Clark et al, 2000). A negative belief effect, the '**nocebo effect**' (Hahn, 1997) is in effect the opposite, that is a negative outcome resulting from the belief that a desired treatment has either not been received, or that a received treatment is harmful.

In the guise of the 'placebo control', the placebo effect has a central role in scientific research. Akin to medicine, a placebo treatment in sports research often serves as a control for the experimental treatment under investigation. For example, in a hypothetical study of the effects of caffeine on concentration among cricketers, the administration to participants in the 'control condition' of a pharmacologically inactive capsule – to all intents indistinguishable from the caffeine capsule administered in the experimental condition – allows the researchers some degree of confidence that any observed effects resulted from the pharmacological action of the caffeine and not from the psychological effect of participants' belief that they had ingested a performance-enhancing substance.

Increasingly, however, researchers in sport and exercise are seeking to study placebo effects directly, rather than simply controlling for them. In more than 30 years between 1967 and 1999, only two studies of the placebo effect in sport or exercise were published (Ariel and Saville, 1972; Desharnais et al, 1993). A further 11 studies have been added in the last eight years (e.g. Beedie et al, 2006; McClung and Collins, 2007; Foad et al, 2008). The results of these investigations demonstrate that the belief that a beneficial treatment has been received is likely to enhance the performance of a significant percentage of athletes. Likewise, in exercise research (e.g. Crum and Langer, 2007), the belief that an activity is healthy or likely to result in increased self-esteem has resulted in improvements in these variables.

This chapter will begin by reviewing several empirical investigations of the placebo effect in sport and exercise, with emphasis on the methodologies and implications. Some of the common assumptions related to the placebo effect in sport and exercise research will be addressed. The role and potential impact of placebo effects in the field will be considered and the ethics surrounding the investigation and use of the placebo effect discussed. Perhaps most controversially, the issue of whether some sports psychological interventions work either wholly or in part via the placebo effect will be raised (see also Chapter 1). Throughout this chapter, readers will be encouraged to think critically about the role and implications of the placebo effect, and beyond this specific phenomenon to the wider issue of the relationship between mind and body, for research and practice in sport and exercise.

Learning outcomes

When you have completed this chapter you should be able to:

1. Describe research that has investigated the placebo effect in sport and exercise.
2. Evaluate the concept of the placebo effect in research.
3. Critically consider the role and implications of the placebo effect for athletes, exercisers and professional practitioners.

Investigatation of the placebo effect in sport and exercise

Placebo effect research in sport

The majority of placebo effect research associated with physical activity has investigated the placebo effects of purported ergogenic aids on sports performance (e.g. Ariel and Saville, 1972; Clark et al, 2000; Maganaris et al, 2000; Foster et al, 2004; Porcari and Foster, 2006; Beedie et al, 2006, 2007; Kalasountas et al, 2007; McClung and Collins, 2007; Foad et al, 2008). The first published study of the placebo phenomenon in this context investigated the placebo effects of anabolic steroid ingestion (Ariel and Saville, 1972). The researchers reported that participants who were deceptively informed that they were receiving the oral anabolic steroid Dianabol, when in fact they were administered a placebo, exhibited substantial strength gains during a four-week period in which they were studied. Maganaris et al (2000) also examined the response to placebos deceptively administered as an anabolic steroid. Notable improvements in performance were observed among 11 competitive power lifters when they believed that they had been administered steroids. However, when five of the participants were informed midway through the experiment that they had in fact received placebos, the improvements amongst this subgroup dissipated rapidly.

Beedie et al (2006) investigated the possibility of a dose–response relationship to placebos presented as 'zero', 'low' and 'high' dose caffeine in 10 kilometre cycling performance. Seven competitive cyclists were informed that, over three experimental trials, they would each receive 0.0 mg/kg, 4.5 mg/kg and 9.0 mg/kg caffeine randomly assigned. An identical placebo was, however, administered in all experimental conditions. Analysis revealed a dose–response relationship in relation to baseline in experimental trials, with participants producing 1.4 per cent *less* power, and 1.3 per cent and 3.1 per cent greater power respectively when they believed they had ingested 0.0 mg/kg, 4.5 mg/kg and 9.0 mg/kg caffeine (the response to the 0.0 mg/kg caffeine was arguably a nocebo effect). Semi-structured interviews were conducted to ascertain how the participants themselves attributed any perceived or observed changes in performance. Five participants believed that they had experienced a placebo effect in one or more of the three experimental trials, and proposed mechanisms such as lower levels of pain and anxiety, as well as deliberate modifications of pacing strategy resulting from the belief that they would produce more power as the result of ingesting caffeine. These data suggested that placebo responses may be associated with changes in psychological variables that indirectly affect performance.

In common with much of the research in sport seeking to investigate the pharmacological effects of a treatment, Beedie et al (2006) (described above) used a blind design to investigate the placebo effect. Participants believed that they could receive caffeine *or* a placebo in each trial. However, several researchers have argued that participants must be certain that they have received the beneficial treatment in order to elicit a placebo effect, and have used a deceptive design, where participants are definitively informed (or misinformed) of their treatment assignment, to investigate placebo effects in sport (e.g. Clark et al, 2000; McClung and Collins, 2007; Foad et al, 2008).

Two recent investigations of placebo and pharmacological effects in sport (e.g. McClung and Collins, 2007; Foad et al, 2008) have employed deceptive procedures in what is called the 'balanced placebo' or 'double disassociation' design (Figure 12.1). This design enables the assessment of each possible combination of what the participant believes they had taken (i.e. placebo or drug) with what they have actually taken (again, placebo or drug).

	Received drug	Received no drug
Inform drug	A Placebo effect + drug effect	B Placebo effect alone
Inform no drug	C Drug effect alone	D Baseline

Figure 12.1 The balanced placebo design.

Source: Adapted from Marlatt & Rohsenow, 1980.

Foad et al (2008) used the balanced placebo design to investigate the placebo and pharmacological effects of caffeine in 40 kilometre cycling performance. Fourteen male competitive cyclists each performed two trials in the following conditions: a) informed caffeine/received caffeine; b) informed caffeine/received placebo; c) informed no treatment/received caffeine; and d) informed no treatment/received no treatment. Results demonstrated that the average power output increased by 3.5 per cent over baseline when participants received caffeine, regardless of whether participants *knew* that they were receiving caffeine or not. The belief that caffeine had been received did not significantly enhance performance, however, a substantial interaction between belief and pharmacology indicated that caffeine exerted a greater effect on performance when participants were informed that they had not ingested it, while belief exerted a greater influence on performance in the absence of caffeine (2.6 per cent). A possibly harmful nocebo effect was observed when participants were correctly informed that they had ingested no caffeine (-1.9 per cent). McClung and Collins (2007) used a similar design to investigate the placebo and pharmacological effects of sodium bicarbonate on 1000 metre run times. The authors reported that not only did the overt administration of sodium bicarbonate improve performance by a substantial 1.7 per cent over the no treatment condition, but that the expectation of receiving sodium bicarbonate improved performance in the absence of the substance by a not dissimilar 1.5 per cent. They suggest that such an effect could make a significant difference to athletes in competition. More significantly perhaps, they note the lack of a performance effect when participants had ingested sodium bicarbonate but believed that they had not, suggesting what they termed a biochemical 'failure'. Thus, arguably in contrast to the findings of Foad et al with caffeine, McClung and Collins' results demonstrated that the belief that sodium bicarbonate had been ingested resulted in times almost as fast as those associated with consuming the drug itself, while taking the drug without knowledge of having done so yielded no significant performance increment.

In 2000, Clark et al used both deceptive and double-blind protocols in a study of the placebo effects of carbohydrate supplementation on 40 kilometre cycling time trial performance. Forty-three competitive cyclists were randomized to two groups: one received carbohydrate, the other an indistinguishable placebo. Cyclists in each group were further randomized into three subgroups according to whether they were told the drink contained carbohydrate or placebo (deceptive protocol), or had a 50:50 chance of receiving either (double-blind protocol). The two protocols had very different effects on performance. Mean power increased by 4.3 per cent and 0.5 per cent over baseline for those informed that they had received carbohydrate and placebo respectively (values for actual receipt of carbohydrate and placebo were not reported). However, mean power actually decreased by 1.1 per cent in those participants not informed of the content of their drink. Not being told what was in the drink also resulted in substantially larger within-participant variation in performance than those definitively informed about drink content.

Placebo effect research in exercise

The studies described so far have focused on sports performance. However, several studies assessed the effects of belief on exercise, health and well-being (e.g. Desharnais et al, 1993; Plante, Lantis and Checa, 1998; Crum and Langer, 2007). In these studies, the placebo intervention is not an inert pill or capsule as is traditionally the case. Instead, a verbal expectancy for improvement is used as the placebo manipulation.

Desharnais et al (1993) investigated the placebo effects of a combined exercise programme and expectancy modification procedure on perceptions of self-esteem. Forty-eight participants took part in a 10-week exercise programme. Experimental participants were informed that the programme was designed specifically to improve their psychological well-being, while controls were informed that the programme was designed to improve aerobic capacity. Although both groups performed the same exercise programme, and results showed similar increases in physical fitness in the two conditions, participants in the experimental condition showed a significant increase in self-esteem. In a more recent study, Crum and Langer (2007) investigated the effects of beliefs on both subjective and objective measures of health. Eighty-four female room attendants were measured on physiological health variables affected by exercise. Those in the informed condition were told that their work was good exercise and met the Surgeon General's recommendations for an active lifestyle. Participants in the control group were not given this information. Although levels of self-reported 'actual' behaviour did not change, four weeks after the intervention the informed group perceived themselves to be getting significantly more exercise than before. Compared with the control group, they exhibited greater decreases in weight, blood pressure, body fat, waist-to-hip ratio and body mass index over the course of the study. According to Desharnais et al and Crum and Langer, the results of their studies suggest that exercise may affect mental and physical health respectively via the placebo effect, a finding that has implications both for researchers examining the effects of an intervention, and for professional practitioners seeking to enhance the efficacy of an exercise programme.

Activity 12.1

In studies by Desharnais et al (1993) and Crum and Langer (2007), participants were provided with information about the benefits of exercise designed to create an expectancy of improvement. Discuss whether you consider this to be a placebo intervention and whether the observed effects are placebo effects. Can you think of any other explanations for the observed results?

Ojanen (1995) has argued that it is impossible to distinguish between the 'pure' or 'true' effects of exercise and the placebo effects associated with exercise. What do you think?

Knowledge of the placebo effect in sport and exercise is by no means complete – several questions either remain unanswered or require clarification. However, the research described above has provided some interesting findings in relation to the direction, magnitude and frequency of the placebo effect, findings that have major implications for research and practice in sport and exercise. For example, over and above the finding that belief that a beneficial treatment has been received might significantly enhance performance or similar dependent variable, this research has demonstrated that:

- Placebo and experimental effects may interact (i.e. placebo effects in control and experimental conditions may not always be equivalent in magnitude).

- Not all participants are placebo responsive.

- Placebo effects may be experienced both objectively and subjectively.

- Beliefs can have both positive (placebo) and negative (nocebo) effects.

These findings have major implications for practitioners seeking to optimize the effects of an intervention, an individual's experience of physical activity, or an athlete's performance, and for researchers seeking to attain valid and reliable estimates of treatment effects. The following section examines the potential impact of beliefs on the outcome of the **placebo-controlled trial** – the experimental design from which much of our knowledge regarding treatment effects in sport and exercise science is derived.

Activity 12.2

Think of an example in sport or exercise where the placebo effect might impact on performance outcome or a similar dependent variable. Design a study to investigate the placebo effect in this context. Is your study valid and reliable? What problems might you encounter in your design that could confound accurate estimation of the placebo effect?

Evaluating the concept of the placebo effect in research

The placebo condition comprises a fundamental part of research in sport and exercise where it is used to 'control' for the effects of beliefs on the outcome of an intervention. By subtracting the mean effect observed in the placebo condition from the mean effect observed in the experimental condition, an estimate of the true mean effect is calculated. Several assumptions are implicit within this model: 1) the placebo control is an 'inactive' condition; 2) placebo effects are always positive in direction; and 3) placebo and experimental effects are additive, not interactive. If these assumptions are correct, valid approximations of experimental effects may be obtained. However, if these assumptions are incorrect, interpretation of *both* placebo and experimental effects becomes problematic.

Assumption 1

The placebo control is an 'inactive' condition. The notion of the placebo control as an inactive condition is understandable given that placebos and placebo effects are so often associated with words such as 'inert', 'sham' and 'non-specific'. What is often overlooked, however, is that the placebo condition represents an active psychological treatment which, as has been demonstrated above, may in itself elicit significant effects. These effects are likely of significance to sports performers and practitioners, but are all too often overlooked in research, in which a null finding is often described in terms such as 'the experimental treatment performed no better than a placebo control'. As has been suggested many times, just because a treatment works no better than a placebo, it does not mean that it does not work. It simply suggests that the mechanisms might be more psychological than biological.

Assumption 2

Placebo effects are always positive in direction. Given common definitions of the placebo effect as a 'positive outcome', it is not surprising that the effects of individuals' beliefs in the placebo-controlled trial are often assumed to be positive in relation to baseline or no-treatment conditions. However, as recent research by Beedie et al (2007) has indicated, if participants hold negative beliefs about an intervention, the scenario might be quite different. The authors allocated 42 team sport athletes into two groups and, following 3 3 30 metre baseline sprints, provided group 1 with positive information about a hypothetical new ergogenic aid (a placebo) while group 2 were provided with negative information about the same substance. The sprint protocol was repeated. In group 1, a significant linear trend towards greater speed in experimental trials suggested that positive belief exerted a positive effect on performance. However, performance in group 2 was significantly slower than baseline suggesting that negative belief exerted a negative effect on performance. Beedie et al's findings indicate that in a placebo-controlled trial, negative beliefs about an intervention may elicit a negative or 'nocebo' effect whereby performance in the placebo condition dips below baseline. In the experimental condition, the effect of the intervention may still be evident, but the effect over baseline is reduced in relation to trials in which participants believed the substance to be effective. While the reported experimental effect would remain the same as when participants held positive beliefs about the intervention, it would be an overestimate of the true increase over baseline. Inclusion of a baseline measure or no-treatment control condition to the standard placebo-controlled design is therefore essential if valid approximations of both placebo and experimental effects are to be made.

Assumption 3

Placebo and experimental effects are additive, not interactive. An important assumption made when evaluating the results of a placebo-controlled trial is that the effects of the experimental treatment and the placebo are separable, additive, linear and stable. However, this model may be too simplistic because it does not account for the possibility of interactions between experimental and placebo effects. Research has in fact demonstrated that a placebo effect may operate differently in the presence of an active substance to when one is not present, and that an active substance may act differently when participants believe that they have ingested it to when participants believe that they have not (McLung and Collins, 2007; Foad et al, 2008). The placebo effect associated with the simple act of ingesting a substance believed by the participant to be ergogenic may potentiate the physiological effect of that substance (de la Fuente-Fernández et al, 2002). Different interventions may mobilize different mechanisms (e.g. psychological, biological, pharmacological) to different degrees, and these mechanisms can be additive for only so long as they are truly independent and not constrained by ceiling effects. Thus it is possible that the magnitude of the true experimental effect may well be constrained by interventions that are particularly effective at mobilizing psychological mechanisms, or in particularly placebo-responsive individuals. Evidence of such complex interactions suggests that deriving true effects by subtracting placebo from experimental effects is much too simple an equation.

Resolving the efficacy conundrum depends almost entirely on our methodological ability to parcel out the different components of treatment. Given the small magnitude of many treatment effects in research in sport and exercise, and the difficulty in obtaining large sample sizes and/or conducting repeated trials which may strengthen the reliability of estimates of effect, any fluctuation in the magnitude and valence of placebo effects between placebo and experimental conditions may significantly confound precise assessments of outcome. A greater understanding of the nature of placebo effects may therefore help to strengthen the reliability and validity of research in sport and exercise, and to better clarify the mechanisms underlying observed effects.

The role and implications of the placebo effect

The convention of the placebo-controlled trial suggests that sport and exercise scientists recognize the potential for placebo effects to impact on the outcomes of research. Indeed, data from empirical investigations are increasing our knowledge of the magnitude, valence, frequency and variability of this effect in research. Some authors (e.g. Clark et al, 2000) have questioned whether placebo effects might simply be artefacts of the research setting, effects that would be over-ridden in the real world, particularly in the motivational climate of competitive sport. It is, however, not only in research that such effects have been reported. The anecdotal reports of athletes, coaches and practitioners such as Vogt (1999) and Gallagher (1970) indicate that placebo effects are not just artefacts of the placebo-controlled trial, but may impact significantly on outcomes in the field, as this quote from Vogt (1999) suggests.

> That day he rode the time trial of his life, finishing second on the stage to Ullrich. The German started 3 minutes after Richard and caught him, after which the pair had a memorable ding-dong battle all the way to the finish. "God I felt good! That stuff's just amazing" he bubbled. "We must get hold of it." Of course his result did have something to do with the magic capsule – but there is one thing he doesn't know, unless he reads this. I had got rid of the fabulous potion and swapped it for one which contained a small amount of glucose. There is no substitute for self belief ... (Vogt, 1999: 104).

Activity 12.3

Vogt (1999) reported an instance of the placebo effect in competitive sports performance (above). Could the validity of such a quote be questioned? What alternative explanations might there be for such apparently placebo-enhanced performance? If a placebo effect was responsible, what do you think was the most likely mechanism?

Sport and exercise psychology interventions and the placebo effect

Many of the key constructs of sport and exercise psychology are beliefs: self-confidence is the *belief* we have in our own or our team's ability, anxiety is the *belief* that we might not have the resources to meet an upcoming challenge. Furthermore, confidence and anxiety are often catalysed by *beliefs* about our opponent's ability or similar environmental factors (see Chapters 3 and 4). Likewise, in exercise, many people participate because they *believe* that it makes them feel better, or because they believe that they are unhealthy. Sport psychologists often have to modify the beliefs of their clients to enable those clients to perform to a higher level. For example, an under-confident athlete who might suffer from tunnel vision might require a confidence-boosting strategy while an over-confident athlete who is perhaps not focused enough on the task in hand might need reminding of the seriousness of the challenge ahead and of the potential threat that the opponent poses. It could be argued that, by modifying organic (that is, naturally occurring) levels of confidence or anxiety, a sport psychologist is actually catalysing a false belief to bring about a positive outcome. Sound familiar? In other words, many interventions in sport and exercise psychology might operate via a placebo effect.

Surprising though this might sound, the issue has been the subject of research in clinical and counselling psychology for many years. In fact, the charge that psychotherapy might exert its effect via a placebo mechanism is not the worst to be aimed at it; that is, it has not only been suggested that many forms of psychotherapy are no better than a placebo, but that they may even be no better than no treatment (see Evans, 2003, Chapter 8, for discussion).

In medicine it is often quite easy to test an active drug against a placebo (via two pills identical in appearance but different in content). It is also possible in psychotherapy; for example, Strupp and Hadley (1979) compared the effects on clinical patients of psychotherapy delivered by trained/qualified therapists and untrained/unqualified psychologists. The authors reported that both groups improved by the same degree (a finding later replicated by Stein and Lambert, 1984). The suggestion is that years of training, and strict adherence to one framework, be it psychodynamic, humanistic, gestalt or cognitive behavioural, makes little difference in the real world. However, research elsewhere, in medicine for example, has demonstrated that the beliefs of the practitioner about a treatment might be a significant factor in the success of that treatment. That is, in any therapeutic setting, the magnitude of any placebo effect might be driven by the beliefs of both practitioner and patient/client. This has often been cited as the mechanism underlying many examples of 'faith healing'.

It is fair to say that, in many respects, whether an intervention operates via what we term 'real' or what we term 'placebo' mechanisms is not important. If it works, it works. If an athlete runs faster because they believe that they have ingested 450 mg of caffeine when they have not, or if the same athlete runs faster because they believe that their sport psychologist has resolved their anxiety issues, the athlete is *still running faster*. Perhaps the placebo effect and many sports psychology interventions operate in the same gap between what is currently being achieved and what is achievable?

Activity 12.4

Using research evidence, suggest what might happen should an athlete be referred to a sport psychologist, but do so believing that the sport psychologist is likely to have a negative effect on the athlete's performance. Describe the possible mechanisms underlying the outcome and suggest what a sport psychologist could do to prevent any negative response.

Implications of placebo responsiveness for the athlete/exerciser and practitioner

Potential ways in which the individual's beliefs might impact on the outcome of research findings are described above. But what are the implications of placebo responsiveness for the athlete or exerciser themselves, and for practitioners working with these individuals? The following sections describe how placebo responsiveness may manifest itself in sport and exercise settings, and suggest ways in which such responsiveness may be identified by the practitioner to optimize the athlete or exerciser's experience.

Placebo effects are traditionally viewed as a positive phenomenon. Indeed, the common sense model of the placebo effect is one in which an individual *benefits* from false information such as 'the tablet I am about to give you will enhance your power output in the upcoming competition'. However, experiential data from Beedie et al (2006) revealed that enhanced performance in placebo trials was often coupled with positive changes in psychological factors such as confidence, motivation and arousal. These findings suggest that the placebo effect may be reflective of a suboptimal psychological status whereby the belief that a beneficial treatment has been received optimizes psychological variables, subsequently enabling the athlete to perform to their full potential. If this is in fact the case, then sport and exercise practitioners would perhaps be better to address such deficiencies, as opposed to attempting to bridge the gap by means of a false belief. This is particularly germane given the evidence that an individual susceptible to a false *positive* belief may be equally susceptible to a false *negative* belief (Beedie et al, 2006, 2007), and therefore the potential for belief effects to impact both positively and negatively on performance.

Identification of placebo-responsive athletes

While not *all* individuals will be placebo responsive in *all* situations, the understanding and prevention of placebo/nocebo responses should be the concern of sport and exercise practitioners. But how does the practitioner know if their athlete/exerciser is placebo responsive? Is placebo responsiveness a function of personality? Or is it more of a contextual situational phenomenon?

Early attempts to identify a relationship between placebo effects and personality indicated that certain psychological variables such as anxiety (Shapiro and Shapiro, 1984), extraversion (Lasagna, 1986), self-esteem

(Gelfand, 1962) and agreeableness (McNair et al, 1979) could be related to placebo responding. These findings were, however, equivocal, and the general consensus of early research was that the placebo effect was more a contextual situational phenomenon than an enduring personality trait. However, recent research in social psychology (e.g. Geers et al, 2005) suggests that personality characteristics may predispose an individual to respond to a placebo, but that situational factors are likely to interact with these traits to determine the degree of response exhibited. The challenge of future research may be to unravel the multitude of situational and personality factors, or combinations of factors, that determine placebo responding. For now, psychometric assessment of personality to identify potentially placebo-responsive traits such as anxiety or extraversion, and assessment of beliefs and expectations regarding a particular intervention, may help to alert sport and exercise practitioners to the potential for placebo responsiveness and facilitate appropriate counsel.

Possible mechanisms

If the placebo effect works, it does so via one or more mechanisms. Data from studies in sport suggest that the mechanisms might be related to reduced pain, reduced anxiety, increased motivation and changes in strategy. These are relatively simply explained; for example, placebo-driven pain reduction – a phenomenon well-documented in the medicine literature – would be expected to reduce an athlete's perception of stress and fatigue and might be interpreted by the athlete as a sign that they have more headroom in which to perform (in other words, they can push a bit harder). A placebo effect manifest as reduced anxiety, again a phenomenon documented in the medicine and psychology literature, might work via a different mechanism. Given that muscle tension is often associated with anxiety, and that muscle tension is costly in terms of oxygen to initiate, maintain and overcome, placebo-driven reductions in anxiety might facilitate more efficient performance by reducing that tension. Both placebo mechanisms above might result in baseline levels of performance at a lower physiological cost to the athlete or a greater level of performance at baseline physiological cost. Increased motivation and revised strategy, resulting from the belief that an intervention might raise the level of performance, might be expected to be associated with both increased performance and increased physiological cost, and as such represent more of a conceptual problem. That is, both might result in substantial declines in performance if associated with unsustainable physiological responses such as blood lactate accumulation or metabolic fatigue. Thus, the mechanisms that underlie an observed positive placebo response in one participant might be the same that underlie a negative placebo response in another (the latter would not be correctly described as a nocebo response as the initial belief and expectation was positive).

In fact, to extend the above, it is possible that there are a substantial number of mechanisms underlying placebo effects on performance, as is almost certainly the case in medicine. In fact, if, as has often been proposed, placebos mimic the effects of the drug they purport to be, logically there must be almost as many different placebo effects as there are drug effects! Certainly, in the same sense that in medicine it is doubtful that all individuals and all conditions are placebo responsive, in sport, perhaps only a few key mechanisms can operate in a few situations; a placebo designed to reduce anxiety will not work on a low anxiety athlete whereas one that is designed to increase motivation might. The converse might also hold true.

Ethics of the use of deception in research and in the field

The placebo effect is complex to investigate and represents something of a paradox to researchers. That is, if a participant is aware that they are taking a placebo they are unlikely to experience a placebo effect. To illustrate, if I know I have been given a sugar pill I am likely to respond in accordance with that belief. However, if I believe that the sugar pill is in fact a painkiller, and that painkiller might make me feel better, it is possible that a number of psychological or biological processes might initiate a positive response, irrespective of the source of that belief (Evans, 2003).

The ethical codes governing research are in place to ensure that the mental and physical health, as well as the dignity of participants participating in such research is not in any way undermined. Research ethics committees scrutinize research proposals to ensure that ethical guidelines will be followed in research studies. Deception, although unlikely to undermine physical or mental health, could be seen to undermine the dignity of participants, and thus is likely to concern an ethics committee. However, several areas of human behaviour, including the placebo effect, are highly problematic to investigate empirically without some form of deception. In such cases, ethics committees generally require that the researcher provide a strong rationale for the use of such procedures. Specifically, the researcher must demonstrate: first, that they are aware of the ethical issues surrounding the use of deception in research; second, that they have carefully considered these issues in relation to their own research question; third, that the possible benefits of their research outweigh any risks to participants; and finally, that effective non-deceptive procedures are not feasible. There are specific guidelines aimed at reconciling the use of deception with the ethical norms of human participant research provided by the American Psychological Association (2002).

Deceptive methods are rarely used in sports research, but this is perhaps more due to the lack of a perceived need than any specific ethical objections. However, what is and what is not acceptable is not just a function of law and guidelines, but of what ethics committees and journal editors deem appropriate methods for addressing often increasingly complex questions. Historical trends in research ethics suggest that due to changes in law, culture or knowledge, practices considered legitimate at one point in time may not be so at a later date (and arguably vice versa). For example, several years ago the elimination of placebo-responsive participants from clinical drug trials might have been deemed unethical as such a practice constituted a self-selecting sample, deprived participants of potentially effective treatment and inflated observed drug effects. However, the practice has become increasingly widespread as drug companies strive to derive ever less ambiguous findings from increasingly expensive and time-consuming drug trials. The ethics of research will to a certain extent always be guided by the shifting balance between the need to protect participants on the one hand, and the need to provide society with reliable information about the effects of interventions on the other.

The use of the placebo effect as a therapeutic intervention in medicine is well documented. Several examples of the deliberate use of false beliefs in real world sport can be found. Australian swimming coach Harry Gallagher (1970), for example, described how he used to doctor the watches and clocks at swimming pools to provide athletes with false negative feedback, ensuring that they swam 'faster' in competition than in training and providing a sense of psychological momentum at competitive events. However, deliberate use of the placebo effect in sport is arguably unethical, largely unrepeatable over time, and likely counter-productive. An athlete falsely led to believe that they have ingested a powerful ergogenic aid might produce a better performance than usual, however, that athlete – upon being either debriefed or inadvertently finding out – might have less trust in their coach in future. In any coaching relationship, although the drive for improvement and success is powerful, the need for trust and honesty is a critical factor.

Activity 12.5

Imagine you are the coach of a team of national-level swimmers. You are looking at ways in which to enhance the team's performance and are considering using a placebo intervention to this effect. Discuss the factors that would influence your decision whether to use the placebo effect as part of your coaching strategy.

Conclusions

The placebo effect has been recognized as a factor in medicine for several centuries. During that time, its status has evolved from that of a superstitious and mercurial phenomenon, through experimental artefact to be controlled for, to that of a legitimate psychological construct in its own right. This process has recently been reflected in sport and exercise, where after many years of being widely acknowledged but little understood, it is finally the focus of systematic research. Recent research in sport and exercise has demonstrated that the placebo effect can elicit substantial and significant positive and negative effects on a number of dependent variables. Furthermore, many such changes are similar, if not equal, in magnitude to those associated with the intervention the placebo was designed to mimic (for example placebo caffeine in Beedie et al, 2006, and placebo sodium bicarbonate in McClung and Collins, 2007).

The placebo effect is, however, not simply an interesting and potentially useful psychological construct. Although it has much in common with other complex sports psychological processes such as flow states or automaticity, the placebo effect presents the sport psychologist with practical and ethical questions; for example, to what extent can the placebo effect be utilized to enhance performance? If it is possible to enhance performance via placebo mechanisms, is it ethical to do so? If an athlete is highly placebo responsive, are they likely nocebo responsive also? Is placebo responsiveness a desirable or an undesirable trait for an athlete? Can placebo/nocebo responsiveness be modified via sport psychology interventions? Answers to these questions will require not only a substantial and systematic research initiative, but – as is arguably required in contemporary medicine also – a concurrent and equally systematic interrogation of the ethical implications of that research.

Over and above the questions above, however, the placebo effect presents perhaps a greater challenge to practitioners. It is quite likely, as has been the case in medicine and psychotherapy, that a substantial number of interventions used in sport psychology might operate, at least in part, via placebo mechanisms. With the increased scientific and ethical scrutiny of such professions that characterizes contemporary medical and related professional practice, such mechanisms will need to be investigated and either discounted or acknowledged and addressed accordingly.

Sport and exercise science should be an evidence-based practice. With the increasing emphasis in medicine, science and the media on mind–body interactions, the placebo effect and related research and therapeutic approaches such as psychoneuroimmunology (e.g. Ader and Cohen, 1993) have become the focus of medical research, academic enquiry and media speculation. Greater knowledge of the placebo effect per se resulting from this process will not only enhance our understanding of the interaction between mind and body – possibly increasing our understanding of the therapeutic effects of processes such as hypnosis and even exercise – but will likely enhance our understanding of the findings of the clinical trials and experimental studies that form the foundation of the evidence base alluded to above. This will allow researchers in a wide range of scientific and academic disciplines to make more reliable estimates of the effects of the interventions under investigation.

Despite the attempts of many scientists to argue otherwise (e.g. Hróbjartsson and Gøtzsche, 2001), the placebo effect is likely, perhaps like many other aspects of human psychology, an evolved adaptive mechanism. As with many other adaptive mechanisms, evidence suggests that we, or those from whom we seek help or advice, may be able to 'tap in' to this mechanism when a certain set of environmental conditions are met. Such a set of environmental conditions is, for example, when there is a desired state (e.g. a certain level of health or performance), a difference between our current state and our desired state (an illness or low level of performance). This mechanism we believe may enhance our chances of reaching the desired state (e.g. a course of antibiotics or a sport psychology intervention and the belief that the intervention has been received). This does not in any way discount the effectiveness of either antibiotics or sport psychology interventions, it merely highlights that a treatment in which an individual holds a strong and positive belief is more likely to elicit a positive placebo response. Whether this placebo response only operates in the absence of the intervention in question (the classic placebo effect), or whether it can also add to a legitimate biological or psychological intervention is a question for future research.

Future directions

Research to date in sport and exercise has demonstrated that the placebo effect might impact on some people some of the time. Identification of the environmental and individual difference factors that might explain such responses is perhaps the primary area for future research. The use of multi-method and multidisciplinary approaches will almost certainly be required to achieve this aim. Finally, analysis of the ethical aspects of placebo effect investigation, most notably in the area of the need for deception, must accompany any empirical research.

Key concepts and terms

Nocebo effect

Placebo effect

Placebo-controlled trial

Sample essay titles

- With reference to theory and research, discuss the contention that the placebo effect is a resource that might be exploited by sport psychologists.
- The placebo control has been fundamental to empirical research in medicine, psychology and sports science for over 50 years. Describe a hypothetical placebo-controlled experiment and highlight why the placebo control is necessary. Provide a detailed example of how a placebo control could be used in a study of a sport psychology intervention.
- The placebo effect represents a problem for sport psychology. Discuss.
- It has been suggested that the placebo effect might account for a significant percentage of the observed effects of psychotherapy (e.g. Evans, 2003). Using ethical and scientific principles as guides, discuss the contention that, if the same is true of applied sport psychology, the end still justifies the means.

Further reading

Books

Evans, D. (2003). *Placebo: The Belief Effect*. London: HarperCollins.

Journal articles

Benedetti, F., Maggi, G., Lopiano, L., et al. (2003). Open versus hidden medical treatments: The patient's knowledge about a therapy affects the therapy outcome. *Prevention and Treatment*, 6, 1–16. www.journals.apa.org/prevention/volume6/pre0001a.html

Kaptchuk, T.J. (2001). The double-blind, randomized, placebo-controlled trial. Gold standard or golden calf? *Journal of Clinical Epidemiology*, 54, 541–549.

Kirsch, I., and Weixel, L.J. (1988). Double-blind versus deceptive administration of a placebo. *Behavioural Neuroscience*, 102, 319–323.

References

Ader, R., and Cohen, N. (1993). Psychoneuroimmunology: conditioning and stress. *Annual Review of Psychology*, 44, 53–85.

Alderman, R.B. (1984). 'The future of sport psychology.' In: J.M. Silva and R.S. Weinberg (Eds), *Psychological Foundations for Sport*. Champaign, IL: Human Kinetics, 45–54.

Allport, G.W. (1937). *Personality: A Psychological Interpretation*. New York: Holt.

American Psychiatric Association (1995). *Diagnostic and Statistical Manual of Mental Disorders*, (4th Ed.), Washington, DC: American Psychiatric Association.

American Psychological Association (2002). Ethical principles of psychologists and code of conduct. www.apa.org/ethics/code2002.pdf

Anderson, K. (1993). *Getting What You Want: How to Reach Agreement and Resolve Conflict Every Time*. New York: Penguin-Puttnam/Dutton.

Anshel, M.H., and Delany, J. (2001). Sources of acute stress, cognitive appraisals, and coping strategies of male and female child athletes. *Journal of Sport Behavior*, 24, 329–353.

Anshel, M.H., and Mansouri, H. (2005). Influences of perfectionism on motor performance, affect, and causal attributions in response to critical information feedback. *Journal of Sport Behavior*, 28, 99–124.

Anshel, M.H., and Marisi, D.Q. (1978). Effects of music and rhythm on physical performance. *Research Quarterly*, 49, 109–113.

Arathoon, S.M., and Malouff, J.M. (2004). The effectiveness of a brief cognitive intervention to help athletes cope with competitive loss. *Journal of Sport Behavior*, 27, 213–229.

Ariel, G., and Saville, W. (1972). Anabolic steroids: The physiological effects of placebos. *Medicine and Science in Sports and Exercise*, 4, 124–126.

Atkinson, G., Wilson, D., and Eubank, M. (2004). Effects of music on work-rate distribution during a cycle time trial. *International Journal of Sports Medicine*, 62, 413–419.

Azjen, I., and Fishbein, M. (1977). Attitude-behavior relations: A theoretical analysis and review of empirical research. *Psychological Bulletin*, 84, 888–918.

Bacon, C., Myers, T., and Karageorghis, C.I. (in press). Effect of movement-music synchrony and tempo on exercise oxygen consumption.

Baker, S.B. (2001). Coping-skills training for adolescents: Applying cognitive behavioral principles to psychoeducational groups. *Journal for Specialists in Group Work*, 26, 219–227.

Baker, T.B., Piper, M.E., McCarthy, D.E., Majeskie, M.R., and Fiore, M.C. (2004). Addiction motivation reformulated: an affective processing model of negative reinforcement. *Psychological Review*, 111, 33–51.

Bandura, A. (1997). *Self-Efficacy: The Exercise of Control*. New York: Freeman.

Bandura, A., and Wood, R.E. (1989). Effect of perceived controllability and performance standards on self-regulation of complex decision making. *Journal of Personality and Social Psychology*, 56, 805–814.

Barwood, M.J., Datta, A., Thelwell, R., and Tipton, M.J. (2007). Breath-hold performance during cold-water immersion: Effects of habituation with psychological skills training. *Aviation, Space and Environmental Medicine*, 78, 1029–1034.

Bass, B.M. (1990). From transactional to transformational leadership: Learning to share the vision. *Organisational Dynamics*, 18, 19–31.

Baumeister, R.F. (1984). Choking under pressure: Self-consciousness and paradoxical effects of incentives on skilful performance. *Journal of Personality and Social Psychology*, 46, 610–620.

Beam, J.W., Serwatka, T.S., and Wilson, W.J. (2004). Preferred leadership of NCAA Division I and II intercollegiate student-athletes. *Journal of Sport Behavior*, 27, 3–17.

Beauchamp, P.H., Hallwell, W.R., Fournier, J.F., and Koestner, R. (1996). Effects of cognitive-behavioural psychological skills training on motivation, preparation and putting performance of novice golf players. *The Sport Psychologist*, 10, 157–170.

Beedie, C.J. (2007). The placebo effect in competitive sport: Qualitative data. *Journal of Sport Science and Medicine*, 6, 21–28.

Beedie, C.J., Terry, P.C., and Lane, A.M. (2000). The profile of mood states and athletic performance: Two meta-analyses. *Journal of Applied Sport Psychology*, 12, 49–68.

Beedie, C.J., Terry, P.C., and Lane, A.M. (2005). Distinguishing mood from emotion. *Cognition and Emotion*, 19, 847–878.

Beedie, C.J., Stuart, E.M., Coleman, D.A., and Foad, A.J. (2006). Placebo effects of caffeine in cycling performance. *Medicine and Science in Sports and Exercise*, 38, 2159–2164.

Beedie, C.J., Coleman, D.A., and Foad, A.J. (2007). Positive and negative placebo effects resulting from the deceptive administration of an ergogenic aid. *International Journal of Sports Nutrition and Exercise Metabolism*, 17, 259–269.

Benedetti, F., Maggi, G., Lopiano, L., et al. (2003). Open versus hidden medical treatments: The patient's knowledge about a therapy affects the therapy outcome. *Prevention and Treatment*, 6, 1–16.

Berglas, S., and Jones, E.E. (1978). Drug choice as a self-handicapping strategy in response to noncontigent success. *Journal of Personality and Social Psychology*, 36, 405–417.

Berlyne, D.E. (1971). *Aesthetics and Psychobiology*. New York: Appleton Century Crofts.

Biddle, S.J.H., and Mutrie, N. (2007). *Psychology of Physical Activity*. London: Routledge.

Billings, A.G., and Moos, R.H. (1984). Coping, stress, and social resources among adults with unipolar depression. *Journal of Personality and Social Psychology*, 46, 877–891.

Binsinger, C., Laure, P., and Ambard, M-F. (2006). Regular extra curricular sports practice does not prevent moderate or severe variations in self-esteem or trait anxiety in early adolescents. *Journal of Sports Science and Medicine*, 5, 123–129.

Bishop, D.T., Karageorghis, C.I., and Loizou, G. (2007). A grounded theory of young tennis players' use of music to manipulate emotional state. *Journal of Sport & Exercise Psychology*, 29, 584–607.

Bonny, H.L. (1987). Music the language of immediacy. *Arts in Psychotherapy*, 14, 255–261.

Bozarth, M.A. (1994). 'Pleasure systems in the brain.' In: D.M. Warburton (Ed.), *Pleasure: The Politics and the Reality*. New York: John Wiley and Sons, 5–14.

Brosschot, J.F., de Ruiter, C., and Kindt, M. (1999). Processing bias in anxious subjects and repressors, measured by emotional Stroop interference and attentional allocation. *Personality and Individual Differences*, 26, 777–793.

Brown, P. (1979). An enquiry into the origins and nature of tempo behavior: II. Experimental work. *Psychology of Music*, 9, 32–43.

Brown, R.I.F. (1993). 'Some contributions of the study of gambling to the study of other addictions.' In: W.R. Eadington and J.A. Cornelius (Eds), *Gambling Behavior and Problem Gambling*. Reno: University of Nevada Press, 241–272.

Burton, D. (1988). Do anxious swimmers swim slower? Reexamining the elusive anxiety-performance relationship. *Journal of Sport & Exercise Psychology*, 10, 45–61.

Burton, D., and Naylor, S. (1997). Is anxiety really facilitative? Reaction to the myth that cognitive anxiety always impairs sport performance. *Journal of Applied Sport Psychology*, 9, 295–302.

Burton, D., Naylor, S., and Holliday, B. (2001). 'Goal setting in sport: Investigating the goal effectiveness paradox.' In: R.N. Singer, H.A. Hausenblas, and C.M. Janelle (Eds), *Handbook of Sport Psychology*. New York: Wiley, 497–528.

Butler, R. (1995). Athlete assessment: The performance profile. *Coaching Focus*, 29, 18–20.

Butler, R. (1997). 'Performance profiling: Assessing the way forward.' In: R.J. Butler (Ed.), *Sports Psychology in Performance*. Oxford: Butterworth-Heinemann, 33–48.

Butler, R.J. (1989). 'Psychological preparation of Olympic boxers.' In: J. Kremer and W. Crawford (Eds), *The Psychology of Sport: Theory and Practice*. Belfast: BPS Northern Ireland Branch, occasional paper, 74–84.

Butler, R.J., and Hardy, L. (1992). The performance profile: Theory and application. *The Sport Psychologist*, 6, 253–264.

Butler, R.J., Smith, M., and Irwin, I. (1993). The performance profile in practice. *Journal of Applied Sports Psychology*, 5, 48–63.

Butt, J., Weinberg, R., and Horn, T. (2003). The intensity and directional interpretation of anxiety: Fluctuations throughout competition and relationship to performance. *The Sport Psychologist*, 17, 35–54.

Carmack, M.A., and Martens, R. (1979). Measuring commitment to running: A survey of runners' attitudes and mental states. *Journal of Sport Psychology*, 1, 25–42.

Carron, A.V., and Hausenblas, H.A. (1998). *Group Dynamics in Sport*, (2nd Ed.). Morgantown, WV: Fitness Information Technology.

Carron, A.V., Colman, M.M., Wheeler, J., and Stevens, D. (2002). Cohesion and performance in sport: A meta-analysis. *Journal of Sport & Exercise Psychology*, 24, 168–188.

Carver, C.S. (1997). You want to measure coping but your protocol's too long: Consider the Brief COPE. *International Journal of Behavioral Medicine*, 4, 92–100.

Carver, C.S., and Scheier, M.F. (1998). *On the Self-Regulation of Behavior*. New York: Cambridge University Press.

Carver, C.S., Pozo, C., Harris, S.D., et al. (1993). How coping mediates the effect of optimism on distress: A study of women with early stage breast cancer. *Journal of Personality and Social Psychology*, 65, 375–390.

Cashmore, E. (2002). *Sport Psychology*. London: Routledge.

Cerin, E., Szabo, A., Hunt, N., and Williams, C. (2000). Temporal patterning of competitive emotions: A critical review. *Journal of Sports Sciences*, 18, 605–626.

Chapman, C.L., and De Castro, J.M. (1990). Running addiction: Measurement and associated psychological characteristics. *The Journal of Sports Medicine and Physical Fitness*, 30, 283–290.

Chelladurai, P. (1980). Leadership in sports organizations. *Canadian Journal of Applied Sport Sciences*, 5, 226–231.

Chelladurai, P. (1990). Leadership in sports: A review. *International Journal of Sport Psychology*, 21, 328–354.

Chelladurai, P. (2001). *Managing Organisations for Sport and Physical Activity: A Systems Perspective*. Scottsdale, AZ: Holcomb Hathaway.

Chelladurai, P. (2007). 'Leadership in Sports.' In: G. Tenenbaum, and R.C. Eklund (Eds), *Handbook of Sport Psychology* (3rd Ed.). Hoboken, NJ: John Wiley and Sons, 113–135.

Chelladurai, P., and Riemer, H. (1998). 'Measurement of leadership in sports.' In: J.L. Duda (Ed.), *Advances in Sport and Exercise Psychology Measurement*. Morgantown, WV: Fitness Information Technology, 227–253.

Chelladurai, P., and Saleh, S.D. (1980). Dimensions of leader behaviour in sports: Development of a leadership scale. *Journal of Sport Psychology*, 2, 34–45.

Chelladurai, P., Malloy, D., Imamura, H., and Yamaguchi, Y. (1987). A cross-cultural study of preferred leadership in sports. *Canadian Journal of Sport Sciences*, 12, 106–110.

Clark, V.R., Hopkins, W.G., Hawley, J.A., and Burke, L.M. (2000). Placebo effect of carbohydrate feeding during a 40-km cycling time trial. *Medicine and Science in Sports and Exercise*, 32, 1642–1647.

Cockerill, I.M., and Riddington, M.E. (1996). Exercise dependence and associated disorders: a review. *Counselling Psychology Quarterly*, 9, 119–129.

Cockerill, I.M., Nevill, A.M., and Lyons, N. (1991). Modelling mood states in athletic performance. *Journal of Sports Sciences*, 9, 205–212.

Cohane, G.H., and Pope, H.G. (2001). Body image in boys: A review of the literature. *International Journal of Eating Disorders*, 29, 373–379.

Collins, D., Jones, B., Fairweather, M., Doolan, S., and Priestley, N. (2001). Examining anxiety associated changes in movement patterns. *International Journal of Sport Psychology*, 31, 223–242.

Colmar Brunton Social Research (April, 2003). Ethics in Sport. Report prepared for the Australian Sports Commission: Canberra.

Conboy, J.K. (1994). The effects of exercise withdrawal on mood states of runners. *Journal of Sport Behavior*, 17, 188–203.

Connaughton, D., Wadey, R., Hanton, S., and Jones, G. (2008). The development and maintenance of mental toughness: Perceptions of elite performers. *Journal of Sports Sciences*, 26, 83–95.

Cooley, C.H. (1902). *Human Nature and the Social Order*. New York: Scriber's.

Copeland, B.L., and Franks, B.D. (1991). Effects of types and intensities of background music on treadmill endurance. *Journal of Sports Medicine and Physical Fitness*, 31, 100–103.

Cormier, S., and Cormier, B. (1998). *Interviewing strategies for helpers: Fundamental skills and cognitive-behavioural interventions* (4th Ed.). Pacific Grove, CA: Brooks/Cole.

Cox, R.H., Martens, M.P., and Russell, W.D. (2003). Measuring anxiety in athletics: The revised competitive state anxiety inventory-2. *Journal of Sport & Exercise Psychology*, 25, 519–533.

Craft, L.L., Magyar, M., Becker, B.J., and Feltz, D.L. (2003). The relationship between the Competitive State Anxiety Inventory-2 and sport performance: A meta-analysis. *Journal of Sport & Exercise Psychology*, 25, 44–65.

Cresswell, S., and Hodge, K. (2004). Coping skills: Role of trait sport confidence and trait anxiety. *Perceptual and Motor Skills*, 98, 433–438.

Crews, D.J., Lochbaum, M.R. and Landers, D.M. (2004). Aerobic physical activity effects on psychological well-being in low-income Hispanic children. *Perceptual and Motor Skills*, 1, 319–324.

Crocker, P.R.E., Eklund, R.C., and Kowalski, K.C. (2000). Children's physical activity and self-perceptions. *Journal of Sports Sciences*, 18, 383–394.

Crum, A.J., and Langer, E.J. (2007). Mind-set matters: Exercise and the placebo effect. *Psychological Science*, 18, 165–171.

Crust, L., and Clough, P.J. (2006). The influence of rhythm and personality in the endurance response to motivational asynchronous music. *Journal of Sports Sciences*, 24, 187–195.

Culver, D.M., and Trudel, P. (2006). 'Cultivating coaches' communities of practice: Developing the potential for learning through interactions.' In: R.L. Jones (Ed.), *The Sports Coach As Educator: Re-Conceptualising Sports Coaching*. London: Routledge.

Cumming, J., and Ste-Marie, D.M. (2001). The cognitive and motivational effects of imagery training: A matter of perspective. *The Sport Psychologist*, 15, 276–288.

Cumming, J., Nordin, S., Horton, R., and Reynolds, S. (2006). Examining the direction of imagery and self-talk on dart-throwing performance and self-efficacy. *The Sport Psychologist*, 20, 257–274.

Cushion, C. (2006). 'Mentoring: Harnessing the power of experience.' In: R.L. Jones (Ed.), *The Sports Coach As Educator: Re-Conceptualising Sports Coaching*. London: Routledge.

Cutrona, C.E., and Russell, D.W. (1990). 'Type of social support and specific stress: Toward a theory of optimal matching.' In: B.R. Sarason, I.G. Sarason, and G.R. Pierce (Eds), *Social Support: An Interactional View*. New York: John Wiley and Sons, 319–366.

D'Urso, V., Petrosso, A., and Robazza, C. (2002). Emotions, perceived qualities, and performance of rugby players. *The Sport Psychologist*, 16, 173–199.

Dale, G.A., and Wrisberg, C.A. (1996). The use of a performance profile technique in a team setting: Getting the athletes and coach on the 'same page'. *The Sport Psychologist*, 10, 261–277.

Danielson, R.R. (1976). Contingency model of leadership effectiveness: an empirical investigation of its application in sport. In: Proceedings – International Congress on Physical Activity Sciences, Quebec City, July 11–16, Vol. 7, 345–354.

Davis, C. (2000). Exercise abuse. *International Journal of Sport Psychology*, 31, 278–289.

Davis, M., Eschelman, E.R., and McKay, M. (1988). *The Relaxation and Stress Reduction Workbook*, (3rd Ed.). Oakland, CA: New Harbinger.

De Coverley Veale, D.M.W. (1987). Exercise dependence. *British Journal of Addiction*, 82, 735–740.

de la Fuente-Fernández, R., Schulzer, M., and Stoessl, A.J. (2002). The placebo effect in neurological disorders. *Lancet Neurology*, 1, 85–91.

Decety, J. (1996). Do imagined and executed actions share the same neural substrate? *Cognitive Brain Research*, 3, 87–93.

Decety, J., and Michel, F. (1989). Comparative analysis of actual and mental movement times in two graphic tasks. *Brain Cognition*, 11, 87–97.

Decety, J., Philippon, B., and Invgar, D.H. (1988). rCBF landscapes during motor performance and motor ideation of a graphic gesture. *European Archives of Psychiatry in Neurological Science*, 238, 33–38.

Decety, J., Jeannerod, M., Germain, M., and Pastène, J. (1991). Vegetative response during imagined movement is proportional to mental effort. *Behavioural Brain Research*, 42, 415–426.

Decety, J., Jeannerod, M., Durozard, D., and Baverel, G. (1993). Central attraction of autonomic effectors during mental simulation of motor actions. *Journal of Physiology*, 461, 549–563.

Deci, E.F., and Ryan, R.M. (1985). *Intrinsic Motivation and Self Determination in Human Behavior*. New York: Plenum Press.

Desharnais, R., Jobin, J., Cote, C., Levesque, L., and Godin, G. (1993). Aerobic exercise and the placebo effect: A controlled study. *Psychosomatic Medicine*, 55, 149–154.

Devonport, T.J., Biscomb, K., Lane, A.M., Mahoney, C.M., and Cassidy, T. (2005a). Stress and coping in elite junior netball. *Journal of Sports Sciences*, 22, 162–163.

Devonport, T.J., Lane, A.M., and Hanin, Y. (2005b). Affective state profiles of athletes prior to best, worst and performance-induced injury outcomes. *Journal of Sports Science and Medicine*, 4, 382–394.

Diener, E., Sadnvik, E., and Pavot, W.G. (1991). 'Happiness is the frequency, not the intensity of positive vs negative affect.' In: F. Strack, M. Argyle, and N. Schwarz (Eds), *Subjective Well Being: An Interdisciplinary Perspective*. Oxford: Pergamon Press, 119–139.

Dodge, A., and Robertson, B. (2004). Justifications for unethical behaviour in sport: The role of the coach. *Canadian Journal for Women and Coaching Online*, 4.

Dowthwaite, P.K., and Armstrong, M.R. (1984). An investigation into the anxiety levels of soccer players. *International Journal of Sport Psychology*, 15, 149–159.

Doyle, J., and Parfitt, G. (1996). Performance profiling and predictive validity. *Journal of Applied Sport Psychology*, 8, 160–170.

Doyle, J., and Parfitt, G. (1999). The effect of induced mood states on performance profile areas of perceived need. *Journal of Sports Sciences*, 17, 115–127.

Doyle, J.M., and Parfitt, G. (1997). Performance profiling and constructive validity. *The Sport Psychologist*, 11, 411–425.

Dreidiger, M., Hall, C., and Callow, N. (2006). Imagery use by injured athletes: A qualitative analysis. *Journal of Sports Sciences*, 24, 261–271.

Driskell, J.E., Copper, C., and Moran, A. (1994). Does mental practice improve performance? *Journal of Applied Psychology*, 79, 481–492.

Duffy, E. (1962). Activation and behavior. New york: Wiley.

Duncan, M., Al-Nakeeb, Y., Jones, M., and Nevill, A. (2006). Body dissatisfaction, body fat and physical activity in British children. *International Journal of Pediatric Obesity*, 1, 89–95.

Dupuis, M., Bloom, G.A., and Loughead, T.M. (2006). Team captains' perceptions of athlete leadership. *Journal of Sport Behavior*, 29, 60–78.

Eberle, S.G. (2004). Compulsive exercise: Too much of a good thing? National Eating Disorders Association. Retrieved October 23, 2007 from: www.uhs.berkeley.edu/edaw/CmpvExc.pdf

Edworthy, J., and Waring, H. (2006). The effects of music tempo and loudness level on treadmill exercise. *Ergonomics*, 49, 1597–1610.

Ekeland, E., Heian, F., and Hagen, K.B. (2005). Can exercise improve self-esteem in children and young people? A systematic review of randomised control trials. *British Journal of Sports Medicine*, 39, 792–798.

Eklund, R., Gould, D., and Jackson, S. (1993). Psychological foundations of Olympic wrestling excellence: Reconciling individual differences and nomothetic characterization. *Journal of Applied Sport Psychology*, 5, 35–47.

Eklund, R.C., Whitehead, J.R., and Welk, G.J. (1997). Validity of the children and youth physical self-perception profile: A confirmatory factor analysis. *Research Quarterly for Exercise and Sport*, 68, 249–256.

Elliott, D., Carr, S., and Savage, D. (2004). Effects of motivational music on work output and affective responses during sub-maximal cycling of a standardized perceived intensity. *Journal of Sport Behavior*, 27, 134–147.

Erickson, K., Côté, J., and Fraser-Thomas, J. (2007). Sport experiences, milestones and educational activities associated with high-performance coaches' development. *The Sport Psychologist*, 21, 302–316.

Estok, P.J., and Rudy, E.B. (1986). Physical, psychosocial, menstrual changes/risks and addiction in female marathon and nonmarathon runners. *Health Care for Women International*, 7, 187–202.

Evans, D. (2003). *Placebo: The Belief Effect.* London: HarperCollins.

Evans, M.G. (1970). The effects of supervisory behaviour on the path-goal relationship. *Organisational Behavior and Human Performance*, 5, 277–298.

Evening Standard (2000). Case history: Jackie's tale. Retrieved October 23, 2007 from: www.thisislondon.co.uk/newsarticle-953584-details/Case+history%3A+Jackie%27s+tale/article.do

Eys, M.A., Loughead, T.M., and Hardy, J. (2007). Athlete leadership dispersion and satisfaction in interactive sport teams. *Psychology of Sport and Exercise*, 8, 281–296.

Eysenck, M.W., and Calvo, M.G. (1992). Anxiety and performance: The processing efficiency theory. *Cognition and Emotion*, 6, 409–434.

Farnsworth, P.R. (1969). *The Social Psychology of Music.* Ames, IA: Iowa State University Press.

Fazey, J., and Hardy, L. (1988). 'The inverted-U hypothesis: A catastrophe for sport psychology?' In: Bass Monograph No 1. Leeds, UK: British Association of Sports Sciences and National Coaching Foundation.

Feltz, D.L., and Landers, D.M. (1983). The effects of mental practice on motor skill learning and performance: A meta-analysis. *Journal of Sport Psychology*, 5, 25–57.

Feltz, D.L., and Lirgg, C.D. (2001). 'Self-efficacy beliefs of athletes, teams and coaches.' In: R.N. Singer, H.A. Hausenblas, and C.M. Janelle (Eds), *Handbook of Sport Psychology*. New York: John Wiley and Sons, 304-361.

Feltz, D.L., and Riessinger, C.A. (1990). Effects of in vivo emotive imagery and performance feedback on self-efficacy and muscular endurance. *Journal of Sport & Exercise Psychology*, 12, 132–143.

Fiedler, F.E. (1967). *A Theory of Leadership Effectiveness.* New York: McGraw-Hill.

Filby, W.C.D., Maynard, I.W., and Graydon, J.K. (1999). The effect of multiple goal strategies on performance outcomes in training and competition. *Journal of Applied Sport Psychology*, 11, 230–246.

Fletcher, D., and Hanton, S. (2001). The relationship between psychological skills usage and competitive anxiety responses. *Psychology of Sport and Exercise*, 2, 89–101.

Flett, G.L., and Hewitt, P.L. (2005). The perils of perfectionism in sports and exercise. *Current Directions in Psychological Science*, 14, 14–18.

Foad, A.J., Beedie, C.J., and Coleman, D.A. (2008). Pharmacological and psychological effects of caffeine ingestion in 40-km cycling performance. *Medicine and Science in Sports and Exercise*, 40(1): 158–65.

Folkman, S., Lazarus, R.S., Dunkel-Schetter, C., De Longis, A., and Gruen, R.J. (1986). The dynamics of a stressful encounter: Cognitive appraisal, coping, and encounter outcomes. *Journal of Personality and Social Psychology*, 50, 992–1003.

Foster, C., Felker, H., Porcari, J.P., Mikat, R.P., and Seebach, E. (2004). The placebo effect on exercise performance. *Medicine and Science in Sport and Exercise*, 36, Supplement S171.

Fox, K.R. (1997). 'The physical self and processes in self-esteem development.' In: K.R. Fox (Ed.), *The Physical Self*. Champaign, IL: Human Kinetics, 111–140.

Fox, K.R. (2000). Self-esteem, self-perceptions and exercise. *International Journal of Sport Psychology*, 31, 228–240.

Fox, K.R., and Corbin, C.B. (1989). The Physical Self-Perception Profile: Development and preliminary validation. *Journal of Sport & Exercise Psychology*, 11, 408–430.

Fox, P.T., Pardo, J.V., Petersen, S.E., and Raichle, M.E. (1987). Supplementary motor and premotor responses to actual and imagined hand movements with positron emission tomography. *Society for Neuroscience Abstracts*, 13, 1433.

Frank, I. (1986). 'Psychology as a science: Resolving the idiographic-nomothetic controversy.' In: J. Valsiner (Ed.), *The Individual Subject and Scientific Psychology*. New York: Plenum Press, 17–36.

Fransella, F. (1981). 'Personal construct psychology and repertory grid technique.' In: F. Fransella (Ed.) *Personality: Theory, Measurement and Research*. London: Methuen.

Frederick, C.M., Morrison, C.S., and Manning, T. (1996). Motivation to participate, exercise affect, and outcome behaviours toward physical activity. *Perceptual and Motor Skills*, 82, 691–701.

Frederickson, B.L. (2001). The role of positive emotions in positive psychology. *American Psychologist*, 56, 218–226.

Frey, M., Laguna, P.L., and Ravizza, K. (2003). Collegiate athletes' mental skill use and perceptions of success: An exploration of the practice and competition settings. *Journal of Applied Sport Psychology*, 15, 115–128.

Frydenberg, E. (2002). *Beyond Coping: Meeting Goals, Visions, and Challenges*. Oxford: Oxford University Press.

Frydenberg, E., and Brandon, C. (2002). *The Best of Coping: Developing Coping Skills*. Melbourne: OzChild.

Frydenberg, E., and Lewis, R. (1993). Boys play sport and girls turn to others: Age gender and ethnicity as determinants of coping. *Journal of Adolescence*, 16, 252–266.

Frydenberg, E., and Lewis. R. (2002). 'Adolescent well-being: Building young people's resources.' In: E. Frydenberg (Ed.), *Beyond Coping: Meeting Goals, Visions, and Challenges*. Oxford: Oxford University Press, 175–194.

Frydenberg, E., and Lewis, R. (2004). Adolescents least able to cope: How do they respond to their stresses? *British Journal of Guidance and Counselling*, 32, 25–37.

Furnham, A., Badmin, N., and Sneade, I. (2002). Body image dissatisfaction: Gender differences in eating attitudes, self esteem and reasons for exercise. *The Journal of Psychology*, 136, 581–596.

Furst, D.M., and Germone, K. (1993). Negative addiction in male and female runners and exercisers. *Perceptual and Motor Skills*, 77, 192–194.

Gallagher, H. (1970). *On Swimming*. London: Pelham, 33–38.

Geers, A.L., Helfer, S.G., Kosbab, K., Weiland, P.E., and Landry, S.J. (2005). Reconsidering the role of personality in placebo effects: Dispositional optimism, situational expectations, and the placebo response. *Journal of Psychosomatic Research*, 58, 121–127.

Gelfand, D.M. (1962). The influence of self-esteem on rate of verbal conditioning and social matching behaviour. *Journal of Abnormal Social Psychology*, 65, 259–265.

Gfeller, K. (1988). Musical components and styles preferred by young adults for aerobic fitness activities. *Journal of Music Therapy*, 25, 28–43.

Giacobbi, P.R., and Weinberg, R.S. (2000). An examination of coping in sport: Individual trait anxiety differences and situational consistency. *The Sport Psychologist*, 14, 42–62.

Gilbert, D.T., Driver-Linn, E., and Wilson, T.D. (2002). 'The trouble with Vronsky: Impact bias in the forecasting of future affective states.' In: L.F. Barrett and P. Salovey (Eds), *The Wisdom in Feeling: Psychological Processes in Emotional Intelligence*. New York: Guilford, 114–143.

Gilbert, W., and Trudel, P. (2006). 'The coach as a reflective practitioner.' In: R.L. Jones (Ed.) *The Sports Coach As Educator: Re-Conceptualising Sports Coaching*. London: Routledge.

Gill, D.L. (1988). Gender differences in competitive orientation and sport participation. *International Journal of Sport Psychology*, 19, 145–159.

Glaser, B., and Strauss, A. (1967). *The Discovery of Grounded Theory*. Chicago, IL: Aldine.

Glasser, W. (1976). *Positive Addiction*. New York, NY: Harper and Row.

Glenn, S.D., and Horn, T.S. (1993). Psychological and personal predictors of leadership behavior in female soccer athletes. *Journal of Applied Sport Psychology*, 5, 17–34.

Gluch, P.D. (1993). The use of music in preparing for sport performance. *Contemporary Thought*, 2, 33–53.

Goodman, A. (1990). Addiction: definition and implications. *British Journal of Addiction*, 85, 1403–1408.

Gould, D., Petchlikoff, L., and Weinberg, R.S. (1984). Antecedents of temporal changes in, and relationships between CSAI-2 subcomponents. *Journal of Sport Psychology*, 6, 289–304.

Gould, D., Tammen, V., Murphy, S., and May, J. (1989). An examination of the US Olympic sport psychology consultants and the services they provide. *The Sport Psychologist*, 3, 300–312.

Gould, D., Eklund, R.C., and Jackson, S.A. (1993). Coping strategies used by more or less successful U.S. Olympic wrestlers. *Research Quarterly for Exercise and Sport*, 64, 83–93.

Gould, D., Udry, E., Bridges, D., and Beck, L. (1997). Coping with season ending injuries. *The Sport Psychologist*, 11, 379–399.

Gould, D., Guinan, D., Greenleaf, C., Medbury, R., and Peterson, K. (1999a). Factors affecting Olympic performance. Perceptions of athletes and coaches from more and less successful teams. *The Sport Psychologist*, 13, 371–394.

Gould, D., Medbury, R., Damarjian, N., and Lauer, L. (1999b). An examination of mental skills training in junior tennis coaches. *The Sport Psychologist*, 13, 371–395.

Gould, D., Dieffenbach, K., and Moffett, A. (2002a). Psychological characteristics and their development in Olympic champions. *Journal of Applied Sport Psychology*, 14, 172–204.

Gould, D., Greenleaf, C., and Krane, V. (2002b). 'Arousal-anxiety in sport.' In: T. Horn (Ed.), *Advances in Sport Psychology* (2nd Ed.). Champaign, IL: Human Kinetics, 207–241.

Graen, G.B., and Uhl-Bien, M. (1995). Relationship-based approach to leadership: Development of a leader-member exchange (LMX) theory of leadership over 25 years: Applying a multi-level multi-domain perspective. *Leadership Quarterly*, 6, 219–247.

Greenleaf, C., Gould, D., and Dieffenbach, K. (2001). Factors influencing Olympic performance: Interviews with Atlanta and Nagano U.S. Olympians. *Journal of Applied Sport Psychology*, 13, 154–184.

Greenspan, M.J., and Feltz, D.L. (1989). Psychological interventions with athletes in competitive situations: A review. *The Sport Psychologist*, 3, 219–236.

Gregg, M., Hall, C., and Nederhof, E. (2005). The imagery ability, imagery use, and performance relationship. *The Sport Psychologist*, 19, 93–99.

Griffiths, M.D. (1996). Behavioural addiction: an issue for everybody? *Journal of Workplace Learning*, 8, 19–25.

Griffiths, M.D. (1997). Exercise addiction: a case study. *Addiction Research*, 5, 161–168.

Griffiths, M.D. (2002). *Gambling and Gaming Addictions in Adolescence*. Leicester: British Psychological Society/Blackwell.

Grint, K. (2005). *Leadership: Limits and Possibilities*. Hampshire, UK: Palgrave Macmillan.

Gross, J.J. (1998). Antecedent- and response-focussed emotion regulation: Divergent consequences for experience, expression, and physiology. *Journal of Personality and Social Psychology*, 74, 224–237.

Gruber, J. (1986). 'Physical activity and self-esteem development in children: A meta-analysis.' In: G. Stull, and H. Eckem (Eds), *Effects of Physical Activity on Children*. Champaign, IL: Human Kinetics, 330–348.

Guinn, B., Semper, T., and Jorgensen, L. (1997). Mexican American female adolescent self-esteem: The effect of body image, exercise behaviour and body fatness. *Hispanic Journal of Behavioral Sciences*, 19, 517–526.

Hagborg, W. (1993). The Rosenberg self-esteem scale and Harter's self perception profile for adolescents: A concurrent validity study. *Psychology and The Schools*, 30, 132–136.

Hahn, R.A. (1997). The nocebo phenomenon: Concept, evidence, and implications for public health. *Preventative Medicine*, 26, 607–611.

Hailey, B.J., and Bailey, L.A. (1982). Negative addiction in runners: A quantitative approach. *Journal of Sport Behavior*, 5, 150–153.

Hall, A., and Terry, P.C. (1995). Predictive capability of pre-performance mood profiling at the 1993 World Rowing Championships, Roundnice, the Czech Republic. *Journal of Sports Sciences*, 13, 56–57.

Hall, C., Mack, D., Paivio, A., and Hausenblas, H. (1998). Imagery use by athletes: Development of the Sport Imagery Questionnaire. *International Journal of Sport Psychology*, 28, 1–17.

Hamilton, S.A., and Fremouw, W.J. (1985). Cognitive-behavioral training for college basketball free-throw performance. *Cognitive Therapy and Research*, 9, 479–483.

Hammermeister, J., and Burton, D. (2001). Stress, appraisal, and coping revisited: Examining the antecedents of competitive state anxiety with endurance athletes. *The Sport Psychologist*, 15, 66–90.

Hanin, Y.L. (1997). Emotions and athletic performance: Individual zones of optimal functioning model. *European Yearbook of Sport Psychology*, 1, 29–72.

Hanin, Y.L. (2000). 'Individual zones of optimal functioning (IZOF) model: Emotion-performance relationships in sport.' In: Y.L. Hanin (Ed.), *Emotions in Sport*. Champaign, IL: Human Kinetics, 65–89.

Hanton, S., and Jones, G. (1999). The effects of a multimodal intervention programme on performers: II. Training the butterflies to fly in formation. *The Sport Psychologist*, 13, 22–41.

Hanton, S., Thomas, O., and Maynard, I.W. (2004). Competitive anxiety response in the week leading up to competition: The role of intensity, direction and frequency dimensions. *Psychology of Sport and Exercise*, 5, 169–181.

Hardy, J. (2006). Speaking clearly: A critical review of the self-talk literature. *Psychology of Sport & Exercise*, 7, 81–97.

Hardy, L. (1990). 'A catastrophe model of performance in sport.' In: J.G. Jones, and L. Hardy (Eds), *Stress and Performance in Sport*. Chichester: John Wiley and Sons, 81–106.

Hardy, L. (1996b). A test of catastrophe models of anxiety and sports performance against multidimensional theory models using the method of dynamic differences. *Anxiety, Stress and Coping: An International Journal*, 9, 69–86.

Hardy, L., and Callow, N. (1999). Efficacy of external and internal visual imagery perspectives for the enhancement of performance on tasks in which form is important. *Journal of Sport & Exercise Psychology*, 21, 95–112.

Hardy, L., and Parfitt, G. (1991). A catastrophe model of anxiety and performance. *British Journal of Psychology*, 82, 163–178.

Hardy, L., Parfitt, G., and Pates, J. (1994). Performance catastrophes in sport: A test of the hysteresis hypothesis. *Journal of Sports Sciences*, 12, 327–334.

Hardy, L., Woodman, T., and Carrington, S. (2004). Is self-confidence a bias factor in higher-order catastrophe models? An exploratory analysis. *Journal of Sport & Exercise Psychology*, 26, 359–368.

Hardy, L., Beattie, S., and Woodman, T. (2007). Anxiety induced performance catastrophes: investigating effort required as an asymmetry factor. *British Journal of Psychology*, 98, 15–31.

Hargreaves, D.J., and North, A.C. (Eds) (1997). *The Social Psychology of Music*. Oxford: Oxford University Press.

Harter, S. (1985). 'Competence as a dimension of self-evaluation: Toward a comprehensive model of self-worth.' In: R.E. Leahy (Ed.), *The Development of the Self*. Orlando, FL: Academic Press, 55–121.

Harwood, C., Cumming, J., and Fletcher, D. (2004). Motivational profiles and psychological skills use within elite youth sport. *Journal of Applied Sport Psychology*, 16, 318–332.

Hatzigeorgiadis, A. (2006). Approach and avoidance coping during task performance in young men: The role of goal attainment expectancies. *Journal of Sports Sciences*, 24, 299–307.

Hatzigeorgiadis, A., Zourbanos, N., and Theodorakis, Y. (2007). The moderating effects of self-talk content on self-talk functions. *Journal of Applied Sport Psychology*, 19, 240–251.

Hausenblas, H.A., and Symons Downs, D. (2002). How much is too much? The development and validation of the exercise dependence scale. *Psychology and Health*, 17, 387–404.

Hayakawa, Y., Miki, H., Takada, K., and Tanaka, K. (2000). Effects of music on mood during bench stepping exercise. *Perceptual and Motor Skills*, 90, 307–314.

Hays, K., Thomas, O., Maynard, I., and Bawden, M. (2005). Sport confidence in successful and unsuccessful world class performances: A comparison of affect, behaviour and cognition. *Journal of Sports Sciences*, 23, 1289–1290.

Hays, K., Thomas, O., Maynard, I.W., and Butt, J. (2006). Profiling confidence for sport. Research poster presented at the Association for the Advancement of Applied Sport Psychology Annual Conference, Miami, September, 2006.

Hays, K., Maynard, I., Thomas, O., and Bawden, M. (2007). Sources and types of confidence identified by world class sport performers. *Journal of Applied Sport Psychology*, 19, 434–456.

Hecker, J.E., and Kaczor, L.M. (1988). Application of imagery theory to sport psychology: some preliminary findings. *Journal of Sport & Exercise Psychology*, 10, 363–373.

Hernandez-Peon, R. (1961). The efferent control of afferent signals entering the central nervous system. *Annals of New York Academy of Science*, 89, 866–882.

Hewston, R., Lane, A.M., Karageorghis, C.I., and Nevill, A.M. (2005). The effectiveness of music as a strategy to regulate mood [Abstract]. *Journal of Sports Sciences*, 22, 181–182.

Hinshaw, K.E. (1991). The effects of mental practice on motor skill performance: Critical evaluation and meta-analysis. *Imagination, Cognition and Personality*, 11, 3–35.

Hirt, E.R., Melton, R.J., McDonald, H.E., and Harackiewics, J.M. (1996). Processing goals, task interest, and the mood-performance relationship: A mediational analysis. *Journal of Personality and Social Psychology*, 71, 245–261.

Hoar, S.D., Kowalski, K.C., Gadreau, P., and Crocker, P.R.E. (2006). 'A review of coping in sport.' In: S. Hanton, and S. Mellalieu (Eds), *Literature Reviews in Sport Psychology*. Hauppauge, NY: Nova Science, 53–103.

Holmes, P.S., and Collins, D.J. (2001). The PETTLEP approach to motorimagery: a functional equivalence model for sport psychologists. *Journal of Applied Sport Psychology*, 13, 60–83.

Holmes, P.S., and Collins, D.J. (2002). 'Functional equivalence solutions for problems with motor imagery.' In: I. Cockerill (Ed). *Solutions in Sport Psychology*. London: Thompson, 120–140.

Holt, N.L. (2003). Coping in professional sport: A case study of an experienced cricket player. Athletic insight, 5, (1). Available at: www.athleticinsight.com/Vol5Iss1/CricketPlayerCoping.htm

Holt, N.L., and Dunn, J.G.H. (2004). Longitudinal idiographic analysis of appraisal and coping responses in sport. *Psychology of Sport and Exercise*, 5, 213–222.

Horn, T.S. (2002). *Advances in Sport Psychology*, (2nd Ed.). Leeds, UK: Human Kinetics.

Hróbjartsson, A., and Gøtzsche, P.C. (2001). Is the placebo powerless? An analysis of clinical trials comparing placebo treatment with no treatment. *New England Journal of Medicine*, 344, 1594–1602.

Isrealasvili, M. (2002). Fostering adolescents' coping skills: An action approach. *Canadian Journal of Counselling*, 36, 211–220.

Iwanaga, I. (1995a). Relationship between heart rate and preference for tempo of music. *Perceptual and Motor Skills*, 81, 435–440.

Iwanaga, I. (1995b). Harmonic relationship between preferred tempi and heart rate. *Perceptual and Motor Skills*, 81, 67–71.

Jackson, S.A., and Eklund, R.C. (2002). Assessing flow in physical activity: The Flow State Scale-2 and Dispositional Flow Scale-2. *Journal of Sport & Exercise Psychology*, 24, 133–150.

James, W. (1950). *The Principles of Psychology*. New York: Dover.

Johnson, J.J.M., Hrycaiko, D.W., Johnson, G.V., and Halas, J.M. (2004). Self-talk and female youth soccer performance. *The Sport Psychologist*, 18, 44–59.

Johnson, R. (1995). Exercise dependence: When runners don't know when to quit. *Sports Medicine and Arthroscopy Review*, 3, 267–273.

Jones, G. (1990). 'A cognitive perspective on the processes underlying the relationship between stress and performance in sport.' In: J.G. Jones and L. Hardy (Eds), *Stress and Performance in Sport*. Chichester: Wiley, 17–42.

Jones, G. (1993). The role of performance profiling in cognitive behavioural interventions in sport. *The Sport Psychologist*, 7, 160–172.

Jones, G., and Hanton, S. (2001). Pre-competitive feeling states and directional anxiety interpretations. *Journal of Sports Sciences*, 19, 385–395.

Jones, G., Hanton, S., and Connaughton, D. (2002). What is this thing called mental toughness? An investigation of elite sport performers. *Journal of Applied Sport Psychology*, 14, 205–218.

Jones, G., Hanton, S., and Connaughton, D. (2007). A framework of mental toughness in the world's best performers. *The Sport Psychologist*, 21, 23–264.

Jones, G., Swain, A.B.J., and Cale, A. (1991). Gender differences in precompetition temporal patterning and antecedents of anxiety and self-confidence. *Journal of Sport & Exercise Psychology*, 13, 1–15.

Jones, G.J., and Hardy, L. (1990). 'Stress in elite sport: Experiences of some elite performers.' In: G.J. Jones, and L. Hardy (Eds), *Stress and Performance in Sport*. New York: John Wiley and Sons, 247–277.

Jones, J.G. (1995). More than just a game: Research developments and issues in competitive state anxiety in sport. *British Journal of Psychology*, 86, 449–478.

Jones, J.G., and Swain, A.B.J. (1992). Intensity and direction dimensions of competitive anxiety and relationships with competitiveness. *Perceptual and Motor Skills*, 74, 467–472.

Jones, J.G., Swain, A., and Hardy, L. (1993). Intensity and direction dimensions of competitive state anxiety and relationships with performance. *Journal of Sports Sciences*, 11, 525–532.

Jones, M.V. (2003). Controlling emotions in sport. *The Sport Psychologist*, 14, 471–486.

Jones, M.V., and Uphill, M. (2004). Responses to the Competitive State Anxiety Inventory-2 (d) by athletes in anxious and excited scenarios. *Psychology of Sport and Exercise*, 5, 201–212.

Jones, M.V., Lane, A.M., Bray, S.R., Uphill, M., and Catlin, J. (2005). Development of the Sport Emotions Questionnaire. *Journal of Sport & Exercise Psychology*, 27, 407–431.

Jones, R.L. (Ed.). *The Sports Coach As Educator: Re-Conceptualising Sports Coaching*. London: Routledge.

Jowdy, D.P., Murphy, S.M., and Durtschi, S. (1989). *An assessment of the use of imagery by elite athletes: Athlete, coach and psychological perspectives*. Colorado Springs, CO: United States Olympic Committee.

Juslin, P.N., and Sloboda, J.A. (2001). *Music and Emotion: Theory and Research*. Oxford: Oxford University Press.

Kalasountas, V., Reed, J., and Fitzpatrick, J. (2007). The effect of placebo-induced changes in expectancies on maximal force production in college students. *Journal of Applied Sport Psychology*, 19, 116–124.

Kaptchuk, T.J. (2001). The double-blind, randomized, placebo-controlled trial. Gold standard or golden calf? *Journal of Clinical Epidemiology*, 54, 541–549.

Karageorghis, C.I., and Lee, J. (2001). Effects of asynchronous music and imagery on an isometric endurance task. Proceedings of the World Congress of Sport Psychology. International Society of Sport Psychology: Skiathos, Greece, Vol. 4, 37–39.

Karageorghis, C.I., and Terry, P.C. (1997). The psychophysical effects of music in sport and exercise: A review. *Journal of Sport Behavior*, 20, 54–68.

Karageorghis, C.I., and Terry, P.C. (1999). Affective and psychophysical responses to asynchronous music during submaximal treadmill running. Proceedings of the 1999 European College of Sport Science Congress, Rome, Italy, 218.

Karageorghis, C.I., Drew, K.M., and Terry, P.C. (1996). Effects of pretest stimulative and sedative music on grip strength. *Perceptual and Motor Skills*, 83, 1347–1352.

Karageorghis, C.I., Terry, P.C., and Lane, A.M. (1999). Development and initial validation of an instrument to assess the motivational qualities of music in exercise and sport: The Brunel Music Rating Inventory. *Journal of Sports Sciences*, 17, 713–724.

Karageorghis, C.I., Jones, L., and Low, D.C. (2006a). Relationship between exercise heart rate and music tempo preference. *Research Quarterly for Exercise and Sport*, 26, 240–250.

Karageorghis, C.I., Priest, D.L., Terry, P.C., Chatzisarantis, N.L.D., and Lane, A.M. (2006b). Redesign and initial validation of an instrument to assess the motivational qualities of music in exercise: The Brunel Music Rating Inventory-2. *Journal of Sports Sciences*, 24, 899–909.

Karageorghis, C.I., Mouzourides, D.A., Sasso, T.A., Morrish, D.J., Walley, C.L., and Priest, D.L. (2007). Psychophysical and ergogenic effects of synchronous music during treadmill walking. Unpublished manuscript, Brunel University, West London.

Karageorghis, C.I., Jones, L., and Stuart, D.P. (in press). Psychological effects of music tempi during exercise. *International Journal of Sports Medicine*.

Kelly, G.A. (1955). *The Psychology of Personal Constructs*. New York: Norton, Vols 1 and 2.

Kerr, J.H. (1997). *Motivation and Emotion in Sport: Reversal Theory*. Hove, East Sussex: Psychology Press.

Kirsch, I., and Weixel, L.J. (1988). Double-blind versus deceptive administration of a placebo. *Behavioral Neuroscience*, 102, 319–323.

Kirschenbaum, D.S., and Bale, R.M. (1984). 'Cognitive behavioral skills in sports: Applications to golf and speculations about soccer.' In: W.F. Straub and J.M. Williams (Eds), *Cognitive Sport Psychology*. Lansing, NY: Sport Science Associates, 275–278.

Kogler Hill, S.E. (2001). 'Team leadership.' In: P.G. Northouse (Ed.), *Leadership: Theory and Practice*. London: Sage.

Krane, V. (1994). The mental readiness form as a measure of competitive state anxiety. *The Sport Psychologist*, 8, 189–202.

Kreider, R.B., Fry, A.C., and O'Toole, M.L. (1998). *Overtraining in Sport*. Champaign, IL: Human Kinetics.

Kuczka, K.K., and Treasure, D.C. (2004). Self-handicapping in competitive sport: Influence of the motivational climate, self-efficacy and perceived importance. *Psychology of Sport and Exercise*, 6, 539–550.

Kyllo, L.B., and Landers, D.M. (1995). Goal setting in sport and exercise: A research synthesis to resolve the controversy. *Journal of Sport & Exercise Psychology*, 17, 117–137.

Lane, A.M. (2007a). 'The rise and fall of the iceberg: Development of a conceptual model of mood-performance relationships.' In: A.M. Lane (Ed.), *Mood and Human Performance: Conceptual, Measurement, and Applied Issues*. Hauppauge, NY: Nova Science, 1–34.

Lane, A.M. (Ed.), (2007b). *Mood and Human Performance: Conceptual, Measurement, and Applied Issues*. Hauppauge, NY: Nova Science.

Lane, A.M. (2007c). 'Developing and validating psychometric tests for use in high performance settings.' In: Boyar, L. (Ed.), *Psychological Tests and Testing Research*. Hauppauge, NY: Nova, 203–213.

Lane, A.M., and Terry, P.C. (1999). The conceptual independence of tension and depression [Abstract]. *Journal of Sports Sciences*, 17, 605–606.

Lane, A.M., and Terry, P.C. (2000). The nature of mood: Development of a conceptual model with a focus on depression. *Journal of Applied Sport Psychology*, 12, 16–33.

Lane, A.M., Sewell, D.F., Terry, P.C., Bartram, D., and Nesti, M.S. (1999a). Confirmatory factor analysis of the Competitive State Anxiety Inventory–2. *Journal of Sports Sciences*, 17, 505–512.

Lane, A.M., Whyte, G.P., Godfrey, R., and Pedlar, C. (2003). Adaptations of psychological state variables to altitude among the Great Britain biathlon team preparing for the 2002 Olympic Games [Abstract]. *Journal of Sports Sciences*, 21, 281–282.

Lane, A.M., Beedie, C.J., and Stevens, M.J. (2005a). Mood matters: A response to Mellalieu. *Journal of Applied Sport Psychology*, 17, 319–325.

Lane, A.M., Nevill, A.M., Bowes, N., and Fox, K.R. (2005b). Investigating indices of stability using the task and ego orientation questionnaire. *Research Quarterly for Exercise and Sport*, 76, 339–346.

Lane, A.M., Whyte, G.P., Godfrey, R., and Pedlar, C. (2005). Relationships between mood and perceived exertion among elite biathletes at altitude. International Society of Sport Psychology (ISSP) 11th World Congress of Sport Psychology, 15–19 August 2005, Syndey Convention and Exhibition Centre, Syndey, Australia.

Lanzillo, J.J., Burke, K.L., Joyner, A.B., and Hardy, C.J. (2001). The effects of music on the intensity and direction of pre-competitive cognitive and somatic state anxiety and state self-confidence in collegiate athletes. *International Sports Journal*, 5, 101–110.

Lasagna, L. (1986). The placebo effect. *Journal of Allergy and Clinical Immunology*, 78, 161–165.

Lavallee, D., Kremer, J., Moran, A.P., and Williams, M. (2004). *Sport Psychology: Contemporary Themes*. New York: Palgrave MacMillan.

Lazarus, R.S. (1966). *Psychological Stress and the Coping Process*. New York: McGraw-Hill.

Lazarus, R.S. (1991). *Emotion and Adaptation*. Oxford: Oxford University Press.

Lazarus, R.S. (1999). *Stress and Emotion: A New Synthesis*. London: Free Association Books.

Lazarus, R.S. (2000a). 'Cognitive-motivational-relational theory of emotion.' In: Y.L. Hanin (Ed.), *Emotions in Sport*. Champaign, IL: Human Kinetics, 39–63.

Lazarus, R.S. (2000b). How emotions influence performance in competitive sports. *The Sport Psychologist*, 14, 229–252.

Lazarus, R.S. (2001). Stress and emotion: a new synthesis. *Human Relations*, 54, 792–803.

Lazarus, R.S., and Folkman, S. (1984). *Stress Appraisal and Coping*. New York: Springer.

LeBlanc, A. (1982). An interactive theory of music preference. *Journal of Music Therapy*, 19, 28–45.

LeBlanc, A. (1995). Differing results in research in preference for music tempo. *Perceptual and Motor Skills*, 81, 1253–1254.

LeBlanc, A., Coleman, J., McCrary, J., Sherrill, L., and Malin, S. (1988). Tempo preference of different age listeners. *Journal of Research in Music Education*, 36, 156–168.

Levy, S., and Ebbeck, V. (2005). The exercise and self-esteem model in adult women: the inclusion of physical acceptance. *Psychology of Sport and Exercise*, 6, 571–584.

Lewthwaite, R. (1990). Threat perception in competitive trait anxiety: The endangerment of important goals. *Journal of Sport & Exercise Psychology*, 12, 280–300.

Li, F. (1999). The Exercise Motivation Scale: Its multifaceted structure and construct validity. *Journal of Applied Sport Psychology*, 11, 97–115.

Li, F., Harmer, P., Chaumeton, N., Duncan, T., and Duncan, S. (2002). Tai-chi as a means to enhance self-esteem: A randomised controlled trial. *The Journal of Applied Gerontology*, 21, 70–89.

Linney, B.J. (1999). Characteristics of good mentors. *Physician Executive*, 25, 70–82.

Lirgg, C.D. (1991). Gender differences in self-confidence in physical activity: A meta-analysis of recent studies. *Journal of Sport & Exercise Psychology*, 13, 294–310.

Locke, E.A., and Latham, G.P. (1990). *A theory of goal setting and task performance.* Englewood Cliffs, NJ: Prentice-Hall.

Loughead, T.M., and Hardy, J. (2005). An examination of coach and peer leader behaviours in sport. *Psychology of Sport and Exercise*, 6, 303–312.

Loughead, T.M., Hardy, J., and Eys, M.A. (2006). The nature of athlete leadership. *Journal of Sport Behavior*, 29, 142–158.

Lucaccini, L.F., and Kreit, L.H. (1972). 'Music.' In: W.P. Morgan (Ed.), *Ergogenic aids and muscular performance.* New York: Academic Press, 240–245.

MacBride, E.R., and Rothstein, A.L. (1979). Mental and physical practice and the learning and retention of open and closed skills. *Perceptual and Motor Skills*, 49, 359–365.

Maganaris, C.N., Collins, D., and Sharp, M. (2000). Expectancy effects and strength training: Do steroids make a difference? *The Sport Psychologist*, 14, 272–278.

Mahoney, M.J., and Avener, M. (1977). Psychology of the elite athlete: An exploratory study. *Cognitive Therapy and Research*, 1, 135–141.

Mallet, C., and Côté, J. (2006). Beyond winning and losing: Guidelines for evaluating high performance coaches. *The Sport Psychologist*, 20, 213–221.

Marlatt, G.A., and Rohsenow, D.J. (1980). 'Cognitive processes in alcohol use: Expectancy and the balanced placebo design.' In: N. Mello (Ed.), *Advances in Substance Abuse (1).* Greenwich: JAI Press, 159–199.

Marsh, H., Richards, G., Johnson, S., Roche, L., and Tremayne, P. (1994). Physical self-description questionnaires: Psychometric properties and a multi trait-multi method analysis of relations to existing instruments. *Journal of Sport & Exercise Psychology*, 16, 270–305.

Martens, R. (1977). *Sport Competition Anxiety Test.* Champaign, IL: Leisure Press.

Martens, R., Vealey, R., and Burton, D. (1990). *Competitive Sports Anxiety Inventory-2.* Champaign, IL; Human Kinetics.

Martin, G., and Pear, J. (2003). *Behavior Modification: What It Is and How To Do It* (7th Ed.). Englewood Cliffs, NJ: Prentice-Hall.

Martin, G.L., Thompson, K., and Regehr, K. (2004). Studies using single-subject designs in sport psychology: 30 years of research. *The Behavior Analyst*, 27, 263–280.

Masters, R.S.W. (1992). Knowledge, knerves and know-how: the role of explicit versus implicit knowledge in the breakdown of a complex motor skill under pressure. *British Journal of Psychology*, 83, 343–358.

Matud, M.P. (2004). Gender differences in stress and coping styles. *Personality and Individual Differences*, 37, 1401–1415.

Maynard, I.W., Hemmings, B., and Warwick-Evans, L. (1995). The effects of somatic intervention strategy on competitive state anxiety in semi-professional soccer players. *The Sport Psychologist*, 9, 51–64.

McAuley, E., Blissmer, B., Katula, J., Duncan, S.C., and Mihalko, S. (2000). Physical activity, self-esteem and self-efficacy relationships in older adults: A randomised control trial. *Annals of Behavioral Medicine*, 22, 131–139.

McAuley, E., Elavsky, S., Motl, R.W., Konopack, J.F., Hu, L., and Marquez, D.X. (2005). Physical activity, self-efficacy and self-esteem: Longitudinal relationships in older adults. *Journal of Gerontology: Psychological Sciences*, 60B, 268–275.

McClung, M., and Collins, D. (2007). 'Because I know it will!': placebo effects of an ergogenic aid on athletic performance. *Journal of Sport & Exercise Psychology*, 29, 382–394.

Mcdonald, D.J., and Hodgdon, J.A. (1991). *Psychological Effects of Aerobic Fitness Training.* New York: Springer.

McNair, D.M., Lorr, M., and Droppleman, L.F. (1971). Manual for the Profile of Mood States. San Diego, CA: Educational and Industrial Testing Services.

McNair, D.M., Gardos, G., Haskell, D.S., and Fisher, S. (1979). Placebo response, placebo effect and two attributes. *Psychopharmacology*, 63, 245–250.

Mead, G.H. (1934). *Mind, Self and Society from the Standpoint of a Social Behaviourist*. Chicago: University of Chicago Press.

Mellalieu, S.D. (2003). Mood matters: But how much? A comment on Lane and Terry (2000). *Journal of Applied Sport Psychology*, 15, 99–114.

Mellalieu, S.D., Hanton, S., and Jones, G. (2003). Emotional labelling and competitive anxiety in preparation and competition. *The Sport Psychologist*, 17, 157–174.

Mendelson, B.K., and White, D.R. (1982). Relation between body-esteem and self-esteem of obese and normal children. *Perceptual and Motor Skills*, 54, 899–905.

Mendelson, B.K., McLaren, L., Gauvin, L., and Steiger, H. (2002). The relationship of self-esteem and body esteem in women with and without eating disorders. *International Journal of Eating Disorders*, 31, 318–323.

Mendoza, D.W., and Wichman, H. (1978). 'Inner' darts: Effects of mental practice on the performance of dart throwing. *Perceptual and Motor Skills*, 47, 1195–1199.

Michel, W., and Wanner, H.U. (1973). Einfuss der musik auf die sportliche leistung [Effect of music on sports performance]. *Schweizerische Zeitschrift für Sportmedizin*, 23, 141–159.

Miller, B. (1997). *Gold Minds: Psychology of Winning in Sport*. Malborough: Crowood Press.

Miller, B.P. (1997). 'Developing team cohesion and empowering individuals.' In: R.J. Butler (Ed.), *Sports Psychology in Performance*. Oxford: Butterworth-Heinemann, 105–125.

Miller, W.R., and Rollnick, S. (2002). *Motivational Interviewing: Preparing People for Change* (2nd Ed.). New York: Guilford.

Moran, A. (2004). *Sport and Exercise Psychology: A Critical Introduction*. London: Routledge.

Moran, A.P., and MacIntyre, T. (1998). 'There's more to an image than meets the eye': A qualitative study of kinaesthetic imagery and elite canoe-slalomists. *The Irish Journal of Psychology*, 19, 406–423.

Morgan, W.P. (1979). Negative addiction in runners. *The Physician and Sportmedicine*, 7, 57–71.

Morgan, W.P. (1980). Test of Champions: The iceberg profile. *Psychology Today*, 14, 92–108.

Morris, M. (1989). Running round the clock. *Running*, 104, 44–45.

Murphy, S.M. (1990). Models of imagery in sport psychology: A review. *Journal of Mental Imagery*, 14, 153–172.

Murphy, S.M., and Jowdy, D.P. (1992). 'Imagery and mental practice.' In: Horn, T. (Ed.), *Advances in Sport Psychology*. Champaign, IL: Human Kinetics.

Murphy, S.M., Greenspan, M., Jowdy, D., and Tammen, V. (1989). Development of a brief rating instrument of competitive anxiety: comparisons with the Competitive State Anxiety Inventory-2. Proceedings of the Association for the Advancement of Applied Sport Psychology. Seattle, WA: Association for the Advancement of Applied Sport Psychology, 82.

Murray, N.M., and Janelle, C.M. (2003). Anxiety and performance: A visual search examination of processing efficiency theory. *Journal of Sport & Exercise Psychology*, 25, 171–187.

Naito, E., and Matsumura, M. (1994). Movement-related slow potentials during motor imagery and motor suppression in humans. *Cognitive Brain Research*, 2, 131–137.

Nelson, L.J., Cushion, C.J., and Potrac, P. (2006) Formal, nonformal and informal coach learning: A holistic conceptualisation. *International Journal of Sports Science and Coaching*, 1, 247–259.

Nethery, V.M. (2002). Competition between internal and external sources of information during exercise: Influence on RPE and the impact of the exercise load. *Journal of Sports Medicine and Physical Fitness*, 42, 172–178.

Nicholls, A.R., Holt, N.L., and Polman, R.C.J. (2005). A phenomenological analysis of coping effectiveness in golf. *The Sport Psychologist*, 19, 111–130.

Nicholls, A.R., Holt, N.L., Polman, R.C.J., Bloomfield, J. (2006). Longitudinal analyses of stress and coping among professional rugby players. *The Sport Psychologist*, 20, 314–329.

Nisbett, R., and Ross, L. (1980). *Human Inference: Strategies and Shortcomings of Social Judgement*. Englewood Cliffs, NJ: Prentice-Hall.

Nordin, S.M., and Cumming, J. (2005). Professional dancers describe their imagery: Where, when, what, why, and how. *The Sport Psychologist*, 19, 295–416.

Norman, D.A. (1988). *The Psychology of Everyday Things*. New York: Basic.

North, A.C., and Hargreaves, D.J. (1997). The musical milieu: Studies of listening in everyday life. *The Psychologist*, 10, 309–312.

Northouse, P.G. (2007). *Leadership: Theory and Practice*. London: Sage.

Noteboom, J.T., Barnholt, K.R., and Enoka, R.M. (2001a). Activation of the arousal response and impairment of performance increase with anxiety and stressor intensity. *Journal of Applied Physiology*, 91, 2093–2101.

Noteboom, J.T., Fleshner, M., and Enoka, R.M. (2001b). Activation of the arousal response can impair performance on a simple motor task. *Journal of Applied Physiology*, 91, 821–831.

Ntoumanis, N., and Biddle, S.J.H. (1998). The relationship of coping and its perceived effectiveness to positive and negative affect in sport. *Personality and Individual Differences*, 24, 773–778.

Ochsner, K.N., and Gross, J.J. (2007). 'The neural architecture of emotion regulation.' In: J.J. Gross (Ed.), *Handbook of Emotion Regulation*. London: Guilford Press, 87–109.

Ojanen, M. (1995). Can the true effects of exercise on psychological variables be separated from placebo effects? *International Journal of Sport Psychology*, 25, 63–80.

Orlick, T., and Partington, J. (1988). Mental links to excellence. *The Sport Psychologist*, 2, 105–130.

Oxendine, J.B. (1969). Effect of mental and physical practice on the learning of three motor skills. *Research Quarterly*, 40, 755–763.

Palladino-Green, S., and Pritchard, M.E. (2003). Predictors of body image dissatisfaction in adult men and women. *Social Behaviour and Personality*, 31, 215–222.

Palmer, C., Burwitz, L., Collins, D., Campbell, E., and Hern, J. (1996). Performance profiling: Construct validity and utilization. *Journal of Sports Sciences*, 14, 41–42.

Parfitt, C.G., Jones, J.G., and Hardy, L. (1990). 'Multidimensional anxiety and performance.' In: J.G. Jones and L. Hardy (Eds), *Stress and Performance in Sport*. New York: John Wiley and Sons, 43–80.

Parfitt, G., Hardy, L., and Pates, J. (1995). Somatic anxiety and physiological arousal: Their effects upon a high anaerobic, low memory demand task. *International Journal of Sport Psychology*, 26, 196–213.

Parkinson, B., Totterdell, P., Briner, R.B., and Reynolds, S. (1996). *Changing Moods: The Psychology of Mood and Mood Regulation*. London: Longman.

Parrott, W.G. (2001). *Emotions in Social Psychology*. Hove, East Sussex: Psychology Press.

Paskevich, D.M., Estabrooks, P.A., Brawley, L.R., and Carron, A.V. (2001). 'Group cohesion in sport and exercise.' In: R.N. Singer, H.A. Hausenblas, and C.M. Janelle (Eds), *Handbook of Sport Psychology*. New York: Wiley, 472–494.

Pasman, L., and Thompson, J.K. (1988). Body image and eating disturbance in obligatory runners, obligatory weightlifters, and sedentary individuals. *International Journal of Eating Disorders*, 7, 759–777.

Pates, J., Karageorghis, C.I., Fryer, R., and Maynard, I. (2003). Effects of asynchronous music on flow states and shooting performance among netball players. *Psychology of Sport and Exercise*, 4, 413–427.

Pelletier, L.G., Fortier, M.S., Vallerand, R.J., Tuson, K.M., Brière, N.M., and Blais, M.R. (1995). Toward a new measure of intrinsic motivation, extrinsic motivation, and amotivation in sports: The Sport Motivation Scale (SMS). *Journal of Sport & Exercise Psychology*, 17, 35–53.

Pensgaard, A.M., and Duda, J.L. (2003). Sydney 2000: The interplay between emotions, coping, and the performance of Olympic level athletes. *The Sport Psychologist*, 17, 253–267.

Perry, C., and Morris, T. (1995). 'Mental imagery in sport.' In: T. Morris, and J. Summers (Eds), *Sport Psychology: Theory, Applications and Issues*. John Wiley and Sons, Singapore.

Pierce, E.F. (1994). Exercise dependence syndrome in runners. *Sports Medicine*, 18, 149–155.

Plante, T.G., Lantis, A., and Checa, G. (1998). The influence of perceived versus aerobic fitness on psychological health and physiological stress responsivity. *International Journal of Stress Management*, 5, 141–156.

Poczwardowski, A., and Conroy, D.E. (2002). Coping responses to failure and success among elite athletes and performing artists. *Journal of Applied Sport Psychology*, 14, 313–329.

Porcari, J., Foster, C. (2006). Mind over body. ACE FitnessMatters 2006 May/June [online]. Available from URL: www.acefitness.org/getfit/PlaceboStudy2006.pdf [Accessed 2006 Dec 5th]

Prapavessis, H., and Carron, A.V. (1997). Cohesion and work output. *Small Group Research*, 28, 294–301.

Prapavessis H., and Grove, J.R. (1998). Self-handicapping and self-esteem. *Journal of Applied Sport Psychology*, 10, 175–184.

Prapavessis, H., Maddison, R., and Fletcher, R. (2005). Further examination of the factor integrity of the Sport Anxiety Scale. *Journal of Sport & Exercise Psychology*, 27, 253–260.

Priest, D.L., Karageorghis, C.I., and Sharp, N.C.C. (2004). The characteristics and effects of motivational music in exercise settings: The possible influence of gender, age, frequency of attendance, and time of attendance. *Journal of Sports Medicine and Physical Fitness*, 44, 77–86.

Ptacek, J., Smith, R., and Dodge, K. (1994). Gender differences in coping with stress. *Personality and Social Psychology Bulletin*, 20, 421–430.

Pujol, T.J., and Langenfeld, M.E. (1999). Influence of music on Wingate anaerobic test performance. *Perceptual and Motor Skills*, 88, 292–296.

Rees, T., and Hardy, L. (2004). Matching social support with stressors: Effects on factors underlying performance in tennis. *Psychology of Sport and Exercise*, 5, 319–337.

Rejeski, W.J. (1985). Perceived exertion: An active or passive process? *Journal of Sport Psychology*, 75, 371–378.

Renger, R. (1993). A review of the Profile of Mood States (POMS) in the prediction of athletic success. *Journal of Applied Sport Psychology*, 5, 78–84.

Richardson, A. (1967a). Mental practice: a review and discussion (Part 1). *Research Quarterly*, 38, 95–107.

Richardson, A. (1967b). Mental practice: a review and discussion (Part 2). *Research Quarterly*, 38, 263–273.

Riemer, H.A. (2007). 'Multidimensional model of coach leadership.' In: S. Jowett and D. Lavallee (Eds), *Social Psychology of Sport*. Leeds: Human Kinetics, 57–74.

Riemer, H.A., and Chelladurai, P. (1995). Leadership and satisfaction in athletics. *Journal of Sport & Exercise Psychology*, 17, 276–293.

Riemer, H.A., and Toon, K. (2001). Leadership and satisfaction in tennis: Examination of congruence, gender and ability. *Research Quarterly for Exercise and Sport*, 72, 243–256.

Riley, P. (1994). *The Winner Within*. New York: Berkley.

Rivers, D. (2005). The seven challenges workbook – web page edition. Available at: http://newconversations.net/communication_skills_worksbook_summary_and_toc.htm accessed 11th July 2006.

Robins, R., Hendin, H., and Trezsniewski, K. (2001). Measuring global self-esteem: Construct validation of a single item measure and the Rosenberg Self-Esteem Scale. *Personality and Social Psychology Bulletin*, 27, 151–161.

Rogerson, L.J., and Hrycaiko, D.W. (2002). Enhancing competitive performance of ice-hockey goaltenders using centering and self-talk. *Journal of Applied Sport Psychology*, 14, 14–26.

Rosario, M., Shinn, M., Morch, H., and Huckabee, C.B. (1988). Gender differences in coping and social support: Testing socialization and role constraint theories. *Journal of Community Psychology*, 16, 55–69.

Roseman, I.J. (1991). Appraisal determinants of discrete emotions. *Cognition and Emotion*, 5, 161–200.

Rosenberg, M. (1965). *Society and the Adolescent Self-Image*. Princeton, NJ: Princeton University Press.

Rowley, A.J., Landers, D.M., Kyllo, L.B., and Etnier, J.L. (1995). Does the Iceberg Profile discriminate between successful and less successful athletes? A meta-analysis. *Journal of Sport & Exercise Psychology*, 16, 185–199.

Rozin, P., and Stoess, C. (1993). Is there a general tendency to become addicted? *Addictive Behaviors*, 18, 81–87.

Rudy, E.B., and Estok, P.J. (1989). Measurement and significance of negative addiction in runners. *Western Journal of Nursing Research*, 11, 548–558.

Rushall, B.S. (1984). 'The content of competition thinking.' In: W.F. Straub, and J.M. Williams (Eds), *Cognitive Sport Psychology*. Lansing, NY: Sport Science Associates, 51–62.

Rushall, B.S., Hall, M., Sasseville, J., and Rushall, A.C. (1988). Effects of three types of thought content instructions on skiing performance. *The Sport Psychologist*, 2, 283–297.

Sachs, M.L. (1981). 'Running addiction.' In: M. Sacks and M. Sachs (Eds), *Psychology of Running*. Champaign, IL: Human Kinetics, 116–126.

Sachs, M.L., and Pargman, D. (1984). 'Running addiction.' In: M.L. Sachs, and G.W. Buffone (Eds), *Running as Therapy: An Integrated Approach*. Lincoln, NE: University of Nebraska Press, 231–252.

Sandler, I.N., Wolchick, S.A., MacKinnon, D., Ayers, T.S., and Roosa, M.W. (1997). 'Developing linkages between theory and intervention in stress and coping processes.' In: S.A. Wolchick, and I.N. Sandler (Eds), *Principles and Practice of Stress Management*. New York: Guilford Press, 373–406.

Schachter, S. (1964). 'The interaction of cognitive and physiological determinants of emotional state.' In: L. Berkowitz (Ed.), *Advances in Experimental and Social Psychology*. New York: Academic Press, 49–80.

Shapiro, A.K., and Shapiro, E. (1984). 'Patient-provider relationships and the placebo effect.' In: J.D. Matarazzo, S.M. Weiss, J.A. Heird, and N.E. Miller (Eds), *Behavioural Health: Handbook of Health Enhancement and Disease Prevention*. New York: Wiley, 371–383.

Simon, J.A., and Martens, R. (1977). 'SCAT as a predictor of A-states in varying competitive situations.' In: D.M. Landers, and R.W. Christina (Eds), *Psychology of Motor Behavior and Sport*. Champaign, IL: Human Kinetics, Vol 2, 146–156.

Simpson, S.D., and Karageorghis, C.I. (2006). The effects of synchronous music on 400-m sprint performance. *Journal of Sports Sciences*, 24, 1095–1102.

Sinclair, G.D., and Sinclair, D.A. (1994). Developing reflective performers by integrating mental management skills with the learning process. *The Sport Psychologist*, 8, 13–27.

Sinclair, R.C., and Mark, M.M. (1992). 'The influence of mood state on judgement and action: Effects on persuasion, categorisation, social justice, person perception, and judgmental accuracy.' In: L.L. Martin, and A. Tesser (Eds), *The Construction of Social Judgement*. Hillsdale, NJ: Erlbaum, 165–193.

Skinner, N., and Brewer, N. (2004). Adaptive approaches to competition: Challenge appraisals and positive emotion. *Journal of Sport & Exercise Psychology*, 26, 283–305.

Smith, C.A., and Ellsworth, P.C. (1985). Patterns of cognitive appraisal in emotion. *Journal of Personality and Social Psychology*, 48, 813–838.

Smith, D., and Collins, D. (2004). Mental practice, Motor performance, and the late CNV. *Journal of Sport & Exercise Psychology*, 26, 412–426.

Smith, D., Collins, D., and Hale, B. (1998). Imagery perspectives and karate performance. *Journal of Sports Sciences*, 16, 103–104.

Smith, D., Wright, C.J., Allsopp, A., and Westhead, H. (2007). It's all in the mind: PETTLEP-based imagery and sports performance. *Journal of Applied Sport Psychology*, 19, 80–92.

Smith, D.J. (2003). A framework for understanding the training process leading to elite performance. *Sports Medicine*, 33, 1103–1126.

Smith, R.E. (1999). Generalization effects in coping skills training. *Journal of Sport & Exercise Psychology*, 21, 189–204.

Smith, R.E., Smoll, F.E., and Hunt, E.B. (1977). A system for the behavioral assessment of athletic coaches. *Research Quarterly*, 48, 401–407.

Smith, R.E., Smoll, F.L., and Curtis, B. (1979). Coach Effectiveness Training: A Cognitive-Behavioral Approach to Enhancing Relationship Skills in Youth Sport Coaches. *Journal of Sport Psychology*, 1, 59–75.

Smith, R.E., Smoll, F.L., and Schutz, R.W. (1990a). Measurements and correlates of sport-specific cognitive and somatic trait anxiety. *Anxiety Research*, 2, 263–280.

Smith, R.E., Smoll, F.L., and Ptacek, J.T. (1990b). Conjunctive moderator variables in vulnerability and resilience research: Life stress, social support, and coping skills, and adolescent sport injuries. *Journal of Personality and Social Psychology*, 58, 360–370.

Smith, R.E., Smoll, F.L., Cumming, S.P., and Grossbard, J.R. (2006). Measurement of multidimensional sport performance anxiety in children and adults: The Sport Anxiety Scale-2. *Journal of Sport & Exercise Psychology*, 28, 479–501.

Smoll, F.L., and Schultz, R.W. (1978). Relationships among measures of preferred tempo and motor rhythm. *Perceptual and Motor Skills*, 46, 883–894.

Smoll, F.L., and Smith, R.E. (1980). Techniques for improving self-awareness of youth sports coaches. *Journal of Physical Education and Recreation*, 51, 46–49; 52.

Smoll, F.L., and Smith, R.E. (Eds). (1996). *Children and Youth in Sport: A Biopsychosocial Perspective*. Dubuque, IA: Brown and Benchmark.

Sonstroem, R., Harlow, L., Gemma, L., and Osbourne, S. (1992). Tests of structural relationships with a proposed exercise and self-esteem model. *Journal of Personality Assessment*, 56, 348–364.

Sonstroem, R., Harlow, L., and Salisbury, K. (1993). Path analysis of a self-esteem model across a competitive swim season. *Research Quarterly for Exercise and Sport*, 64, 335–342.

Sonstroem, R.J. (1997). 'The Physical Self-System: A mediator of exercise and self-esteem.' In: K.R. Fox (Ed.), *The Physical Self*. Champaign, IL: Human Kinetics, 3–26.

Sonstroem, R.J., and Morgan, W.P. (1989). Exercise and self-esteem: Rationale and model. *Medicine and Science in Sports and Exercise*, 21, 329–337.

Sonstroem, R.J., Harlow, L.L., and Josephs, L. (1994). Exercise and self-esteem: Validity of model expansion and exercise associations. *Journal of Sport & Exercise Psychology*, 16, 29–42.

Spence, J.C., McGannon, K.R., and Poon, P. (2005). The effect of exercise on global self-esteem: A quantitative review. *Journal of Sport & Exercise Psychology*, 27, 311–334.

Spielberger, C.D. (1966). 'Theory and research on anxiety.' In: C.S. Spielberger (Ed.), *Anxiety and Behavior*. New York: Academic Press, 3–20.

Spielberger, C.D. (1991). *Manual for the State-Trait Anger Expression Inventory*. Odessa, FL: Psychological Assessment Resources.

Stein, D.M., and Lambert, M.J. (1984). On the relationship between therapist experience and psychotherapy outcome. *Clinical Psychology Review*, 4, 1–16.

Stephan, K.M., and Frackowiak, R.S.J. (1996). Motor imagery – anatomical representation and electrophysiological characteristics. *Neurochemical Research*, 21, 1105–1116.

Stice, E. (2002). Risk and maintenance factors for eating pathology: A meta-analytic review. *Psychological Bulletin*, 128, 825–848.

Stoeber, J., Otto, K., Pescheck, E., Becker, C., and Stoll, O. (2007). Perfectionism and competitive anxiety in athletes: Differentiating striving for perfection and negative reactions to imperfection. *Personality and Individual Differences*, 42, 959–969.

Stoll, O. (1997). Endorphine, Laufsucht und Runner's High. Aufstieg und Niedergang eines Mythos. *Leipziger Sportwissenschaftliche Beiträge*, 38, 102–121.

Strauss, R.S., Rodzilsky, D., Burack, G. and Colin, M. (2001). Psychosocial correlates of physical activity in healthy children. *Archives of Pediatrics and Adolescent Medicine*, 155, 897–902.

Strupp, H.H., and Hadley, S.W. (1979). Specific versus nonspecific factors in psychotherapy: A controlled study of outcome. *Archives of General Psychiatry*, 36, 1125–1136.

Summers, J.J., and Hinton, E.R. (1986). 'Development of scales to measure participation in running.' In: Unestahl, L.E. (Ed.), *Contemporary Sport Psychology*. Veje: Sweden, 73–84.

Swain, A., and Jones, G. (1995). Effects of goal-setting interventions on selected basketball skills: A single-subject design. *Research Quarterly for Exercise and Sport*, 66, 51–63.

Swain, A.B.J., and Jones, J.G. (1993). Intensity and frequency dimensions of competitive state anxiety. *Journal of Sports Sciences*, 11, 533–542.

Szabo, A. (1995). The impact of exercise deprivation on well-being of habitual exercisers. *The Australian Journal of Science and Medicine in Sport*, 27, 68–75.

Szabo, A. (2000). 'Physical activity as a source of psychological dysfunction.' In: S.J.H. Biddle, K.R. Fox, and S.H. Boutcher (Eds), *Physical Activity and Psychological Well-Being*. London: Routledge, 130–153.

Szabo, A. (2001). The dark side of sports and exercise: Research dilemmas. Paper presented at the 10th World Congress of Sport Psychology, 30th May 2001, Skiathos, Greece.

Szabo, A., Frenkl, R., and Caputo, A. (1996). Deprivation feelings, anxiety, and commitment to various forms of physical activity: A cross-sectional study on the Internet. *Psychologia*, 39, 223–230.

Szabo, A., Frenkl, R., and Caputo, A. (1997). Relationships between addiction to running, commitment to running, and deprivation from running. *European Yearbook of Sport Psychology*, 1, 130–147.

Szabo, A., Small, A., and Leigh, M. (1999). The effects of slow- and fast-rhythm classical music on progressive cycling to physical exhaustion. *Journal of Sports Medicine and Physical Fitness*, 39, 220–225.

Szmedra, L., and Bacharach, D.W. (1998). Effect of music on perceived exertion, plasma lactate, norepinephrine and cardiovascular hemodynamics during treadmill running. *International Journal of Sports Medicine*, 19, 32–37.

Taylor, J. (1995). A conceptual model for integrating athletes' needs and sport demands in the development of competitive mental preparation strategies. *The Sport Psychologist*, 9, 339–357.

Tenenbaum, G. (2001). 'A social-cognitive perspective of perceived exertion and exercise tolerance.' In: R.N. Singer, H.A. Hausenblas, and C. Janelle (Eds), *Handbook of Sport Psychology*. New York: Wiley, 810–822.

Tenenbaum, G., Lidor, R., Lavyan, N., et al. (2004). The effect of music type on running perseverance and coping with effort sensations. *Psychology of Sport and Exercise*, 5, 89–109.

Terry, A., Szabo, A., and Griffiths, M.D. (2004). The exercise addiction inventory: A new brief screening tool. *Addiction Research and Theory*, 12, 489–499.

Terry, P.C. (1993). 'Mood state profile as indicators of performance among Olympic and World Championship athletes.' In: S. Serpa, J. Alves, V. Ferreira, and A. Paulo-Brito (Eds), *Proceedings of the VIIIth ISSP World Congress of Sport Psychology*. Lisbon: ISSP, 963–967.

Terry, P.C. (1995a). The efficacy of mood state profiling among elite competitors: A review and synthesis. *The Sport Psychologist*, 9, 309–324.

Terry, P.C. (1995b). Discriminant capability of preperformance mood state profiles during the 1993–1994 World Cup Bobsleigh [Abstract]. *Journal of Sports Sciences*, 13, 77–78.

Terry, P.C. (2004). 'Mood and emotions in sport.' In: T. Morris and J. Summers (Eds), *Sport Psychology: Theory, Applications and Issues*, (2nd Ed.). Brisbane: Wiley, 31–57.

Terry, P.C., and Karageorghis, C.I. (2006). 'Psychophysical effects of music in sport and exercise: An update on theory, research and application.' In: Katsikitis, M. (Ed.), *Psychology Bridging the Tasman: Science, Culture and Practice*. Proceedings of the Joint Conference of the Australian and Psychological Society and the New Zealand Psychological Society. Melbourne, VIC: Australian Psychological Society, 415–419.

Terry, P.C., and Slade, A. (1995). Discriminant capability of psychological state measures in predicting performance outcome in karate competition. *Perceptual and Motor Skills*, 81, 275–286.

Terry, P.C., Lane, A.M., Lane, H.J., and Keohane, L. (1999). Development and validation of a mood measure for adolescents: POMS-A. *Journal of Sports Sciences*, 17, 861–872.

Terry, P.C., Dinsdale, S.L., Karageorghis, C.I., and Lane, A.M. (2006). 'Use and perceived effectiveness of pre-competition mood regulation strategies among athletes.' In: Katsikitis, M. (Ed.), *Psychology Bridging the Tasman: Science, Culture and Practice*. Proceedings of the Joint Conference of the Australian and Psychological Society and the New Zealand Psychological Society. Melbourne, VIC: Australian Psychological Society, 420–424.

Thaxton, L. (1982). Physiological and psychological effects of short term exercise addiction on habitual runners. *Journal of Sport Psychology*, 4, 73–80.

Thelwell, R.C., and Maynard, I.W. (2003). The effects of a mental skills package on 'repeatable good performance' in cricketers. *Psychology of Sport and Exercise*, 4, 377–396.

Thelwell, R.C., Weston, N.J.V., and Greenlees, I.A. (2005). Defining and understanding mental toughness within soccer. *Journal of Applied Sport Psychology*, 17, 326–332.

Thelwell, R.C., Greenlees, I.A., and Weston, N. (2006). Using psychological skills training to develop soccer performance. *Journal of Applied Sport Psychology*, 18, 254–270.

Thoits, P.A. (1995). Stress, coping, and social support processes: Where are we? What next? *Journal of Health and Social Behavior*, Extra issue, 53–79.

Thomas, L.F. (1979). 'Construct, reflect and converse: The conventional reconstruction of social realities.' In: P. Stringer, and D. Bannister (Eds), *Constructs of Sociality and Individuality*. London: Academic Press, 49–72.

Thompson, J.K., and Blanton, P. (1987). Energy conservation and exercise dependence: A sympathetic arousal hypothesis. *Medicine and Science in Sports and Exercise*, 19, 91–97.

Thornton, E.W., and Scott, S.E. (1995). Motivation in the committed runner: Correlations between self-report scales and behaviour. *Health Promotion International*, 10, 177–184.

Tice, D.M. (1991). Esteem protection or enhancement? Self-handicapping motives and attributions differ by trait self-esteem. *Journal of Personality and Social Psychology*, 60, 711–725.

Tiggemann, M., and Wilson-Barratt, E. (1998). Children's figure ratings: Relationship to self-esteem and negative stereotyping. *International Journal of Eating Disorders*, 23, 83–88.

Trail, G.T. (2004). Leadership, cohesion, and outcomes in scholastic sports. *International Journal of Sport Management*, 4, 111–132.

Uphill, M.A., and Jones, M.V. (2004). 'Coping with emotions in sport: A cognitive motivational relational theory perspective.' In: D. Lavallee, J. Thatcher, and M.V. Jones (Eds), *Coping and Emotion in Sport*. New York: Nova Science, 75–89.

Uphill, M.A., and Jones, M.V. (2007a). Antecedents of emotions in elite athletes: A cognitive motivational relational perspective. *Research Quarterly for Exercise and Sport*, 78, 79–89.

Uphill, M.A., and Jones, M.V. (2007b). '"When running is something you dread": A cognitive-behavioural intervention with a club runner.' In: A.M. Lane (Ed.), *Mood and Human Performance: Conceptual, Measurement and Applied Issues*. New York: Nova Science, 271–295.

Uppal, A.K., and Datta, U. (1990). Cardiorespiratory response of junior high school girls to exercise performed with and without music. *Journal of Physical Education and Sport Science*, 2, 52–56.

Vallée, C.N., and Bloom, G.A. (2005). Building a successful university program: Key and common elements of expert coaches. *Journal of Applied Sport Psychology*, 17, 179–196.

Van de Vliet, P., Van Coppenolle, H.V., and Knapen, J. (2002). Physical measures, perceived physical ability and body acceptance of adult psychiatric patients. *Adapted Physical Activity Quarterly*, 16, 113–125.

Vandell, R.A., Davis, R.A., Clugston, H.A. (1943). The function of mental practice in the acquisition of motor skills. *Journal of General Psychology*, 29, 243–250.

Vealey, R. (1994). Current status and prominent issues in sport psychology interventions. *Medicine and Science in Sports and Exercise*, 26, 495–502.

Vealey, R.S. (1986). Conceptualization of sport-confidence and competitive orientation: Preliminary investigation and instrument development. *Journal of Sport Psychology*, 8, 221–246.

Vealey, R.S. (2001). 'Understanding and enhancing self-confidence in athletes.' In: R.N. Singer, H.A. Hausenblas, and C.M. Janelle (Eds), *Handbook of Sport Psychology*. New York: John Wiley and Sons, 550–565.

Vealey, R.S., and Garner-Holman, M. (1998). 'Measurement issues in applied sport psychology.' In: J.L. Duda (Ed.), *Advances in Sport and Exercise Psychology Measurement*. Morgantown, WV: Fitness Information Technology, 247–268.

Vealey, R.S., and Walter, S.M. (1993). 'Imagery training for performance enhancement and personal development.' In: J.M. Williams (Ed.), Applied Sport Psychology: Personal Growth to Peak Performance (2nd Ed.). Mountain View, CA: Mayfield, 200–221.

Vealey, R.S., Hayashi, S.W., Garner-Holman, M., and Giacobbi, P. (1998). Sources of sport-confidence: Conceptualization and instrument development. *Journal of Sport & Exercise Psychology*, 21, 54–80.

Velasquez, M.M., Von Sternberg, K., Dodrill, C.L., Kan, L.Y., and Parsons, J.T. (2005). The transtheoretical model as a framework for developing substance abuse interventions. *Journal of Addictions Nursing*, 16, 31–40.

Vogt, W. (1999). *Breaking the Chain: Drugs and Cycling, the True Story* (trans. William Fotherington). London: Random House.

Weinberg, R.S., and Comar, W. (1994). The effectiveness of psychological interventions in competitive sports. *Sports Medicine Journal*, 18, 406–418.

Weinberg, R.S., and Gould, D. (1999). *Foundations of Sport and Exercise Psychology* (2nd Ed.). Champaign, IL: Human Kinetics.

Weinberg, R.S., and Gould, D. (2003). *Foundations of Sport and Exercise Psychology* (3rd Ed.). Champaign, IL: Human Kinetics.

Weinberg, R.S., and Gould, D. (2007). *Foundations of Sport and Exercise Psychology* (4th Ed.). Champaign, IL: Human Kinetics.

Weinberger, D.A., Schwarz, G.E., and Davidson, R.J. (1979). Low-anxious, high-anxious and repressive coping styles: Psychometric patterns and behavioural and physiological responses to stress. *Journal of Abnormal Psychology*, 88, 369–380.

Welk, G.J., and Eklund, B. (2005). Validation of the children and youth physical self perceptions profile for young children. *Psychology of Sport and Exercise*, 6, 51–65.

Wenzlaff, R.M., and LePage, J.P. (2000). The emotional impact of chosen and imposed thoughts. *Personality and Social Psychology Bulletin*, 26, 1502–1514.

Weston, N.J.V. (2005). The impact of Butler and Hardy's (1992) performance profiling technique in sport. Doctorial Thesis, University of Southampton.

Weston, N.J.V., Greenlees, I., and Graydon, J. (2004a). The impact of repeated group performance profiling on the intrinsic motivation of collegiate soccer players. *Journal of Sport & Exercise Psychology*, S197.

Weston, N., Greenlees, I.A., Graydon, J., and Thelwell, R.C. (2004b). Sport psychology consultant perceptions of the usefulness and impacts of performance profiling within a group setting. *Journal of Sport & Exercise Psychology*, S198.

Wethington, E., and Kessler, R.C. (1991). 'Situations and processes of coping.' In: J. Eckenrode (Ed.), *The Social Context of Coping*. New York: Plenum Press, 13–29.

Whetstone, T.S. (1995). Enhancing psychomotor skill development through the use of mental practice. Journal of Industrial Teacher Education, 32, http://scholar.lib.vt.edu/ejournals/JITE/v32n4/whetstone.html.

White, A., and Hardy, L. (1995). Use of different imagery perspectives on the learning and performance of different motor skills. *British Journal of Psychology*, 86, 169–180.

Whitehead, J.R. (1995). A study of children's physical self-perceptions using an adapted physical self-perception questionnaire. *Pediatric Exercise Science*, 7, 132–151.

Wichmann, S., and Martin, D.R. (1992). Exercise excess. *The Physician and Sportsmedicine*, 20, 193–200.

Wilkinson, J. (2004). *My World*. London: Headline.

Williams, A.M., Vickers, J., and Rodrigues, S. (2002). The effects of anxiety on visual search, movement kinematics, and performance in table tennis: A test of Eysenck and Calvo's processing efficiency theory. *Journal of Sport & Exercise Psychology*, 24, 438–455.

Wills, T.A. (1990). 'Social support and interpersonal relationships.' In: M.S. Clark (Ed.), *Review of Personality and Social Psychology*. Newbury Park, CA: Sage, 265–289.

Wilson, M., Smith, N.C., Chattington, M., Ford, M., and Marple-Horvat, D.E. (2006). The role of effort in moderating the anxiety-performance relationship: Testing the prediction of processing efficiency theory in simulated rally driving. *Journal of Sports Sciences*, 24, 1223–1233.

Wilson, M., Chattington, M., Marple-Horvat, D.E., and Smith, N.C. (2007). A comparison of self-focus versus attentional explanations of choking. *Journal of Sport & Exercise Psychology*, 29, 439–456.

Wilson, R.C., Sullivan, P.J., Myers, N.D. and Feltz, D. (2004). Sources of sport confidence of master athletes. *Journal of Sport & Exercise Psychology*, 26, 369–384.

Wilson, R.M.F., and Davey, N.J. (2002). Musical beat influences corticospinal drive to ankle flexor and extensor muscles in man. *International Journal of Psychophysiology*, 44, 177–184.

Woodman, T., and Hardy, L. (2001a). 'Stress and anxiety.' In: R.N. Singer, H.A. Hausenblas, and C.M. Janelle (Eds), *Handbook of Sport Psychology* (2nd Ed.). Chichester: Wiley, 290–318.

Woodman, T., and Hardy, L. (2001b). A case study of organisational stress in elite sport. *Journal of Applied Sport Psychology*, 13, 207–238.

Woodman, T., and Hardy, L. (2003). The relative impact of cognitive anxiety and self-confidence upon sport performance: A meta analysis. *Journal of Sports Sciences*, 21, 443–457.

Wright, A., and Côté, J. (2003). A retrospective analysis of leadership development through sport. *The Sport Psychologist*, 17, 268–291.

Wuyam, R., Moosari, S.H., Decety, J., Adams, L., Lansing, R.W., and Guz, A. (1995). Imagination of dynamic exercise produced ventilatory responses which were more apparent in competitive sportsmen. *Journal of Physiology*, 482, 713–724.

Young, R.A., and Valach, L. (2000). 'Reconceptualising career theory and research: An action-theoretical perspective.' In: A. Collin, and R.A. Young (Eds), *The Future of Career*. Cambridge: Cambridge University Press, 181–196.

Yukelson, D. (1998). 'Communicating effectively.' In: J.M. Williams (Ed.), *Applied Sport Psychology: Personal Growth to Peak Performance*. Mountain View, CA: Mayfield, 142–157.

Zeidner, M. (1990). Life events and coping resources as predictors of stress symptoms of adolescents. *Personality and Individual Differences*, 11, 693–703.

Zeidner, M., Matthews, G., and Roberts, R.D. (2004). Emotional intelligence in the workplace: A critical review. *Applied Psychology: An International Review*, 53, 371–399.

Zeigler, S.G. (1987). Effects of stimulus cueing on the acquisition of ground strikes by beginning tennis players. *Journal of Applied Behavioral Analysis*, 20, 405–411.

Zhang, J., Jensen, B.E., and Mann, B.L. (1997). Modification and revision of the Leadership Scale for Sport. *Journal of Sport Behavior*, 20, 105–121.

Zinsser, N., Bunker, L., and Williams, J.M. (2001). 'Cognitive techniques for building confidence and enhancing performance.' In: J.M. Williams (Ed.), *Applied Sport Psychology: Personal Growth to Peak Performance*. Mountain View, CA: Mayfield, 284–311.

Index